I0010751

Cardboard VR Projects for Android

Develop mobile virtual reality apps using the native
Google Cardboard SDK for Android

Jonathan Linowes

Matt Schoen

[PACKT] open source*
PUBLISHING   community experience distilled

BIRMINGHAM - MUMBAI

Cardboard VR Projects for Android

Copyright © 2016 Packt Publishing

All rights reserved. No part of this book may be reproduced, stored in a retrieval system, or transmitted in any form or by any means, without the prior written permission of the publisher, except in the case of brief quotations embedded in critical articles or reviews.

Every effort has been made in the preparation of this book to ensure the accuracy of the information presented. However, the information contained in this book is sold without warranty, either express or implied. Neither the authors, nor Packt Publishing, and its dealers and distributors will be held liable for any damages caused or alleged to be caused directly or indirectly by this book.

Packt Publishing has endeavored to provide trademark information about all of the companies and products mentioned in this book by the appropriate use of capitals. However, Packt Publishing cannot guarantee the accuracy of this information.

First published: May 2016

Production reference: 1120516

Published by Packt Publishing Ltd.
Livery Place
35 Livery Street
Birmingham B3 2PB, UK.

ISBN 978-1-78588-787-1

www.packtpub.com

Credits for the Cover Image:

Custom Illustration designed by eLearning Mind, LLC., www.eLearningMind.com, ELM creates interactive learning experiences using modern brain science and intuitively stunning design.

The DIY Virtual Reality article:
http://elearningmind.com/diy-virtual-reality-world-of-warcraft-thinks-inside-the-box-at-comic-con-2015/

Credits

Authors
Jonathan Linowes
Matt Schoen

Reviewers
Scott Dolim
Oleksandr Popov

Commissioning Editor
Edward Gordon

Acquisition Editor
Reshma Raman

Content Development Editor
Sachin Karnani

Technical Editor
Siddhi Rane

Copy Editor
Rashmi Sawant

Project Coordinator
Nikhil Nair

Proofreader
Safis Editing

Indexer
Hemangini Bari

Graphics
Kirk D'Penha

Production Coordinator
Shantanu N. Zagade

Cover Work
Shantanu N. Zagade

About the Authors

Jonathan Linowes is the owner of Parkerhill Reality Labs, a start-up VR/AR consultancy firm. He is a VR and 3D graphics enthusiast, full-stack web developer, software engineer, successful entrepreneur, and teacher. He has a fine arts degree from Syracuse University and a master's degree from the MIT Media Lab. He has founded several successful start-ups and held technical leadership positions at major corporations, including Autodesk Inc. He is also the author of the *Unity Virtual Reality Projects* book by Packt Publishing.

Matt Schoen is the cofounder of Defective Studios and has been making VR apps since the early DK1 days. Still in the early stages of his career, he spent most of his time working on Unity apps and games, some for hire and some of his own design. He studied computer engineering at Boston University and graduated with a BS in 2010, at which point he founded Defective with Jono Forbes, a high-school friend. He has been making games and apps ever since. Matt was the technical lead on Defective's debut game, CosmoKnots, and remains involved in Jono's pet project, Archean. This is his first foray into authorship, but he brings with him his experience as an instructor and curriculum designer for Digital Media Academy. Jono and Matt have recently joined Unity's VR Labs division, where they will be helping to create experimental new features which will shape the VR landscape for years to come.

About the Reviewers

Scott Dolim has worked on and off in 3D computer graphics for over 20 years, including a 5-year stint at Walt Disney Feature Animation in the 1990s. More recently, for the last 5 years, he has been actively involved in virtual reality development, mostly with Unity 3D. Scott currently works at Google where he is the lead engineer of the Cardboard SDK for Unity.

Oleksandr Popov is a developer of numerous 3D apps, mainly live wallpapers, for Android devices. His first experience with 3D for Android started in 2012 when with the release of Android 2.2, it became possible to create live wallpapers. Since then, he has released about 15 of them in collaboration with his brother, Dmytro, who is responsible for creating 3D scenes. After releasing each app, he gained more and more experience in OpenGL ES. Basically, he tried almost every new feature of Android where 3D and OpenGL can be applied. He started with live wallpapers in Android 2.2, then he added support of the daydream mode for them in 4.2. He started using some of the features of OpenGL ES 3.0 introduced in Android 4.3. And as soon as Google added support of custom watch faces for Android Wear 5.0, he and his brother created a set of 3D watch faces for smart watches too. Of course, after Google announced Cardboard, he immediately decided to create VR apps for this platform as well.

He and his brother are also coauthors of the *Deconstructing Google Cardboard Apps* book by Bleeding Edge Press.

www.PacktPub.com

eBooks, discount offers, and more

Did you know that Packt offers eBook versions of every book published, with PDF and ePub files available? You can upgrade to the eBook version at www.PacktPub.com and as a print book customer, you are entitled to a discount on the eBook copy. Get in touch with us at customercare@packtpub.com for more details.

At www.PacktPub.com, you can also read a collection of free technical articles, sign up for a range of free newsletters and receive exclusive discounts and offers on Packt books and eBooks.

https://www2.packtpub.com/books/subscription/packtlib

Do you need instant solutions to your IT questions? PacktLib is Packt's online digital book library. Here, you can search, access, and read Packt's entire library of books.

Why subscribe?

- Fully searchable across every book published by Packt
- Copy and paste, print, and bookmark content
- On demand and accessible via a web browser

Table of Contents

Preface	**ix**
Chapter 1: Virtual Reality for Everyone	**1**
Why is it called Cardboard?	**1**
The spectrum of VR devices	**3**
Old fashioned stereoscopes	3
Cardboard is mobile VR	4
Desktop VR and beyond	5
A gateway to VR	**6**
The value of low-end VR	**9**
Cardware!	**11**
Configuring your Cardboard viewer	**14**
Developing apps for Cardboard	**16**
Using Unity	16
Going native	17
An overview to VR best practices	**19**
Summary	**21**
Chapter 2: The Skeleton Cardboard Project	**23**
What's in an Android app?	**23**
APK files	24
A Gradle build process	24
A Java compiler	26
The Android project structure	**26**
Getting started with Android Studio	**29**
Installing Android Studio	29
The Android Studio user interface	29
Creating a new Cardboard project	**33**
Adding the Cardboard Java SDK	**37**

The AndroidManifest.xml file	**40**
The activity_main.xml file	**45**
The MainActivity class	**46**
Default onCreate	48
Building and running	49
Summary	**51**
Chapter 3: Cardboard Box	**53**
Creating a new project	**54**
Hello, triangle!	**55**
Introducing geometry	55
Triangle variables	57
onSurfaceCreated	58
Introducing OpenGL ES 2.0	58
Simple shaders	61
The compileShaders method	63
The prepareRenderingTriangle method	63
onDrawEye	65
Building and running	66
3D camera, perspective, and head rotation	**67**
Welcome to the matrix	67
The MVP vertex shader	70
Setting up the perspective viewing matrices	70
Render in perspective	71
Building and running	73
Repositioning the triangle	**74**
Hello, cube!	**75**
The cube model data	75
Cube code	77
Lighting and shading	**80**
Adding shaders	80
Cube normals and colors	82
Preparing the vertex buffers	84
Preparing the shaders	85
Adding a light source	87
Building and running the app	88
Spinning the cube	**88**
Hello, floor!	**89**
Shaders	89
Floor model data	91
Variables	91

onCreate	92
onSurfaceCreated	92
initializeScene	92
prepareRenderingFloor	93
onDrawEye	94
drawFloor	94
Hey, look at this!	**95**
The isLookingAtObject method	95
Summary	**98**
Chapter 4: Launcher Lobby	**99**
Creating a new project	**100**
Adding Hello Virtual World text overlay	**101**
A simple text overlay	101
Center the text using a child view	103
Create stereoscopic views for each eye	105
Controlling the overlay view from MainActivity	108
Using a virtual screen	**109**
Responding to head look	**111**
Adding an icon to the view	**113**
Listing installed Cardboard apps	**115**
Queries for Cardboard apps	116
Create the Shortcut class for apps	117
Add shortcuts to OverlayView	117
Using view lists in OverlayEye	118
Highlighting the current shortcut	**120**
Using the trigger to pick and launch the app	**122**
Further enhancements	**123**
Summary	**124**
Chapter 5: RenderBox Engine	**125**
Introducing RenderBox – a graphics engine	**126**
Creating a new project	**128**
Creating the RenderBox package folder	129
Creating an empty RenderBox class	130
Adding the IRenderBox interface	132
Materials, textures, and shaders	**133**
Abstract material	134
The Math package	**137**
MathUtils	137
Matrix4	138
Quaternion	138

Vector2	139
Vector3	140
The Transform class	**141**
Parent methods	143
Position methods	144
Rotation methods	146
Scale methods	147
Transform to matrix and draw	148
The Component class	**149**
The RenderObject component	**150**
The Cube RenderObject component	**152**
Vertex color material and shaders	**155**
Vertex color shaders	155
VertexColorMaterial	156
The Camera component	**159**
RenderBox methods	**161**
A simple box scene	**163**
Cube with face normals	**164**
The Light component	**165**
Vertex color lighting material and shaders	**167**
Time for animation	**172**
Detect looking at objects	**174**
Exporting the RenderBox package	**176**
Building the RenderBoxLib module	177
The RenderBox test app	181
Using RenderBox in future projects	182
Summary	**185**
Chapter 6: Solar System	**187**
Setting up a new project	**188**
Creating a Sphere component	**189**
A solid color lighted sphere	**195**
Solid color lighting shaders	195
Solid color lighting material	197
Adding a Material to a Sphere	200
Viewing the Sphere	200
Adding the Earth texture material	**201**
Loading a texture file	202
Diffuse lighting shaders	203
Diffuse lighting material	205
Adding diffuse lighting texture to a Sphere component	209

Viewing the Earth   209
Changing the camera position   211
Day and night material   **212**
Day/night shader   212
The DayNightMaterial class   215
Rendering with day/night   218
Creating the Sun   **219**
Unlit texture shaders   219
Unlit texture material   220
Rendering with an unlit texture   222
Adding the Sun   223
Creating a Planet class   **224**
Formation of the Solar System   **226**
Setting up planets in MainActivity   227
Camera's planet view   230
Animating the heavenly bodies   231
A starry sky dome   **231**
Fine tuning the Earth   **232**
The night texture   233
Axis tilt and wobble   234
Changing the camera location   **234**
Possible enhancements   **235**
Updating the RenderBox library   **236**
Summary   **237**
Chapter 7: 360-Degree Gallery   **239**
Setting up the new project   **240**
Viewing a 360-degree photo   **242**
Viewing a sample photosphere   244
Using the background image   246
Viewing a regular photo   **247**
Defining the Plane component and allocating buffers   247
Adding materials to the Plane component   249
Adding an image screen to the scene   249
Putting a border frame on the image   **252**
Border shaders   252
The border material   254
Using the border material   256
Loading and displaying a photo image   **257**
Defining the image class   258
Reading images into the app   259

Image load texture   260
Showing an image on the screen   262
Rotating to the correct orientation   263
Dimensions to correct the width and height   266
Sample image down to size   267
Loading and displaying a photosphere image   **270**
The image gallery user interface   **272**
Positioning the photo screen on the left   274
Displaying thumbnails in a grid   **274**
The thumbnail image   274
The Thumbnail class   275
The thumbnail grid   276
Gaze to load   **278**
Gaze-based highlights   278
Selecting and showing photos   279
Queue events   280
Using a vibrator   281
Enable scrolling   **282**
Creating the Triangle component   282
Adding triangles to the UI   284
Interacting with the scroll buttons   285
Implementing the scrolling method   286
Stay responsive and use threads   **287**
An explanation of threading and virtual reality   **292**
Launch with an intent   **294**
Showing/hiding the grid with tilt-up gestures   **297**
Spherical thumbnails   **300**
Add a sphere to the Thumbnail class   300
Updating the RenderBox library   **302**
Further possible enhancements   **303**
Summary   **304**
Chapter 8: 3D Model Viewer   **305**
Setting up a new project   **306**
Understanding the OBJ file format   **307**
Creating the ModelObject class   **309**
Parse OBJ models   **310**
buildBuffers   315
Model extents, scaling, and center   **316**
I'm a little teapot   **317**
I'm a little rotating teapot   **319**

Thread safe	**321**
Launch with intent	**322**
Practical and production ready	**324**
Summary	**324**
Chapter 9: Music Visualizer	**325**
Setting up a new project	**326**
Capturing audio data	**327**
A VisualizerBox architecture	**328**
Waveform data capture	**331**
A basic geometric visualization	**332**
2D texture-based visualization	**335**
Texture generator and loader	335
Waveform shaders	337
Basic waveform material	338
Waveform visualization	341
FFT visualization	**343**
Capture the FFT audio data	343
FFT shaders	345
Basic FFT material	346
FFT visualization	347
Trippy trails mode	**348**
Multiple simultaneous visualizations	**351**
Random visualizations	**353**
Further enhancements	**355**
A community invite	356
Summary	**356**
Onward to the future	**357**
Index	**359**

Preface

Google Cardboard is a low-cost, entry-level medium used for experiencing virtual 3D environments. Its applications are as broad and varied as mobile smartphone applications themselves. This book gives you the opportunity to implement a variety of interesting projects for Google Cardboard using the native Java SDK. The idea is to educate you with best practices and methodologies to make Cardboard-compatible mobile VR apps and guide you through making quality content appropriate for the device and its intended users.

What this book covers

Chapter 1, *Virtual Reality for Everyone*, defines Google Cardboard, explores it, and discusses how it's used and how it fits in the spectrum of VR devices.

Chapter 2, *The Skeleton Cardboard Project*, examines the structure of a Cardboard app for Android, takes a tour of Android Studio, and helps you build a starter Cardboard project by introducing the Cardboard Java SDK.

Chapter 3, *Cardboard Box*, discusses how to build a Cardboard Android app from scratch (based on Google's Treasure Hunt sample) with a 3D cube model, transformations, stereoscopic camera views, and head rotations. This chapter also includes discussions of 3D geometry, Open GL ES, shaders, matrix math, and the rendering pipeline.

Chapter 4, *Launcher Lobby*, helps you build an app to launch other Cardboard apps on your phone. Rather than using 3D graphics, this project simulates stereoscopic views in screen space and implements gaze-based selections.

Chapter 5, *RenderBox Engine*, shows you how to create a small graphics engine used to build new Cardboard VR apps by abstracting the low-level OpenGL ES API calls into a suite of the `Material`, `RenderObject`, `Component`, and `Transform` classes. The library will be used and further developed in subsequent projects.

Chapter 6, Solar System, builds a Solar System simulation science project by adding a sunlight source, spherical planets with texture mapped materials and shaders, animating in their solar orbits, and a Milky Way star field.

Chapter 7, 360-Degree Gallery, helps you build a media viewer for regular and 360-degree photos, and helps you load the phone's camera folder pictures into a grid of thumbnail images and use gaze-based selections to choose the ones to view. It also discusses how to add process threading for improved user experience and support Android intents to view images from other apps.

Chapter 8, 3D Model Viewer, helps you build a viewer for 3D models in the OBJ file format, rendered using our RenderBox library. It also shows you how to interactively control the view of the model as you move your head.

Chapter 9, Music Visualizer, builds a VR music visualizer that animates based on waveform and FFT data from the phone's current audio player. We implement a general architecture used to add new visualizations, including geometric animations and dynamic texture shaders. Then, we add a trippy trails mode and multiple concurrent visualizations that transition in and out randomly.

What you need for this book

Throughout the book, we use the Android Studio IDE development environment to write and build Android applications. You can download Android Studio for free, as explained in *Chapter 2, The Skeleton Cardboard Project*. You will need an Android phone to run and test your projects. And it's strongly recommended that you have a Google Cardboard viewer to experience your apps in stereoscopic virtual reality.

Who this book is for

This book is for Android developers who are interested in learning about and developing Google Cardboard apps using the Google Cardboard native SDK. We assume that the reader has some knowledge of Android development and the Java language, but may be new to 3D graphics, virtual reality, and Google Cardboard. Novice developers, or those unfamiliar with the Android SDK, may find it hard to get started with this book. Those who aren't coming from an Android background may be better served by creating cardboard apps with a game engine like Unity.

Conventions

In this book, you will find a number of text styles that distinguish between different kinds of information. Here are some examples of these styles and an explanation of their meaning.

Code words in text, database table names, folder names, filenames, file extensions, pathnames, dummy URLs, user input, and Twitter handles are shown as follows: "Edit the `MainActivity` Java class so that it extends `CardboardActivity` and implements `CardboardView.StereoRenderer`."

A block of code is set as follows:

```
@Override
protected void onCreate(Bundle savedInstanceState) {
    super.onCreate(savedInstanceState);
    setContentView(R.layout.activity_main);

    CardboardView cardboardView = (CardboardView)
    findViewById(R.id.cardboard_view);
    cardboardView.setRenderer(this);
    setCardboardView(cardboardView);
}
```

When we wish to draw your attention to a particular part of a code block, the relevant lines or items are set in bold:

```
@Override
protected void onCreate(Bundle savedInstanceState) {
    super.onCreate(savedInstanceState);
    setContentView(R.layout.activity_main);

    CardboardView cardboardView = (CardboardView)
    findViewById(R.id.cardboard_view);
    cardboardView.setRenderer(this);
    setCardboardView(cardboardView);
}
```

Any command-line input or output is written as follows:

```
git clone https://github.com/googlesamples/cardboard-java.git
```

New terms and **important words** are shown in bold. Words that you see on the screen, for example, in menus or dialog boxes, appear in the text like this: "In Android Studio, select **File** | **New** | **New Module...**. Select **Import .JAR/.AAR Package**."

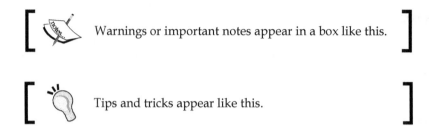

Warnings or important notes appear in a box like this.

Tips and tricks appear like this.

Reader feedback

Feedback from our readers is always welcome. Let us know what you think about this book—what you liked or disliked. Reader feedback is important for us as it helps us develop titles that you will really get the most out of.

To send us general feedback, simply e-mail feedback@packtpub.com, and mention the book's title in the subject of your message.

If there is a topic that you have expertise in and you are interested in either writing or contributing to a book, see our author guide at www.packtpub.com/authors.

Customer support

Now that you are the proud owner of a Packt book, we have a number of things to help you to get the most from your purchase.

Downloading the example code

You can download the example code files for this book from your account at http://www.packtpub.com. If you purchased this book elsewhere, you can visit http://www.packtpub.com/support and register to have the files e-mailed directly to you.

You can download the code files by following these steps:

1. Log in or register to our website using your e-mail address and password.
2. Hover the mouse pointer on the **SUPPORT** tab at the top.
3. Click on **Code Downloads & Errata**.
4. Enter the name of the book in the **Search** box.

5. Select the book for which you're looking to download the code files.
6. Choose from the drop-down menu where you purchased this book from.
7. Click on **Code Download**.

You can also download the code files by clicking on the **Code Files** button on the book's webpage at the Packt Publishing website. This page can be accessed by entering the book's name in the **Search** box. Please note that you need to be logged in to your Packt account.

Once the file is downloaded, please make sure that you unzip or extract the folder using the latest version of:

- WinRAR / 7-Zip for Windows
- Zipeg / iZip / UnRarX for Mac
- 7-Zip / PeaZip for Linux

You can also download the code fles from GitHub at `https://github.com/cardbookvr`.

Downloading the color images of this book

We also provide you with a PDF file that has color images of the screenshots/ diagrams used in this book. The color images will help you better understand the changes in the output. You can download this file from `https://www.packtpub.com/sites/default/files/downloads/CardboardVRProjectsforAndroid_ColorImages.pdf`.

Errata

Although we have taken every care to ensure the accuracy of our content, mistakes do happen. If you find a mistake in one of our books—maybe a mistake in the text or the code—we would be grateful if you could report this to us. By doing so, you can save other readers from frustration and help us improve subsequent versions of this book. If you find any errata, please report them by visiting `http://www.packtpub.com/submit-errata`, selecting your book, clicking on the **Errata Submission Form** link, and entering the details of your errata. Once your errata are verified, your submission will be accepted and the errata will be uploaded to our website or added to any list of existing errata under the Errata section of that title.

To view the previously submitted errata, go to `https://www.packtpub.com/books/content/support` and enter the name of the book in the search field. The required information will appear under the **Errata** section.

Piracy

Piracy of copyrighted material on the Internet is an ongoing problem across all media. At Packt, we take the protection of our copyright and licenses very seriously. If you come across any illegal copies of our works in any form on the Internet, please provide us with the location address or website name immediately so that we can pursue a remedy.

Please contact us at copyright@packtpub.com with a link to the suspected pirated material.

We appreciate your help in protecting our authors and our ability to bring you valuable content.

Questions

If you have a problem with any aspect of this book, you can contact us at questions@packtpub.com, and we will do our best to address the problem.

1

Virtual Reality for Everyone

Welcome to the exciting new world of virtual reality! We're sure that, as an Android developer, you want to jump right in and start building cool stuff that can be viewed using Google Cardboard. Your users can then just slip their smartphone into a viewer and step into your virtual creations. Before we get up to our elbows in the code and tech stuff throughout the rest of this book, let's take an outside-in tour of VR, Google Cardboard, and its Android SDK to see how they all fit together. We will discuss the following topics in this chapter:

- Why is it called Cardboard?
- The spectrum of virtual reality devices
- A gateway to VR
- The value of low-end VR
- Cardware
- Configuring your Cardboard viewer
- Developing apps for Cardboard
- An overview of VR best practices

Why is it called Cardboard?

It all started in early 2014 when Google employees, David Coz and Damien Henry, in their spare time, built a simple and cheap stereoscopic viewer for the Android smartphones. They designed a device that can be constructed from ordinary cardboard, plus a couple of lenses for your eyes, and a mechanism to trigger a button "click." The viewer is literally made from cardboard. They wrote software that renders a 3D scene with a split screen: one view for the left eye, and another view, with offset, for the right eye. Peering through the device, you get a real sense of 3D immersion into the computer generated scene. It worked! The project was then proposed and approved as a "20% project" (where employees may dedicate one day a week for innovations), funded, and joined by other employees.

Two sources of "canonical" facts about the story behind how Cardboard came into existence are as follows:

- `http://www.wired.com/2015/06/inside-story-`
  `googles-unlikely-leap-cardboard-vr/`
- `https://en.wikipedia.org/wiki/Google_Cardboard`

In fact, Cardboard worked so well that Google decided to go forward, taking the project to the next level and releasing it to the public a few months later at Google I/O 2014. The following figure shows a typical unassembled Google Cardboard kit:

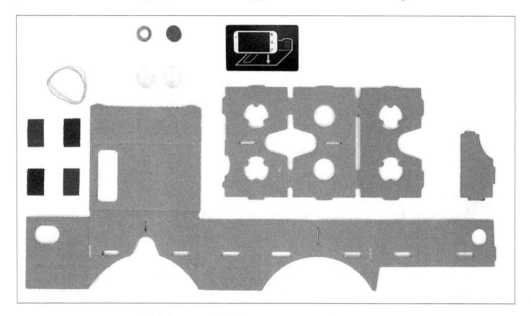

Since its inception, Google Cardboard has been accessible to hackers, hobbyists, and professional developers alike. Google open sourced the viewer design for anyone to download the schematics and make their own, from a pizza box or from whatever they had lying around. One can even go into business selling precut kits directly to consumers. An assembled Cardboard viewer is shown in the following image:

The Cardboard project also includes a **software development kit** (**SDK**) that makes it easy to build VR apps. Google has released continuous improvements to the software, including both a native Java SDK as well as a plugin for the Unity 3D game engine (`https://unity3d.com/`).

Since the release of Cardboard, a huge number of applications have been developed and made available on the Google Play Store. At Google I/O 2015, Version 2.0 introduced an upgraded design, improved software, and support for Apple iOS.

Google Cardboard has rapidly evolved in the eye of the market from an almost laughable toy into a serious new media device for certain types of 3D content and VR experiences. Google's own Cardboard demo app has been downloaded millions of times from the Google Play Store. The New York Times distributed about a million cardboard viewers with its November 8, Sunday issue back in 2015.

Cardboard is useful for viewing 360-degree photos and playing low-fidelity 3D VR games. It is universally accessible to almost anyone because it runs on any Android or iOS smartphone.

Developers are now integrating 3D VR content directly into Android apps. Google Cardboard is a way of experiencing virtual reality that is here to stay.

The spectrum of VR devices

As with most technologies, there is a spectrum of products for virtual reality ranging from the simplest and least expensive to the very advanced.

Old fashioned stereoscopes

Cardboard is at the low end of the VR device spectrum. Well, you could even go lower if you consider the ViewMaster that you may have played with as a child, or even the historic stereoscope viewer from 1876 (B.W. Kilborn & Co, Littleton, New Hampshire), as shown in the following image:

In these old fashioned viewers, a pair of photographs display two separate views for the left and right eyes that are slightly offset to create parallax. This fools the brain into thinking that it's seeing a truly three-dimensional view. The device contains separate lenses for each eye that allow you to easily focus on the photo close up.

Similarly, rendering these side-by-side stereo views is the first job of a Google Cardboard application. (Leveraging their legacy, Mattel recently released a Cardboard-compatible ViewMaster brand VR viewer that uses a smartphone, which can be found at http://www.view-master.com/).

Cardboard is mobile VR

Cardboard's obvious advantages over stereoscopic viewers are like the advantages of digital photographs over traditional ones. Digital media can be dynamically stored, loaded, and manipulated right within our smartphones. That's a powerful leap on its own.

On top of that, Cardboard uses the motion sensors in the phone in such a way that when you turn your head left-right or up-down, the image is adjusted accordingly, effectively obliterating the traditional frame edges of the image. Framing the image is a very important part of traditional visual media, such as painting, photography, and cinematography. For centuries, artists and directors have established a visual language using this rectangular frame.

However, not so much in VR. When you move your head in VR your view direction changes, and the scene is updated as if the camera is rotating along with you, providing a fully immersive view. You can rotate it horizontally 360 degrees as you look side to side and 180 degrees up and down. In other words, you can look anywhere you want. There is no frame in VR! (Albeit your peripheral vision might be limited by the optics and display size, which determine the device's field of view or FOV). In this way, the design considerations may be more akin to sculpture, theatre-in-the-round, or even architectural design. We need to think about the whole space that immerses the visitor.

The Google Cardboard device is simply a casing for you to slip your smartphone into. It uses the smartphone's technology, including the following:

- Display
- CPU (the main processor)
- GPU (the graphics processor)
- IMU (the motion sensor)
- Magnetometer and/or touchscreen (the trigger sensor)

We'll talk more about how all this works a little later.

Using a mobile smartphone for VR means great things, such as ease of use, but also annoying constraints, such as limited battery life, slower graphics processing, and lower accuracy/higher latency motion sensors.

The Samsung Gear VR is a mobile VR headset that is smarter than a simple Cardboard viewer. Android-based but not compatible with Cardboard apps (and only works with specific models of Samsung phones), it has a separate built-in higher precision IMU (motion sensor), which increases the accuracy of the head motion tracking and helps reduce the motion-to-pixel latency when updating the display. It's also ergonomically designed for more extended use and it includes a strap.

Desktop VR and beyond

At the higher end of consumer virtual reality devices are the Oculus Rift, HTC Vive, and Sony PlayStation VR, among others. These products go beyond what Cardboard can do because they're not limited by the capabilities of a smartphone. Sometimes referred to as "desktop VR," these devices are **head-mounted displays** (**HMD**) tethered to an external PC or console.

On desktop VR, the desktop's powerful CPU and GPU do the actual computation and graphics rendering and send the results to the HMD. Furthermore, the HMD has higher quality motion sensors and other features that help reduce the latency when updating the display at, say, 90 **frames per second** (**FPS**). We'll learn throughout this book that reducing latency and maintaining high FPS are important concerns for all VR development and the comfort of your users on all VR devices, including Cardboard.

Desktop VR devices also add *positional tracking*. The Cardboard device can detect the rotational movement on any of the X, Y, and Z axes, but it unfortunately cannot detect the positional movement (for example, sliding along any of these axes). The Rift, Vive, and PSVR can. The Rift, for example, uses an external camera to track the position using infrared lights on the HMD (*outside-in tracking*). The Vive, on the other hand, uses sensors on the HMD to track a pair of laser emitters placed strategically in the room (*inside-out tracking*). The Vive also uses this system to track the position and rotation of a pair of hand controllers. Both strategies achieve similar results. The user has a greater freedom to move around within the tracked space while experiencing moving around within the virtual space. Cardboard cannot do this.

Note that innovations are continually being introduced. Very likely, at some point, positional tracking will be included with the Cardboard arsenal. For example, we know that Google's Project Tango implements visual-inertial odometry, or VIO, using sensors, gyroscopes, and awareness of the physical space to provide motion and positional tracking to mobile apps. Refer to `https://developers.google.com/project-tango/overview/concepts`. Mobile device companies, such as LG and Samsung, are working hard to figure out how to do mobile positional tracking, but (at the time of this writing) a universal, low-latency solution does not yet exist. Google's Project Tango shows some promise but cannot yet achieve the time-to-pixel latency required for a smooth, comfortable VR experience. Too much latency and you get sick!

At the very high end are industrial and military grade systems that cost thousands or millions of dollars, which are not consumer devices, and I'm sure can do really awesome things. I could tell you more about it, but then I'd have to kill you. Solutions such as these have also been around since the 1980s. VR is not new — consumer VR is new.

The spectrum of VR devices is illustrated in the following diagram:

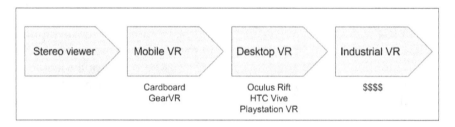

When we develop for Cardboard, it is important to keep in mind the things it can and cannot do relative to other VR devices. Cardboard can display stereoscopic views. Cardboard can track rotational head movement. It cannot do positional tracking. It has limitations of graphics processing power, memory, and battery life.

A gateway to VR

In the very short time it has been available, this generation of consumer virtual reality has demonstrated itself to be instantly compelling, immersive, entertaining, and "a game changer" for just about everyone who tries it. Google Cardboard is especially easy to access with a very low barrier to use. All you need is a smartphone, a low-cost Cardboard viewer (as low as $5 USD), and free apps downloaded from Google Play (or Apple App Store for iOS).

Google Cardboard has been called a **gateway to VR**, perhaps in reference to marijuana as a "gateway drug" to more dangerous illicit drug abuse? We can play with this analogy for a moment, however decadent. Perhaps Cardboard will give you a small taste of VR's potential. You'll want more. And then more again. This will help you fulfill your desire for better, faster, more intense, and immersive virtual experiences that can only be found in higher end VR devices. At this point, perhaps there'll be no turning back; you're addicted!

Yet as a Rift user, I still also enjoy Cardboard. It's quick. It's easy. It's fun. And it really does work, provided I run apps that are appropriately designed for the device.

I brought a Cardboard viewer in my backpack when visiting my family for the holidays. Everyone enjoyed it a lot. Many of my relatives didn't even get past the standard Google Cardboard demo app, especially its 360-degree photo viewer. That was engaging enough to entertain them for a while. Others jumped to a game or two or more. They wanted to keep playing and try new experiences. Perhaps it's just the novelty. Or, perhaps it's the nature of this new medium. The point is that Google Cardboard provides an immersive experience that's enjoyable, useful, and very easily accessible. In short, it is amazing.

Then, show them an HTC Vive or Oculus Rift. Holy Cow! That's really, really amazing! Well, for this book, we're not here to talk about the higher end VR devices, except to contrast them with Cardboard and to keep things in perspective.

Once you try desktop VR, is it hard to "go back" to mobile VR? Some folks say so. But that's almost silly. The fact is that they're really separate things.

As discussed earlier, desktop VR comes with much higher processing power and other high-fidelity features, whereas mobile VR is limited by your smartphone. If a developer were to try and directly port a desktop VR app to a mobile device, there's a good chance that you'll be disappointed.

It's best to think of each as a separate medium. Just like a desktop application or a console game is different from, but similar to, a mobile one. The design criteria may be similar but different. The technologies are similar but different. The user expectations are similar but different. Mobile VR may be similar to desktop VR, but it's different.

To emphasize how different Cardboard is from desktop VR devices, it's worth pointing out that Google has written the following into their manufacturer's specifications and guidelines:

"Do not include a headstrap with your viewer. When the user holds the Cardboard with their hands against the face, their head rotation speed is limited by the torso rotational speed (which is much slower than the neck rotational speed). This reduces the chance of "VR sickness" caused by rendering/IMU latency and increases the immersiveness in VR."

The implication is that Cardboard apps should be designed for shorter, simpler, and somewhat stationary experiences. Throughout this book, we'll illustrate these and other tips and best practices as you develop for the mobile VR medium.

Let's now consider the other ways that Cardboard is a gateway to VR.

We predict that Android will continue to grow as a primary platform for virtual reality in the future. More and more technologies will get crammed into smartphones. And this technology will include features advantageous to VR:

- Faster processors and mobile GPUs
- Higher resolution screens
- Higher precision motion sensors
- Optimized graphics pipelines
- Better software
- Many more VR apps

Mobile VR will not give way to desktop VR; it may even eventually replace it.

Furthermore, we'll soon see dedicated mobile VR headsets that have the guts of a smartphone built-in without the cost of a wireless communications contract. No need to use your own phone. No more getting interrupted while in VR by an incoming call or notification. No more rationing battery life in case you need to receive an important call or otherwise use your phone. All these dedicated VR devices will likely be Android-based.

The value of low-end VR

Meanwhile, Android and Google Cardboard are here today on our phones, in our pockets, in our homes, at the office, and even in our schools.

Google Expeditions, for example, is Google's educational program for Cardboard (`https://www.google.com/edu/expeditions/`), which allows K-12 school children to take virtual field trips to "places a school bus can't," as they say, "around the globe, on the surface of Mars, on a dive to coral reefs, or back in time." The kits include Cardboard viewers and Android phones for each child in a classroom, plus an Android tablet for the teacher. They're connected with a network. The teacher can then guide students on virtual field trips, provide enhanced content, and create learning experiences that go way beyond a textbook or classroom video, as shown in the following image:

In another creative marketing example, in summer of 2015, Kellogg's began selling Nutri-Grain snack bars in a box that transforms into a Google Cardboard viewer. This links to an app that shows a variety of extreme sport 360-degree videos (`http://www.engadget.com/2015/09/09/cereal-box-vr-headset/`), as shown in the following image:

The entire Internet can be considered a world-wide publishing and media distribution network. It's a web of hyperlinked pages, text, images, music, video, JSON data, web services, and much more. It's also teeming with 360-degree photos and videos. There's also an ever growing amount of three-dimensional content and virtual worlds. Would you consider writing an Android app today that doesn't display images? Probably not. There's a good chance that your app also needs to support sound files, videos, or other media. So pay attention. Three-dimensional Cardboard-enabled content is coming quickly. You might be interested in reading this book now because VR looks fun. But, soon enough, it may be a customer-driven requirement for your next app.

Some examples of types of popular Cardboard apps include:

- **360-degree photo viewing**, for example, Google's Cardboard demo (`https://play.google.com/store/apps/details?id=com.google.samples.apps.cardboarddemo`) and Cardboard Camera (`https://play.google.com/store/apps/details?id=com.google.vr.cyclops`)
- **Video and cinema viewing**, for example, a Cardboard theatre (`https://play.google.com/store/apps/details?id=it.couchgames.apps.cardboardcinema`)

- **Roller coasters and thrill rides**, for example, VR Roller Coaster (`https://play.google.com/store/apps/details?id=com.frag.vrrollercoaster`)

- **Cartoonish 3D games**, for example, Lamber VR (`https://play.google.com/store/apps/details?id=com.archiactinteractive.LfGC&hl=en_GB`)

- **First person shooter games**, for example, Battle 360 VR (`https://play.google.com/store/apps/details?id=com.oddknot.battle360vr`)

- **Creepy scary stuff**, for example, Sisters (`https://play.google.com/store/apps/details?id=com.otherworld.Sisters`)

- **Educational experiences**, for example, Titans of Space (`https://play.google.com/store/apps/details?id=com.drashvr.titansofspacecb&hl=en_GB`)

- **Marketing experiences**, for example, Volvo Reality (`https://play.google.com/store/apps/details?id=com.volvo.volvoreality`)

And much more; thousands more. The most popular ones have had hundreds of thousands of downloads (the Cardboard demo app itself has millions of downloads).

The projects in this book are examples of different kinds of Cardboard apps that you can build yourself today.

Cardware!

Let's take a look at the different Cardboard devices that are available. There's a lot of variety.

Obviously, the original Google design is actually made from cardboard. And manufacturers have followed suit, offering cardboard Cardboards directly to consumers — brands such as Unofficial Cardboard, DODOCase, and IAmCardboard were among the first.

Google provides the specifications and schematics free of charge (refer to
`https://www.google.com/get/cardboard/manufacturers/`). For example,
the Version 2.0 Viewer Body schematic is shown as follows:

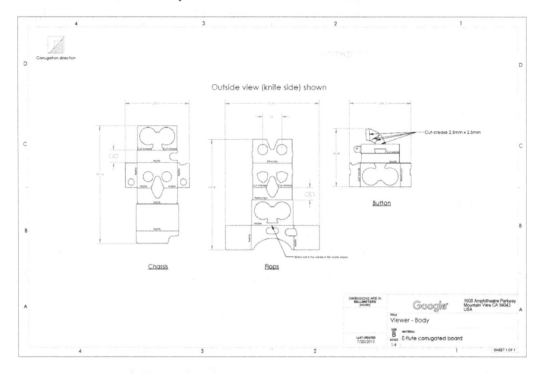

The basic viewer design consists of an enclosure body, two lenses, and an input
mechanism. The *Works with Google Cardboard* certification program indicates
that a given viewer product meets the Google standards and works well with
Cardboard apps.

The viewer enclosure may be constructed from any material: cardboard, plastic,
foam, aluminum, and so on. It should be lightweight and do a pretty good job of
blocking the ambient light.

The lenses (I/O 2015 Edition) are 34 mm diameter aspherical single lenses with
an 80 degree circular FOV (field of view) and other specified parameters.

The input trigger ("clicker") can be one of several alternative mechanisms. The simplest is none, where the user must touch the smartphone screen directly with her finger to trigger a click. This may be inconvenient since the phone is sitting inside the viewer enclosure but it works. Plenty of viewers just include a hole to stick your finger inside. Alternatively, the original Cardboard utilized a small ring magnet attached to the outside of the viewer, held in place by an embedded circular magnet. The user can slide the ring magnet, and the change in magnetic field is sensed by the phone's magnetometer and recognized by the software as a "click". This design is not always reliable because the location of the magnetometer varies among phones. Also, using this method, it is harder to detect a "press and hold" interaction, which means that there is only one type of user input "event" to use within your application.

Cardboard Version 2.0 introduced a button input constructed from a conductive "strip" and "pillow" glued to a Cardboard-based "hammer," like the ones in a grand piano. When the button is pressed, the user's body charge is transferred onto the smartphone screen, as if he'd directly touched the screen with his finger. This clever solution avoids the unreliable magnetometer solution, and instead it uses the phone's native touchscreen input, albeit indirectly.

It is also worth mentioning at this point that, since your smartphone supports Bluetooth, it's possible to use a handheld Bluetooth controller with your Cardboard apps. This is not part of the Cardboard specifications and requires some extra configuration: the use of a third-party input handler or controller support built into the app. A mini Bluetooth controller is shown in the following image:

Cardboard viewers are not necessarily made out of cardboard. Plastic viewers can get relatively costly. While they are more sturdy than cardboard they fundamentally have the same design (assembled). Some devices allow you to adjust the distance from the lenses to the screen, and/or the distance between your eyes (IPD or inter-pupillary distance). The Zeiss VR One, Homido, and Sunnypeak devices were among the first to become popular.

Some manufacturers have gone outside the box (pun intended) with innovations that are not necessarily compliant with Google's specifications but provide capabilities beyond the Cardboard design. A notable example is the Wearality viewer (`http://www.wearality.com/`), which includes a patented 150-degree **field of view** (**FOV**) double Fresnel lens. It's so portable that it folds up like a pair of sunglasses. A pre-release version of the Wearality viewer is shown in the following image:

Configuring your Cardboard viewer

With such a variety of Cardboard devices and variations in lens distance, field of view, distortion, and so on, Cardboard apps must be configured to a specific device's attributes. Google provides a solution to this as well. Each Cardboard viewer comes with a unique QR code and/or NFC chip which you scan to configure the software for that device. If you're interested in calibrating your own device or customizing your parameters, check out the profile generator tools at `https://www.google.com/get/cardboard/viewerprofilegenerator/`.

To configure your phone to a specific Cardboard viewer, open the standard Google Cardboard app, and select the Settings icon in the bottom center section of the screen, as shown in the following image:

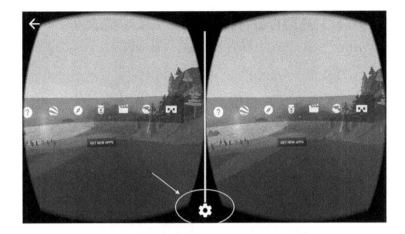

Then point the camera at the QR code for your particular Cardboard viewer:

Your phone is now configured for the specific Cardboard viewer parameters.

Developing apps for Cardboard

At the time of writing this book, Google provides two SDKs for Cardboard:

- Cardboard SDK for Android (`https://developers.google.com/cardboard/android`)
- Cardboard SDK for Unity (`https://developers.google.com/cardboard/unity`)

Let's consider the Unity option first.

Using Unity

Unity (`http://unity3d.com/`) is a popular full-featured 3D game engine, which supports building your games on a wide gamut of platforms, from PlayStation and XBox, to Windows and Mac (and Linux!), to Android and iOS.

Unity consists of many separate tools integrated into a powerful engine under a unified visual editor. There are tools for graphics, physics, scripting, networking, audio, animations, UI, and much more. It includes advanced computer graphics rendering, shading, textures, particles, and lighting with all kinds of options for optimizing performance and fine tuning the quality of your graphics for both 2D and 3D. If that's not enough, Unity hosts a huge Asset Store teeming with models, scripts, tools, and other assets created by its large community of developers.

The Cardboard SDK for Unity provides a plugin package that you can import into the Unity Editor, containing prefabs (premade objects), C# scripts, and other assets. The package gives you what you need in order to add a stereo camera to your virtual 3D scene and build your projects to run as Cardboard apps on Android (and iOS). Unity is planning on integrating the Cardboard SDK directly into the engine, which means that adding support for Cardboard will be possible by just checking a box in the build settings.

 If you're interested in learning more about using Unity to build VR applications for Cardboard, check out another book by Packt Publishing, *Unity Virtual Reality Projects* by Jonathan Linowes (`https://www.packtpub.com/game-development/unity-virtual-reality-projects`).

Going native

So, why not just use Unity for Cardboard development? Good question. It depends on what you're trying to do. Certainly, if you need all the power and features of Unity for your project, it's the way to go.

But at what cost? With great power comes great responsibility (says Uncle Ben Parker). It is quick to learn but takes a lifetime to master (says the Go Master). Seriously though, Unity is a powerful engine that may be overkill for many applications. To take full advantage, you may require additional expertise in modeling, animation, level design, graphics, and game mechanics.

Cardboard applications built with Unity are bulky. An empty Unity scene build for Android generates an .apk file that is a minimum of 23 megabytes. In contrast, the simple native Cardboard application, .apk, that we build in *Chapter 2*, *The Skeleton Cardboard Project*, is under one megabyte.

Along with this large app size comes a long loading time, possibly more than several seconds. It impacts the memory usage and battery use. Unless you've paid for a Unity Android license, your app always starts with the *Made With Unity* splash screen. These may not be acceptable constraints for you.

In general, the closer you are to the metal, the better performance you'll eke out of your application. When you write directly for Android, you have direct access to the features of the device, more control over memory and other resources, and more opportunities for customization and optimization. This is why native mobile apps tend to trump mobile web apps.

Lastly, one of the best reasons to develop with native Android and Java may be the simplest. You're anxious to build something now! If you're already an Android developer, then just use what you already know and love! Take the straightest path from here to there.

If you're familiar with Android development, then Cardboard development will come naturally. Using the Cardboard SDK for Android, you can program in Java, using the Android Studio IDE (integrated development environment), which is based on InteliJ IDEA by Jet Brains.

As we'll see throughout this book, your Cardboard Android app is like other Android apps, including a manifest, resources, and Java code. As with any Android app, you will implement a `MainActivity` class, but yours will extend `CardboardActivity` and implement `CardboardView.StereoRenderer`. Your app will utilize OpenGL ES 2.0 graphics, shaders, and 3D matrix math. It will be responsible for updating the display on each frame, that is, rerendering your 3D scene based on the direction the user is looking at that particular slice in time. It is particularly important in VR, but also in any 3D graphics context, to render a new frame as quickly as the display allows, usually at 60 FPS. Your app will handle the user input via the Cardboard trigger and/or gaze-based control. We'll go into the details of all these topics in the upcoming chapters.

That's what your app needs to do. However, there are still more nitty gritty details that must be handled to make VR work. As noted in the Google Cardboard SDK guide (`https://developers.google.com/cardboard/android/`), the SDK simplifies many of these common VR development tasks, including the following:

- Lens distortion correction
- Head tracking
- 3D calibration
- Side-by-side rendering
- Stereo geometry configuration
- User input event handling

Functions are provided in the SDK to handle these tasks for you.

Building and deploying your applications for development, debugging, profiling, and eventually publishing on Google Play also follow the same Android workflows you may be familiar with already. That's cool.

Of course, there's more to building an app than simply following an example. We'll take a look at techniques such as using data-driven geometric models, abstracting shaders and OpenGL ES API calls, and building user interface elements with gaze-based selection. On top of all this, there are important suggested best practices for making your VR experiences work and avoiding common mistakes.

An overview to VR best practices

More and more is being discovered and written each day about the dos and don'ts when designing and developing for VR. Google provides a couple of resources to help developers build great VR experiences, including the following:

- *Designing for Google Cardboard* is a best practice document that helps you focus on overall usability as well as avoid common VR pitfalls (`http://www.google.com/design/spec-vr/designing-for-google-cardboard/a-new-dimension.html`).

- *Cardboard Design Lab* is a Cardboard app that directly illustrates the principles of designing for VR which you can explore in Cardboard itself. At Vision Summit 2016, the Cardboard team announced that they have released the source (Unity) project for developers to examine and extend (`https://play.google.com/store/apps/details?id=com.google.vr.cardboard.apps.designlab` and `https://github.com/googlesamples/cardboard-unity/tree/master/Samples/CardboardDesignLab`).

VR motion sickness is a real symptom and concern for virtual reality caused in part by a lag in screen updates, or latency, when you're moving your head. Your brain expects the world around you to change exactly in sync with your actual motion. Any perceptible delay can make you feel uncomfortable, to say the least, and possibly nauseous. Latency can be reduced by faster rendering of each frame to maintain the recommended frames per second. Desktop VR apps are held to the high standard of 90 FPS, enabled by a custom HMD screen. On mobile devices, the screen hardware often limits refresh rates to 60 FPS, or in the worst case, 30 FPS.

There are additional causes of VR motion sickness and other user discomforts, which can be mitigated by following these design guidelines:

- Always maintain head tracking. If the virtual world seems to freeze or pause, this may cause users to feel ill.

- Display user interface elements, such as titles and buttons, in 3D virtual space. If rendered in 2D, they'll seem to be "stuck to your face" and you will feel uncomfortable.

- When transitioning between scenes, fade to black. Cut scenes will be very disorienting. Fading to white might be uncomfortably bright for your users.

- Users should remain in control of their movement within the app. Something about initiating camera motion yourself helps reduce motion sickness. Try to avoid "artificially" rotating the camera.

- Avoid acceleration and deceleration. As humans, we feel acceleration but not constant velocity. If you are moving the camera inside the app, keep it at a constant velocity. Rollercoasters are fun, but even in real life they can make you feel sick.

- Keep your users grounded. Being a virtual floating point in space can make you feel sick, whereas feeling like you're standing on the ground or sitting in a cockpit provides a sense of stability.

- Maintain a reasonable distance from the eye for UI elements, such as buttons and reticle cursors. If objects are too close, the user may have to look cross-eyed and can experience eye strain. Some items that are too close may not converge at all and cause "double-vision."

Applications for virtual reality also differ from conventional Android apps in other ways, such as:

- When transitioning from a 2D application into VR, it is recommended that you provide a headset icon for the user to tap, as shown in the following image:

- To exit VR, the user can hit the back button in the system bar (if present) or the home button. The cardboard sample apps use a "tilt-up" gesture to return to the main menu, which is a fine approach if you want to allow a "back" input without forcing the user to remove the phone from the device.

- Make sure that you build your app to run in fullscreen mode (and not in Android's Lights Out mode).

- Do not perform any API calls that will present the user with a 2D dialog box. The user will be forced to remove the phone from the viewer to respond.

- Provide audio and haptic (vibration) feedback to convey information and indicate that the user input is recognized by the app.

So, let's say that you've got your awesome Cardboard app done and it is ready to publish. Now what? There's a line you can put in the `AndroidManifest` file that marks the app as a Cardboard app. Google's Cardboard app includes a Google Play Store browser used to find a Cardboard app. Then just publish it as you would do for any normal Android application.

Summary

In this chapter, we started by defining Google Cardboard and saw how it fits in the spectrum of consumer virtual reality devices. We then contrasted Cardboard with higher end VR devices, such as Oculus Rift, HTC Vive, and PlayStation VR, making the case for low-end VR as a separate medium in its own right. There are a variety of Cardboard viewer devices on the market, and we looked at how to configure your smartphone for your viewer using QR codes. We talked a bit about developing for Cardboard, and considered why and why not to use the Unity 3D game engine versus writing a native Android app in Java with the Cardboard SDK. Lastly we took a quick survey of many design considerations for developing for VR that we'll talk more about throughout the book, including ways to avoid motion sickness and tips for integrating Cardboard with Android apps in general.

In the next chapter we start coding. Yaay! For a common point of reference, we'll spend a little time introducing the Android Studio IDE and reviewing the Cardboard Android classes. Then together we'll build a simple Cardboard app, as we lay the groundwork for the structure and function of other projects throughout the book.

2
The Skeleton Cardboard Project

In this chapter, you will learn how to build a skeleton Cardboard project which can be a starting point for other projects in this book. We will begin with an introduction to Android Studio, the Cardboard SDK, and Java programming. We want to make sure that you're up to speed on the tools and Android projects in general. Then, we will walk you through setting up a new Cardboard project so that we don't need to repeat these details in each project. If some or all of this is already familiar to you, great! You might be able to skim it. In this chapter, we will cover the following topics:

- What's in an Android app?
- The Android project structure
- Getting started with Android Studio
- Creating a new Cardboard project
- Adding the Cardboard Java SDK
- Editing the manifest, layout, and `MainActivity`
- Building and running the app

What's in an Android app?

For our projects, we're going to use the powerful Android Studio IDE (an integrated development environment) to build Google Cardboard virtual reality applications that run on Android devices. *Woot!* Android Studio integrates a number of different tools and processes under one roof.

The result of all your hard work to develop an Android app is an Android application package or an .apk file, which is distributed to users via the Google Play Store or however you choose to distribute your app. This file gets installed on their Android device.

We'll jump to Android Studio itself in a moment. However, in order to shed some light on what's going on here, let's consider this end result .apk file first. What is it really? How'd we get it? Understanding the build process will help.

Keeping this in mind, for fun and to gain perspective, let's start from the end and work our way backward from the APK through the build pipeline to our app source code.

APK files

The APK file is actually a compressed zipped package of a bunch of different files, including the compiled Java code and non-compiled resources, such as images.

An APK file is built for a specific *target* version of Android, but it also indicates a *minimum* version. An app built for an older version of Android, in general, will run on newer Android versions but not vice versa. To build for an older version of Android, however, means that newer features will not be available to the app. You want to choose the minimum version of Android that supports the features you need in order to target as many devices as possible. Or, if you want to support a smaller subset of devices for, say, performance reasons, you might choose an artificially high minimum API version.

To build your project and create an APK file in Android Studio, you need to click on the **Build menu** option and select **Make Project**, (or click on the green arrow icon to build, deploy, and run the app on a device or within an **Android Virtual Device (AVD)**), which kicks off a Gradle build process. You can build a version to develop and debug or build a more optimized release version of the application for distribution. You can choose to do this by clicking on the **Build** menu and selecting **Select Build Variant...**.

A Gradle build process

Android Studio uses a tool named **Gradle** to build the APK file from your project files. The following is a flow diagram of the Gradle build process taken from the Android documentation (http://developer.android.com/sdk/installing/studio-build.html). Actually, most of the illustrated details aren't so important for us. What is important is to see the many pieces and how they fit together.

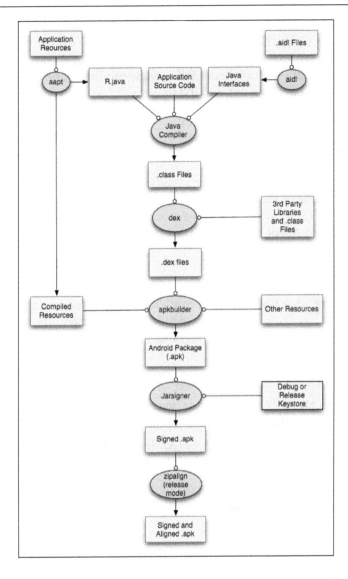

In the bottom-most box in the preceding diagram, you can see that the result of the build is a signed and aligned .apk file, which is the final version of our app that has been compiled (converted from the source code), zipped (compressed), and signed (for authentication) from the earlier build process. The final step, zipalign, aligns the compressed resources along 4-byte boundaries in order to quickly access them at runtime. Basically, this last step makes the app load faster.

In the middle of the diagram, you'll see that the .apk (unsigned, uncompressed) file is assembled from .dex files, compiled Java classes, and other resources (such as images and media files).

A `.dex` file is the Java code, which has been compiled into a format (Dalvik bytecode) that runs on the **Dalvik virtual machine** (**DVM**) on your device. This is an executable file of your program. Any third-party libraries and compiled Java source code files (`.class`) that you have included in your module build are converted to `.dex` files in order to be packaged into the final `.apk` file.

Again, don't sweat the details if this is new to you. The important thing is that we're going to be working with a lot of different files in our Google Cardboard projects. It will be helpful for us to have a context of where they're used in the build process.

For example, the `common.aar` file (binary Android Library Archive) with the Cardboard SDK is one of the third-party libraries which we will use. The contents of your project's `res/` directory, such as `layout/activity_main.xml`, are passed through the **Android Asset Packaging Tool (aapt)**.

A Java compiler

What feeds into the `.dex` file? A Java compiler takes the Java language source code and generates an `.dex` file containing bytecode. By referring to the preceding Gradle build flow diagram, at the top of the diagram, you will see that the inputs to the Java compiler include the following:

- Your application's Java source code

- Your application's XML resources, such as the `AndroidManifest.xml` file, compiled using the **aapt**, and used to generate the `R.java` file

- Your application's Java interfaces (**Android Interface Definition Language** `.aidl` files), compiled using the **aidl** tool

In the rest of this book, we're going to talk a lot about these source code files. That's the stuff you write! That's the place where you do your magic! That's the world where we programmers live.

Let's now take a look at the directory structure of your Android project source code.

The Android project structure

The root directory of your Android project contains various files and subdirectories. Or, should I say, the root folder of your Android project contains various files and *subfolders. Ha ha*. We'll use the words "folder" and "directory" interchangeably throughout this book, just as Android Studio also seems to do (actually, there is a difference, as discussed at `http://stackoverflow.com/questions/29454427/new-directory-vs-new-folder-in-android-studio`).

As shown in the Android hierarchy, in the following sample Cardboard project, the root directory contains an `app/` subdirectory, which, in turn, contains the following subdirectories:

- `app/manifests/`: This contains the `AndroidManifest.xml` manifest file that specifies the components of the application, including activities (UI), device permissions, and other configurations

- `app/java/`: This contains subfolders with your application Java files that implement the application's `MainActivity` and other classes

- `app/res/`: This contains subfolders with resources, including the layout XML definition files, values definitions (`strings.xml`, `styles.xml`, and so on), icons, and other resource files

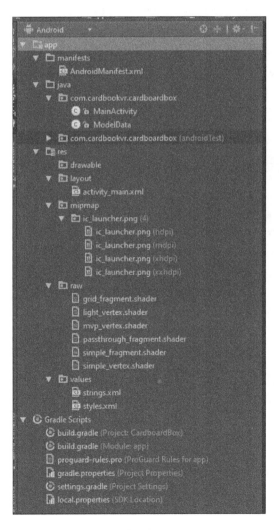

It's not a coincidence that these directories correspond to the boxes in the topmost row of the preceding Gradle build process diagram; they supply the source files that are run through the Java compiler.

Also, there are Gradle scripts under the root directory, which do not need to be edited directly since the Android Studio IDE provides convenient dialog boxes to manage the settings. In some cases, you might find it to be easier to modify these files directly.

Notice that in the upper-left corner of the hierarchy pane is a tab select menu. In the preceding screenshot, it is set to **Android**, which just shows the Android-specific files. There are other views that might also be useful, such as **Project**, which lists all the files and subdirectories under your project root directory, as shown in the following screenshot, for the same app. The **Project** hierarchy shows the files as they are structured on the actual filesystem. The other hierarchies artificially restructure your project to make it easier to work with.

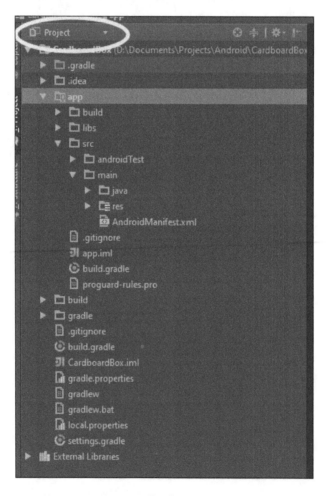

From time to time, you'll need to switch between the **Android** view and **Project** view.

Getting started with Android Studio

When developing Cardboard apps for Android, there's tons of stuff that you need to track, including all your files and folders, Java classes and objects, and functions and variables. You need a properly organized Java program structure and valid language syntax. You need to set options and manage processes to build and debug your applications. *Whew!*

Thank goodness we have Android Studio, a powerful **IDE (integrated development environment)**. It's built on top of IntelliJ IDEA by JetBrains, a popular intelligent Java development suite of tools.

It's intelligent because it actually gives you relevant suggestions as you write your code (*Ctrl + Space*), helps navigate between related references and files (*Ctrl + B, Alt + F7*) as well as automates refactor operations, such as renaming a class or method (*Alt + Enter*). In some ways, it may know what you're trying to do, even if you don't. *How smart is that?*

Installing Android Studio

If you don't already have Android Studio installed on your development machine, what are you waiting for? Head on over to the Android developers page (http://developer.android.com/develop/index.html) and download it to your system. It's available for Windows, Mac OS X, or Linux. You can install the full Android Studio package and not just the SDK tools. Then, obediently follow the installation instructions.

The Android Studio user interface

There's a lot to Android Studio. In most cases, we'll just explain with the help of examples as we go along. But let's take a little time to review a few features, especially the ones that are relevant to Cardboard development. Just make sure that you read the documentation available at the Android developer tools page if needed (http://developer.android.com/tools/studio/index.html).

For a beginner, the Android Studio user interface can seem daunting. And the default interface is only the beginning; editor themes and layouts can be customized to your liking. Worse, it has a tendency to change with new releases, so tutorials can seem out of date. While this can make it challenging for you to find what you need on a particular occasion, the underlying functionality does not change a whole lot. An Android app is an Android app is an Android app, in most cases. We used Android Studio 2.1 for Windows for this book (although some screen captures are from an earlier version, the interface is essentially identical).

While using Android Studio, you may get notifications of the new updates available. We recommend that you do not upgrade in the middle of a project, unless you know that you really need the new improvements. Even so, make sure that you have backups if compatibility issues are introduced.

Let's take a brief tour of the Android Studio window, as shown in the following screenshot:

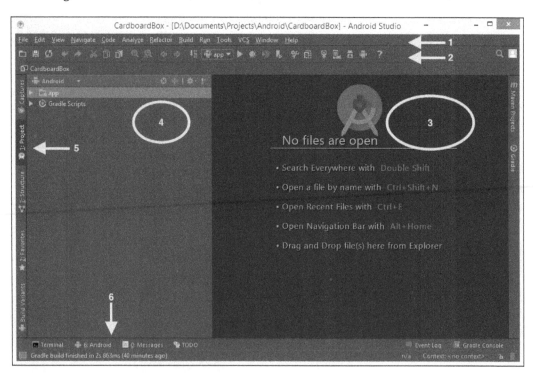

The menus of Android Studio are:

- At the top is the main menu bar (**#1**) with a drop-down menu and pull out menus for just about all the features available.

- Under the menu bar is a convenient main toolbar (**#2**) with shortcuts to common functions. Hovering over an icon shows a tooltip hint of what it does.

- Under the toolbar is the main editor pane (**#3**). When no file is open, it says **No files are open**. The main editor panes are tabbed along the top when multiple files are open.

- The hierarchy navigator pane is on the left-hand side (**#4**).

- The hierarchy navigator pane has tabs along the left-hand side (vertical tabs, **#5**) to select between the various views of your project.

> Notice the select menu on the top left-hand side of the hierarchy pane. In the preceding screenshot, it is set to **Android**, which just shows the Android-specific files. There are other views that might also be useful, such as **Project**, which shows all the files and subdirectories under your project root directory, as mentioned earlier.

- Along the bottom is an additional tool bar (**#6**) used to choose other dynamic tools you might need, including a Terminal window, build messages, debugging information, and even a to-do list. Perhaps the most important one is the Android Monitor **logcat** tab that provides a window to the Android logging system to collect and view the system debug output.

> It will be helpful for you to pay attention to the **Debuggable Application** drop-down menu, **Log Level** and other filters within **logcat** in order to filter out the "log spam" that will make it hard for you to find the output that you are looking for. Also, note that even on a high-end computer with a fast CPU, this log view can slow down Android Studio to a crawl. It is recommended that you hide this view when not in use, especially if you have multiple instances of Android Studio open.

- Controls in the corners of each pane generally pertain to managing the IDE panes themselves.

It can be fun to poke around and browse all the different things Android Studio provides. To learn more, click on the **Help | Help Topics** menu items (or the **?** icon on the toolbar) to open the IntelliJ IDEA help documentation (`https://www.jetbrains.com/idea/help/intellij-idea.html`).

Keep in mind that Android Studio is built on top of the IntelliJ IDE, which can be used for more than just the Android development. So, there's a lot here; some of which you'll never use; others you'll need but might have to hunt for.

 Here's a bit of advice: with great power comes great responsibility (*where have I heard this before?*). Actually, with so many user interface things, a little tunnel vision will come in handy (*yeah, I just made that one up*). Focus on the ones you need to use when you need to use them, and don't sweat the other details.

Before we move on, let's take a glance at the main menu bar. It looks like the following screenshot:

File   Edit   View   Navigate   Code   Analyze   Refactor   Build   Run   Tools   VCS   Window   Help

Reading from left to right, the menu items are organized somewhat parallel to your application development process itself: create, edit, refactor, build, debug, and manage.

- **File**: These are project files and settings
- **Edit**: This includes the cut, copy, paste, and macros options, and so on
- **View**: This allows us to view windows, toolbars, and UI modes
- **Navigate**: This refers to content-based navigation between files
- **Code**: These are code editing shortcuts
- **Analyze**: This is used to inspect and analyze code for errors and inefficiencies
- **Refactor**: This is used to edit code across semantically related files
- **Build**: This builds the project
- **Run**: This is used to run and debug
- **Tools**: This is an interface with external and third-party tools
- **VCS**: The refers to version-control (that is, `git`) commands
- **Window**: This manages the IDE user interface
- **Help**: This includes documentation and help links

There now, was that so scary?

If you haven't already, you might want to try and build the Cardboard Android demo app available from the Google Developers website's Android SDK Getting Started page (refer to `https://developers.google.com/cardboard/android/get-started`).

At the time of writing this book, the demo app is called **Treasure Hunt**, and there are instructions on how to clone the project from its GitHub repository. Just clone it, open it in Android Studio, then click on the green play button to build it, and run it. The rest of the **Getting Started** page walks you through the code that explains the key elements.

Cool! In the next chapter, we will start and rebuild pretty much the same project but from scratch.

Creating a new Cardboard project

With Android Studio installed, let's create a new project. These are the steps you'll follow for any of the projects in this book. We'll just make an empty skeleton and make sure that it can be built and run:

1. After opening the IDE, you'll see a **Welcome** screen, as shown in the following screenshot:

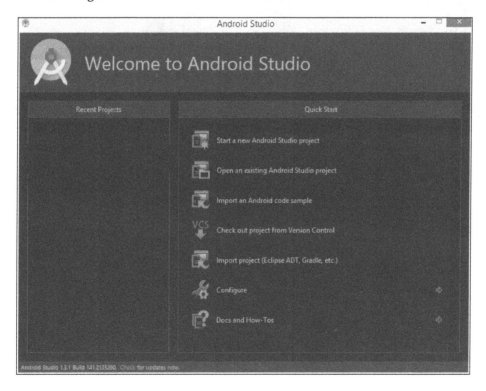

2. Select **Start a new Android Studio project**, and the **New Project** screen appears, as follows:

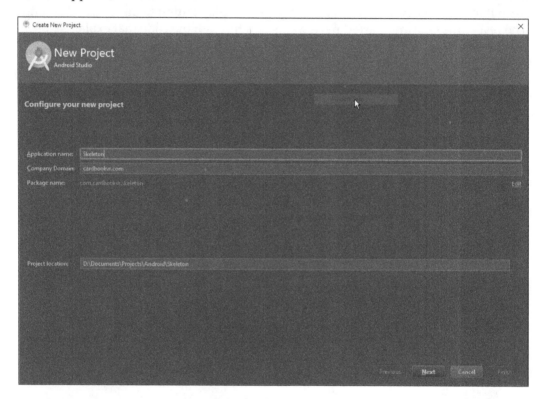

3. Fill in your **Application name:**, such as `Skeleton`, and your **Company Domain:**, for example, `cardbookvr.com`. You can also change the **Project location**. Then, click on **Next**:

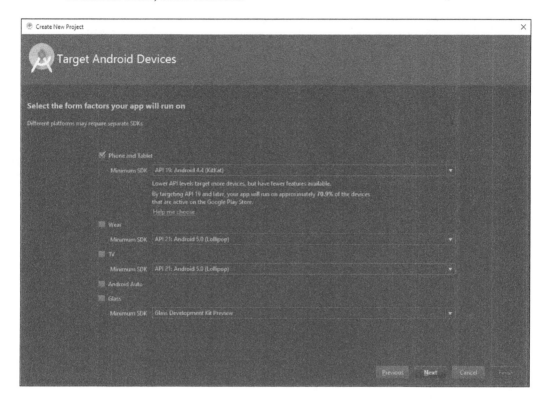

4. On the **Target Android Devices** screen, ensure that the **Phone and Tablet** checkbox is checked. In the **Minimum SDK**, select **API 19: Android 4.4 (KitKat)**. Then, click on **Next**:

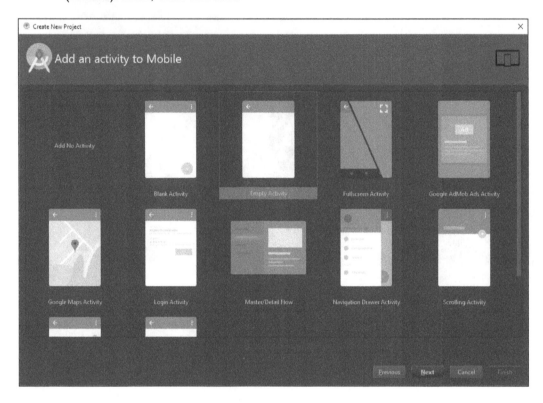

5. On the **Add an activity to Mobile** screen, select **Empty Activity**. We're going to build this project from scratch. Then, click on **Next**:

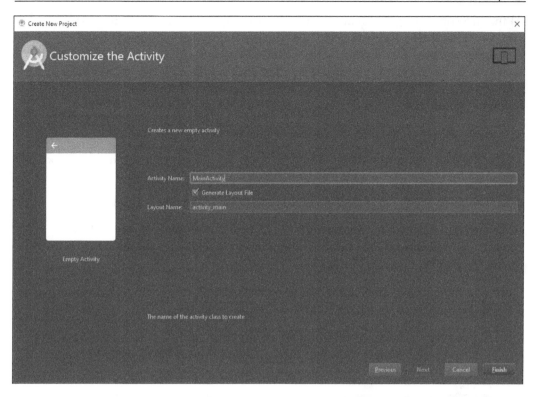

6. Keep the suggested name, `MainActivity`. Then, click on **Finish**.

Your brand new project comes up on Studio. If required, press *Alt + 1* to open the **Project View** (*Command + 1* on the Mac).

Adding the Cardboard Java SDK

Now's a good time to add the Cardboard SDK library `.aar` files to your project. For the basic projects in this book the libraries you need (at the time of writing v0.7) are:

*   `common.aar`
*   `core.aar`

> Note the SDK includes additional libraries that we do not use in the projects in this book but could be useful for your projects. The `audio.aar` file is for spatialized audio support. The `panowidget` and `videowidget` libraries are meant for 2D apps that want to drop-into VR for things such as viewing a 360-degree image or video.

At the time of writing, to obtain the Cardboard Android SDK client libraries, you can clone the `cardboard-java` GitHub repository, as explained on the Google Developers Cardboard Getting Started page, **Start your own project** topic at `https://developers.google.com/cardboard/android/get-started#start_your_own_project`. Clone the `cardboard-java` GitHub repository by running the following command:

```
git clone https://github.com/googlesamples/cardboard-java.git
```

To use the exact commit with the same SDK version 0.7 we're using here, `checkout` the commit:

```
git checkout 67051a25dcabbd7661422a59224ce6c414affdbc -b sdk07
```

Alternatively, the SDK 0.7 library files are included with each of the download projects `.zip` files from Packt Publishing, and on this book's GitHub projects at `https://github.com/cardbookvr`.

Once you have local copies of the libraries, be sure to locate them on your filesystem. To add the libraries to our project, take the following steps:

1. For each of the required libraries, create new modules. In Android Studio, select **File** | **New** | **New Module...**. Select **Import .JAR/.AAR Package**:

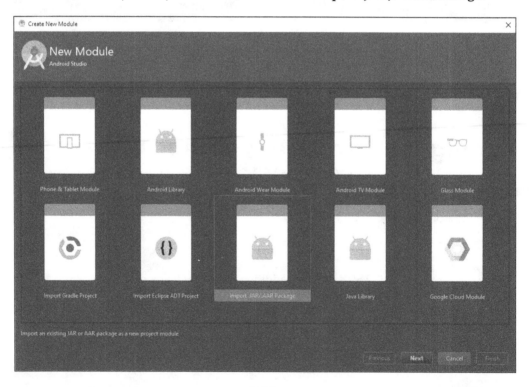

2. Locate one of the AARs and import it.

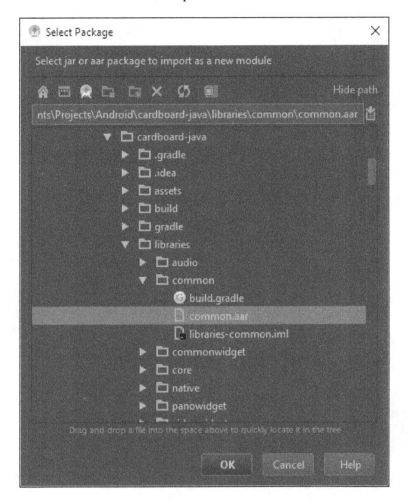

3. Add the new modules as dependencies to your main app by navigating to **File** | **Project Structure** | **Modules** (on the left hand side) | **app** (your app name) | **Dependencies** | **+** | **Module Dependency**:

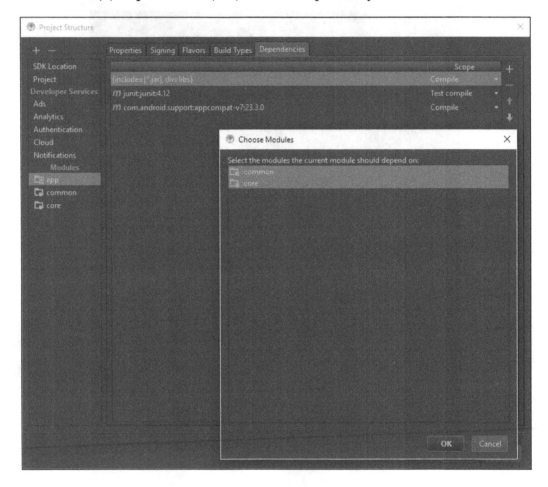

Now we can use the Cardboard SDK in our app.

The AndroidManifest.xml file

The new empty app includes a handful of default files, including the manifests/ AndroidManifest.xml file (this is if you have the **Android** view activated. In the **Project** view, it is in app/src/main). Every application must have an AndroidManifest.xml file in its manifest directory that tells the Android system what it needs in order to run the app's code, along with other metadata.

More information on this can be found at `http://` `developer.android.com/guide/topics/manifest/` `manifest-intro.html`.

Let's set this up first. Open your `AndroidManifest.xml` file in the editor. Modify it to read it as follows:

```xml
<?xml version="1.0" encoding="utf-8"?>
<manifest
    xmlns:android="http://schemas.android.com/apk/res/android"
    package="com.cardbookvr.skeleton" >

    <uses-permission android:name="android.permission.NFC" />
    <uses-permission android:name="android.permission.INTERNET" />
    <uses-permission
    android:name="android.permission.READ_EXTERNAL_STORAGE" />
    <uses-permission
    android:name="android.permission.WRITE_EXTERNAL_STORAGE" />
    <uses-permission android:name="android.permission.VIBRATE" />

    <uses-sdk android:minSdkVersion="16"
    android:targetSdkVersion="19"/>
    <uses-feature android:glEsVersion="0x00020000"
    android:required="true" />
    <uses-feature
    android:name="android.hardware.sensor.accelerometer"
    android:required="true"/>
    <uses-feature android:name="android.hardware.sensor.gyroscope"
    android:required="true"/>

    <application
        android:allowBackup="true"
        android:icon="@mipmap/ic_launcher"
        android:label="@string/app_name"
        android:theme="@style/AppTheme" >
        <activity
            android:name=".MainActivity"

            android:screenOrientation="landscape"
            android:configChanges=
            "orientation|keyboardHidden|screenSize" >

            <intent-filter>
                <action android:name="android.intent.action.MAIN"
                />
```

```
            <category
            android:name="android.intent.category.LAUNCHER" />
            <category
            android:name=
            "com.google.intent.category.CARDBOARD" />
        </intent-filter>
      </activity>
    </application>

  </manifest>
```

The package name show in the preceding listing, `package="com.cardbookvr.skeleton"`, may be different for your project. The `<uses-permission>` tag indicates that the project may be using the NFC sensor, which the Cardboard SDK can use to detect the smartphone that has been inserted into a Cardboard viewer device. The Internet and read/write storage permissions are needed for the SDK to download, read, and write the configure setup options. We will need to do a little more work in order to handle permissions properly, but that happens in another file, which we will discuss later.

The `<uses-feature>` tag specifies that we'll be using the OpenGL ES 2.0 graphics processing library (`http://developer.android.com/guide/topics/graphics/opengl.html`).

It's also strongly recommended that you include the accelerometer and gyroscope sensor `uses-feature` tags. Too many users have phones lacking one or both of these sensors. When the app fails to track their head motions correctly, they may think that the app is to blame rather than their phone. Within the `<application>` tag (the default attributes of which were generated when we created the file), there's an `<activity>` definition named `.MainActivity` and screen settings. Here, we specify the `android:screenOrientation` attribute as our Cardboard app uses the normal (left) landscape orientation. We also specify `android:configChanges` that the activity will handle itself.

These and other attribute settings may vary based on your application's requirements. For example, using `android:screenOrientation="sensorLandscape"` instead will allow either normal or reverse landscape orientations based on the phone's sensor (and trigger the `onSurfaceChanged` callback when the screen flips).

We specify our *intent* metadata in the `<intent-filter>` tag. In Android, an **intent** is a messaging object used to facilitate communication between applications' components. It can also be used to query the apps that are installed and match certain intent filters, as defined in the app's manifest file. For example, an app that wants to take a picture will broadcast an intent with the `ACTION_IMAGE_CAPTURE` action filter. The OS will respond with a list of apps installed which contain activities that can respond to such an action.

Having defined the `MainActivity` class, we'll specify that it can respond to the standard MAIN action and match the LAUNCHER category. MAIN means that this activity is the entry point of the application; that is, when you launch the app, this activity is created. LAUNCHER means that the app should appear in the home screen's launcher as a top-level application.

We've added an intent so that this activity will also match the CARDBOARD category because we want the other apps to see this as a Cardboard app!

Google made major changes to the permissions system in Android 6.0 Marshmallow (API 23). While you still must include the permissions you want within the `AndroidManifest.xml` file, you must now also call a special API function to request permissions at runtime. There are a variety of reasons for this, but the idea is to give the user finer control of app permissions, and avoid having to ask for a long list of permissions during install and at runtime. This new feature also allows users to selectively revoke permissions after they have been granted. This is great for the user, but unfortunate for us app developers, as it means that we need to do significantly more work when we need access to these protected features. Essentially, you need to introduce a step which checks if a particular permission is granted, and prompts the user if it is not. Once the user grants permission, a callback method is called, and you are free to do whatever it was that needed permission. Alternatively, if the permission was granted the whole time, you can proceed to use the restricted feature.

At the time of writing, our project code and the current version of the Cardboard SDK do not implement this new permission system. Instead, we will force Android Studio to build our projects against an older version of the SDK (API 22) so that we side-step the new features. It is possible that, in the future, Android might break backwards compatibility with the old permissions system. However, you can read a very clear guide on how to use the new permissions system in the Android documentation (refer to `http://developer.android.com/training/permissions/requesting.html`). We hope to address this, and any future issues in the online GitHub repositories, but bear in mind that the code in the text, and the provided zip files, may not work on the newest version of Android. Such is the nature of software maintenance.

Let's apply that workaround to build against version 22 of the SDK. Odds are that you just installed Android Studio 2.1 or above, which comes with SDK 23 or above. Whenever you create a new project, Android Studio does ask what minimum SDK you would like to target, but does not let you choose the SDK used for compilation. That's OK, because we can manually set this in the `build.gradle` file. Don't be afraid; the build toolset is big and scary, but we're only tweaking the project settings a little bit. Bear in mind that there are a couple of `build.gradle` files in your project. Each one will be within its corresponding module folder on the filesystem, and will be labeled accordingly within the Gradle scripts section of the Android flavor of the project view. Were looking to change `build.gradle` for the app module. Modify it to look like this:

```
apply plugin: 'com.android.application'

android {
    compileSdkVersion 22

    ...

    defaultConfig {
        minSdkVersion 19
        targetSdkVersion 22

        ...
    }
    ...
}

dependencies {
    compile 'com.android.support:appcompat-v7:22.1.0'
    ...
}
```

The important changes are to compileSdkVersion, minSdkVersion, targetSdkVersion, and that last one in dependencies, where we changed the version of the support repository we are linking to. Technically, we could eliminate this dependency entirely, but the project template includes a bunch of references to it, which are a pain to remove. However, if we leave the default setting, Gradle will most likely yell at us about mismatching versions. Once you've made these changes, there should be a yellow bar at the top of the editor with a link that says **Sync now**. Sync now. If you're lucky, the Gradle sync will finish successfully, and you can go on your merry way. If not, you might be missing the SDK platform or other dependencies. The **Messages** window should have clickable links to install and update the Android system appropriately. If you hit an error, try restarting Android Studio.

From this point on, you might want to avoid updating Android Studio or your SDK platform versions. Pay special attention to what happens when you import your project on another computer or after updates to Android Studio. You will likely need to let the IDE manipulate your Gradle files, and it may modify your compile version. This permissions issue is sneaky, in that it will only reveal itself at runtime on phones running 6.0 and above. Your app may appear to work just fine on a device running an older version of Android, but actually run into trouble on newer devices.

The activity_main.xml file

Our app needs a layout where we'll define a canvas to paint our graphics. The new project created by Android Studio makes a default layout file in the `app/res/layout/` folder (using the Android view or `app/src/main/res/layout` using the **Project** view). Find the `activity_main.xml` file and double-click on it to edit it.

There are two views of a layout file in the Android Studio editor: **Design** versus **Text**, selected by tabs on the lower-left hand side of the window pane. If the **Design** view tab is selected, you'll see an interactive editor with a simulated smartphone image, a palette of UI components on the left-hand side, and a **Properties** editor on the right-hand side. We're not going to use this view. If necessary, select the **Text** tab at the bottom of the `activity_main.xml` editor pane to use text mode.

Cardboard apps should run on the full screen, so we remove any padding. We will also remove the default `TextView` that we're not going to use. Instead, we replace it with a `CardboardView`, as follows:

```xml
<?xml version="1.0" encoding="utf-8"?>
<RelativeLayout
xmlns:android="http://schemas.android.com/apk/res/android"
    xmlns:tools="http://schemas.android.com/tools"
    android:layout_width="match_parent"
    android:layout_height="match_parent"
    tools:context=".MainActivity">

    <com.google.vrtoolkit.cardboard.CardboardView
        android:id="@+id/cardboard_view"
        android:layout_width="fill_parent"
        android:layout_height="fill_parent"
        android:layout_alignParentTop="true"
        android:layout_alignParentLeft="true" />

</RelativeLayout>
```

The `AndroidManifest.xml` file references the main activity named `MainActivity`. Let's take a look at that now.

The MainActivity class

The default project generated with `Empty Activity` also created a default `MainActivity.java` file. In the hierarchy pane, locate the `app/java/` directory that contains a subdirectory named `com.cardbookvr.skeleton`.

 Note, this is different than the `androidTest` version of the directory, we're not using that one! (Your name may vary based on the actual project and domain names given when you created the project.)

In this folder, double-click on the `MainActivity.java` file to open it for editing. The default file looks like this:

```
package com.cardbookvr.skeleton;
import ...
public class MainActivity extends AppCompatActivity {
    @Override
    protected void onCreate(Bundle savedInstanceState) {
        super.onCreate(savedInstanceState);
        setContentView(R.layout.activity_main);
    }
}
```

The first thing you should notice is the extends `AppCompatActivity` class (or `ActionBarActivity`) for the built-in Android action bar. We do not need this. We will rather define the activity to the extends `CardboardActivity` and implements the `CardboardView.StereoRenderer` interfaces. Modify the class declaration line of code, as follows:

```
public class MainActivity extends CardboardActivity implements
CardboardView.StereoRenderer {
```

As this is a Google Cardboard application, we need to define the `MainActivity` class as a child class of the `CardboardActivity` class given by the SDK. We do this using the `extends` keyword.

`MainActivity` needs to also implement, at a minimum, the stereo renderer interface defined as `CardboardView.StereoRender`. We do this using the `implements` keyword.

One of the nice things about Android Studio is how it does work for you as you write the code. When you enter `extends CardboardActivity`, the IDE automatically adds an `import` statement for the `CardboardActivity` class at the top of the file. When you enter `implements CardboardView.StereoRenderer`, it adds an `import` statement to the `CardboardView` class.

As we continue to add code, Android Studio will identify when we need additional import statements and automatically add them for us. Therefore, I won't bother to show you the `import` statements in the code that follows. On occasion it may find the wrong one when, for example, there's multiple `Camera` or `Matrix` classes among your libraries, and you'll need to resolve it to the correct reference.

We'll now fill in the body of the `MainActivity` class with stubs for the functions that we're going to need. The `CardboardView.StereoRenderer` interface that we're using defines a number of abstract methods that we can override, as documented in the Android API Reference for the interface (refer to `https://developers.` `google.com/cardboard/android/latest/reference/com/google/vrtoolkit/` `cardboard/CardboardView.StereoRenderer`).

This is quickly accomplished in Studio in a number of ways. Either use the intellisense context menu (the light bulb icon) or go to **Code | Implement Methods…** (or *Ctrl* + *I*). By placing your cursor at the red error underline and pressing *Alt* + *Enter*, you will also be able to accomplish the same goal. Do it now. You will be asked to confirm the methods to implement, as shown in the following screenshot:

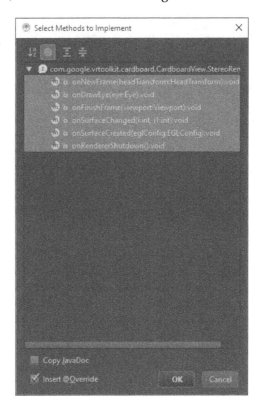

Ensure that all are selected and click on **OK**.

Stubs for the following methods will be added to the `MainActivity` class:

- `onSurfaceCreated`: This is called when the surface is created or recreated. It should create buffers and variables needed to display graphics.

- `onNewFrame`: This is called when a new frame is about to be drawn. It should update the application data that changes from one frame to the next, such as animations.

- `onDrawEye`: This renders the scene for one eye for the current camera viewpoint (called twice per frame, unless you have three eyes!).

- `onFinishFrame`: This is called before a frame is finished.

- `onRenderShutdown`: This is called when the renderer thread is shutting down (rarely used).

- `onSurfaceChanged`: This is called when there is a change in the surface dimensions (for example, when a portrait/landscape rotation is detected).

I've listed these methods in an order that mirrors the life cycle of a Cardboard Android application.

The `@Override` directive means that these functions are originally defined in the `CardboardView.StereoRenderer` interface and we're replacing (overriding) them in our `MainActivity` class here.

Default onCreate

All Android activities expose an `onCreate()` method that is called when the activity is first created. This is where you should do all your normal static setups and bindings. The stereo renderer interface and Cardboard activity class are the foundations of the Cardboard SDK.

The default `onCreate` method makes a standard `onCreate` call to the parent activity. Then, it registers the `activity_main` layout as the current content view.

Edit `onCreate()` by adding the `CardboadView` instance, as follows:

```
@Override
protected void onCreate(Bundle savedInstanceState) {
    super.onCreate(savedInstanceState);
    setContentView(R.layout.activity_main);

    CardboardView cardboardView = (CardboardView)
    findViewById(R.id.cardboard_view);
    cardboardView.setRenderer(this);
    setCardboardView(cardboardView);
}
```

To set up the `CardboardView` instance for the app, we get its instance by looking it up by the resource ID given in `activity_main.xml` and then set it up with a couple of function calls.

This object is going to do the stereoscopic rendering to the display, so we call `setRenderer(this)` to specify it as the receiver of the `StereoRenderer` interface methods.

 Note that your activity doesn't have to implement the interface. You can have any class define these methods, such as an abstracted renderer as we'll see later in this book.

Then we associate the `CardboardView` class with this activity by calling `setCardboardView(cardboardView)` so that we'll be able to receive any required life cycle notifications, including the `StereoRenderer` interface methods, such as `onSurfaceCreated` and `onDrawEye`.

Building and running

Let's build and run it:

1. Go to **Run** | **Run 'app'**, or simply use the green-triangle **Run** icon on the toolbar.

2. If you've made changes, Gradle will do its build thing.

3. Select the **Gradle Console** tab at the bottom of the Android Studio window to view the Gradle build messages. Then, assuming that all goes well, the APK will be installed on your connected phone (it's connected and turned on, right?).

4. Select the **Run** tab at the bottom to view the upload and launch messages.

You shouldn't get any build errors. But of course, the app doesn't actually do anything or draw anything on the screen. Well, that's not entirely true! The Cardboard SDK, via `CardboardView.StereoRenderer`, provides a stereoscopic split screen with a vertical line in between and a gear icon, as shown in the following screenshot:

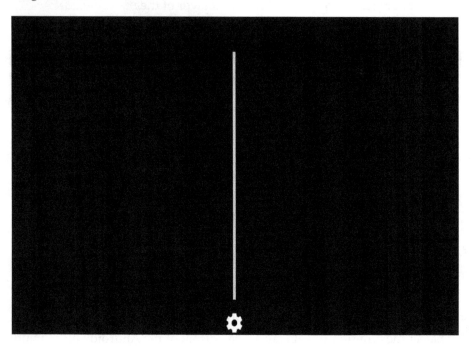

The vertical line will be used to align your phone properly on the Cardboard viewer device.

The gear icon opens the standard configuration settings utility which includes the ability to scan a QR code to configure the SDK for the lenses and other physical attributes of your specific device (as explained in *Chapter 1, Virtual Reality for Everyone*, in the *Configuring your Cardboard viewer* section).

Now, we've built a skeleton Google Cardboard app for Android. You'll follow similar steps to start each project in this book.

Summary

In this chapter, we examined the structure of a Cardboard app for Android and many of the files involved, including the Java source code, XML manifest, .aar libraries, and final built APK, which runs on your Android device. We installed and took a brief tour of the Android Studio development environment. Then, we walked you through the steps to create a new Android project, add the Cardboard Java SDK, and define the `AndroidManifest.xml` file and layout, as well as a stubbed `MainActivity` Java class file. You will follow similar steps to start each Cardboard project in this book.

In the next chapter, we will build a Google Cardboard project from scratch called `CardboardBox` with a scene containing some simple geometry (a triangle and a cube), 3D transformations, and shaders that render graphics to your Cardboard device.

3
Cardboard Box

Remember when you were a kid and happy to just play in a cardboard box? This project might even be more fun than that! Our first Cardboard project will be a simple scene with a box (a geometric cube), a triangle, and a bit of user interaction. Let's call it "CardboardBox." Get it?

Specifically, we're going to create a new project, build a simple app that just draws a triangle, then enhance the app to draw a shaded 3D cube, and illustrate some user interactions by highlighting the cube when you look at it.

In this chapter, you will be:

- Creating a new Cardboard project
- Adding a triangle object to the scene, including geometry, simple shaders, and render buffers
- Using a 3D camera, perspective, and head rotation
- Using model transformations
- Making and drawing a cube object
- Adding a light source and shading
- Spinning the cube
- Adding a floor
- Highlighting the object that the user is looking at

The project in this chapter is derived from an example application provided by the Google Cardboard team called *Treasure Hunt*. Originally, we considered instructing you to simply download Treasure Hunt, and we'd walk you through the code explaining how it works. Instead, we decided to build a similar project from scratch, explaining as we go along. This also mitigates the possibility that Google changes or even replaces that project after this book is published.

The source code for this project can be found on the Packt Publishing website and on GitHub at `https://github.com/cardbookvr/cardboardbox` (with each topic as a separate commit).

The Android SDK version is important to your finished app, but your desktop environment can also be set up in a number of ways. We mentioned earlier that we used Android Studio 2.1 to build the projects in this book. We also used the Java SDK Version 8 (1.8). It will be important for you to have this version installed (you can have many versions installed side by side) in order to import the projects. As with any development environment, any changes made to Java or Android Studio may "break" the import process in the future, but the actual source code should compile and run for many years to come.

Creating a new project

If you'd like more details and explanation about these steps, refer to the *Creating a new Cardboard project* section in *Chapter 2, The Skeleton Cardboard Project*, and follow along there:

1. With Android Studio opened, create a new project. Let's name it `CardboardBox` and target **Android 4.4 KitKat (API 19)** with an **Empty Activity**.

2. Add the Cardboard SDK `common.aar` and `core.aar` library files to your project as new modules, using **File | New | New Module...**.

3. Set the library modules as dependencies to the project app, using **File | Project Structure**.

4. Edit the `AndroidManifest.xml` file as explained in *Chapter 2, The Skeleton Cardboard Project*, being careful to preserve the `package` name for this project.

5. Edit the `build.gradle` file as explained in *Chapter 2, The Skeleton Cardboard Project*, to compile against SDK 22.

6. Edit the `activity_main.xml` layout file as explained in *Chapter 2, The Skeleton Cardboard Project*.

7. Edit the `MainActivity` Java class so that it `extends CardboardActivity` and `implements CardboardView.StereoRenderer`. Modify the class declaration line as follows:

   ```
   public class MainActivity extends CardboardActivity
   implements CardboardView.StereoRenderer {
   ```

8. Add the stub method overrides for the interface (using intellisense implement methods or pressing *Ctrl + I*).

9. At the top of the `MainActivity` class, add the following comments as placeholders for variables that we will be creating in this project:

```
CardboardView.StereoRenderer {
    private static final String TAG = "MainActivity";

    // Scene variables
    // Model variables
    // Viewing variables
    // Rendering variables
```

10. Lastly, edit `onCreate()` by adding the `CardboadView` instance as follows:

```
@Override
protected void onCreate(Bundle savedInstanceState) {
    super.onCreate(savedInstanceState);
    setContentView(R.layout.activity_main);

    CardboardView cardboardView = (CardboardView)
findViewById(R.id.cardboard_view);
    cardboardView.setRenderer(this);
    setCardboardView(cardboardView);
}
```

Hello, triangle!

Let's add a triangle to the scene. Yeah, I know that a triangle isn't even a box. However, we're going to start with super simple tips. Triangles are the building blocks of all 3D graphics and the simplest shapes that OpenGL can render (that is, in triangle mode).

Introducing geometry

Before moving on, let's talk a little about geometry.

Virtual reality is largely about creating 3D scenes. Complex models are organized as three-dimensional data with vertices, faces, and meshes, forming objects that can be hierarchically assembled into more complex models. For now, we're taking a really simple approach—a triangle with three vertices, stored as a simple Java array.

The triangle is composed of three vertices (that's why, it's called a **tri-angle**!). We're going to define our triangle as top (0.0, 0.6), bottom-left (-0.5, -0.3), bottom-right (0.5, -0.3). The first vertex is the topmost point of the triangle and has *X=0.0*, so it's at the center and *Y=0.6* up.

The order of the vertices, or triangle winding, is very important as it indicates the front-facing direction of the triangle. OpenGL drivers expect it to wind in a counter-clockwise direction, as shown in the following diagram:

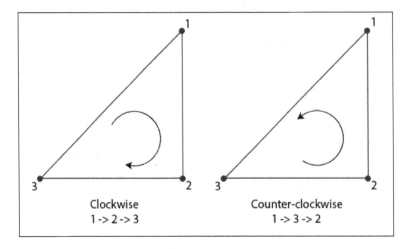

If the vertices are defined clockwise, the shader will assume that the triangle is facing the other direction, away from the camera, and will thus not be visible and rendered. This is an optimization called **culling**, which allows the rendering pipeline to readily throw away geometry that is on the back side of an object. That is, if it is not visible to the camera, don't even bother trying to draw it. Having said this, you can set various culling modes to choose to only render front faces, back faces, or both.

Refer to the creative commons source at `http://learnopengl.com/#!Advanced-OpenGL/Face-culling`.

> *The OpenGL Programming Guide* by Dave Shreiner, Graham Sellers, John M. Kessenich, Bill Licea-Kane, "*By convention, polygons whose vertices appear in a counter-clockwise order on the screen are called front-facing.*" This is determined by a global state mode, and the default value is GL_CCW (`https://www.opengl.org/wiki/Face_Culling`).

Three-dimensional points, or vertices, are defined with x, y, and z coordinate values. A triangle, for example, in 3D space is made up of three vertices, each having an x, y, and z value.

Our triangle lies on a plane parallel to the screen. When we add 3D viewing to the scene (later in this chapter), we'll need a *z* coordinate to place it in 3D space. In anticipation, we'll set the triangle on the *Z=-1* plane. The default camera in OpenGL is at the origin (0,0,0) and looks down at the negative *z* axis. In other words, objects in the scene are looking up the positive *z* axis at the camera. We put the triangle one unit away from the camera so that we can see it at *Z=-1.0*.

Triangle variables

Add the following code snippet to the top of the `MainActivity` class:

```
// Model variables
private static final int COORDS_PER_VERTEX = 3;
private static float triCoords[] = {
    // in counter-clockwise order
    0.0f,   0.6f, -1.0f, // top
   -0.5f,  -0.3f, -1.0f, // bottom left
    0.5f,  -0.3f, -1.0f  // bottom right
};

private final int triVertexCount = triCoords.length /
COORDS_PER_VERTEX;
// yellow-ish color
private float triColor[] = { 0.8f, 0.6f, 0.2f, 0.0f };
private FloatBuffer triVerticesBuffer;
```

Our triangle coordinates are assigned to the `triCoords` array. All the vertices are in 3D space with three coordinates (*x*, *y*, and *z*) per vertex (COORDS_PER_VERTEX). The `triVertexCount` variable, precalculated as the length of the triangle's `triCoords` array, is divided by COORDS_PER_VERTEX. We also define an arbitrary `triColor` value for our triangle, which is composed of R, G, B, and A values (red, green, blue, and alpha (transparency)). The `triVerticesBuffer` variable will be used in the draw code.

For those who are new to Java programming, you might also wonder about the variable types. Integers are declared `int` and floating point numbers are declared `float`. All the variables here are being declared `private`, which means that they'll only be visible and used within this class definition. The ones that are declared `static` will share their data across multiple instances of the class. The ones that are declared `final` are immutable and are not expected to change once they are initialized.

onSurfaceCreated

The purpose of this activity code is to draw stuff on the Android device display. We do this through the OpenGL graphics library, which draws onto a surface, a memory buffer onto which you can draw graphics via a rendering pipeline.

After the activity is created (`onCreate`), a surface is created and `onSurfaceCreated` is called. It has several responsibilities, including initializing the scene and compiling the shaders. It also prepares for rendering by allocating memory for vertex buffers, binding textures, and initializing the render pipeline handles.

Here's the method, which we've broken into several private methods that we're going to write next:

```
@Override
public void onSurfaceCreated(EGLConfig eglConfig) {
    initializeScene();
    compileShaders();
    prepareRenderingTriangle();
}
```

There's nothing to initialize in the scene at this point:

```
private void initializeScene() {
}
```

Let's move on to the shaders and rendering discussions.

Introducing OpenGL ES 2.0

Now is a good time to introduce the *graphics pipeline*. When a Cardboard app draws 3D graphics on the screen, it hands the rendering to a separate graphics processor (GPU). Android and our Cardboard app uses the OpenGL ES 2.0 standard graphics library.

OpenGL is a specification for how applications interact with graphics drivers. You could say that it's a long list of function calls that do things in graphics hardware. Hardware vendors write their drivers to conform to the latest specification, and some intermediary, in this case Google, creates a library that hooks into driver functions in order to provide method signatures that you can call from whatever language you're using (generally, Java, C++, or C#).

OpenGL ES is the mobile, or **Embedded Systems**, version of OpenGL. It follows the same design patterns as OpenGL, but its version history is very different. Different versions of OpenGL ES and even different implementations of the same version will require different approaches to drawing 3D graphics. Thus, your code might differ greatly between OpenGL ES 1.0, 2.0, and 3.0. Thankfully, most major changes happened between Version 1 and 2, and the Cardboard SDK is set up to use 2.0. The `CardboardView` interface also varies slightly from a normal `GLSurfaceView`.

To draw graphics on the screen, OpenGL needs two basic things:

- The graphics programs, or *shaders* (sometimes used interchangeably), which define how to draw shapes
- The data, or *buffers*, which define what is being drawn

There are also some parameters that specify transformation matrices, colors, vectors, and so on. You might be familiar with the concept of a game loop, which is a basic pattern to set up the game environment and then initiate a loop that runs some game logic, renders the screen, and repeats at a semi-regular interval until the game is paused or the program exits. The `CardboardView` sets up the game loop for us, and basically, all that we have to do is implement the interface methods.

A bit more on shaders: at the bare minimum, we need a vertex shader and a fragment shader. The vertex shader is responsible for transforming the vertices of an object from world space (where they are in the world) to screen space (where they should be drawn on the screen).

The fragment shader is called on each pixel that the shape occupies (determined by the raster function, a fixed part of the pipeline) and returns the color that is drawn. Every shader is a single function, accompanied by a number of attributes that can be used as inputs.

A collection of functions (that is, a vertex and a fragment) is compiled by OpenGL into a program. Sometimes, whole programs are referred to as shaders, but this is a colloquialism that assumes the basic knowledge that more than one function, or *shader*, is required to fully draw an object. The program and the values for all its parameters will sometimes be referred to as a *material*, given that it completely describes the material of the surface that it draws.

Shaders are cool. However, they don't do anything until your program sets up the data buffers and makes a bunch of draw calls.

A draw call consists of a **Vertex Buffer Object** (**VBO**), the shaders that will be used to draw it, a number of parameters that specify the transformation applied to the object, the texture(s) used to draw it, and any other shader parameters.

The VBO refers to any and all data used to describe the shape of an object. A very basic object (for example, a triangle) only needs an array of vertices. The vertices are read in order, and every three positions in space define a single triangle. Slightly more advanced shapes use an array of vertices and an array of indices, which define which vertices to draw in what order. Using an index buffer, multiple vertices can be re-used.

While OpenGL can draw a number of shape types (a point, line, triangle, and quad), we will assume that all are triangles. This is both a performance optimization and a matter of convenience. If we want a quad, we can draw two triangles. If we want a line, we can draw a really long, skinny quad. If we want a point, we can draw a tiny triangle. This way, not only can we leave OpenGL in triangle mode, but we can also treat all VBOs in exactly the same manner. Ideally, you want your render code to be completely agnostic to what it is rendering.

To summarize:

- The purpose of the OpenGL graphics library is to give us access to the GPU hardware, which then paints pixels on the screen based on the geometry in a scene. This is achieved through a rendering pipeline, where data is transformed and passed through a series of shaders.

- A shader is a small program that takes certain inputs and generates corresponding outputs, depending on the stage of the pipeline.

- As a program, shaders are written in a special C-like language. The source code is compiled to be run very efficiently on the Android device's GPU.

For example, a *vertex shader* handles processing individual vertices, outputting a transformed version of each one. Another step rasterizes the geometry, after which a *fragment shader* receives a raster fragment and outputs colored pixels.

We'll be discussing the OpenGL rendering pipeline later on, and you can read about it at `https://www.opengl.org/wiki/Rendering_Pipeline_Overview`.

You can also review the Android OpenGL ES API Guide at `http://developer.android.com/guide/topics/graphics/opengl.html`.

For now, don't worry too much about it and let's just follow along.

Note: GPU drivers actually implement the entire OpenGL library on a per-driver basis. This means that someone at NVIDIA (or in this case, probably Qualcomm or ARM) wrote the code that compiles your shaders and reads your buffers. OpenGL is a specification for how this API should work. In our case, this is the GL class that's part of Android.

Simple shaders

Presently, we'll write a couple of simple shaders. Our shader code will be written in a separate file, which is loaded and compiled by our app. Add the following functions at the end of the `MainActivity` class:

```
/**
 * Utility method for compiling a OpenGL shader.
 *
 * @param type - Vertex or fragment shader type.
 * @param resId - int containing the resource ID of the shader
 * code file.
 * @return - Returns an id for the shader.
 */
private int loadShader(int type, int resId){
    String code = readRawTextFile(resId);
    int shader = GLES20.glCreateShader(type);

    // add the source code to the shader and compile it
    GLES20.glShaderSource(shader, code);
    GLES20.glCompileShader(shader);

    return shader;
}


/**
 * Converts a raw text file into a string.
 *
 * @param resId The resource ID of the raw text file about to
 * be turned into a shader.
 * @return The content of the text file, or null in case of
 * error.
 */
private String readRawTextFile(int resId) {
    InputStream inputStream =
    getResources().openRawResource(resId);
    try {
        BufferedReader reader = new BufferedReader(new
        InputStreamReader(inputStream));
        StringBuilder sb = new StringBuilder();
        String line;
        while ((line = reader.readLine()) != null) {
            sb.append(line).append("\n");
        }
        reader.close();
```

```
        return sb.toString();
    } catch (IOException e) {
        e.printStackTrace();
    }
    return null;
}
```

We will call `loadShader` to load a shader program (via `readRawTextFile`) and compile it. This code will be useful in other projects as well.

Now, we'll write a couple of simple shaders in the `res/raw/simple_vertex.shader` and `res/raw/simple_fragment.shader` files.

In the **Project Files** hierarchy view, on the left-hand side of Android Studio, locate the `app/res/` resource folder, right-click on it, and go to **New | Android Resource Directory**. In the **New Resource Directory** dialog box, from **Resource Type:**, select **Raw**, and then click on **OK**.

Right-click on the new `raw` folder, go to **New | File**, and name it `simple_vertex.shader`. Add the following code:

```
attribute vec4 a_Position;
void main() {
    gl_Position = a_Position;
}
```

Similarly, for the fragment shader, right-click on the `raw` folder, go to **New | File**, and name it `simple_fragment.shader`. Add the following code:

```
precision mediump float;
uniform vec4 u_Color;
void main() {
    gl_FragColor = u_Color;
}
```

Basically, these are identity functions. The vertex shader passes through the given vertex, and the fragment shader passes through the given color.

Notice the names of the parameters that we declared: an attribute named a_Position in `simple_vertex` and a uniform variable named u_Color in `simple_fragment`. We'll set these up from the `MainActivity onSurfaceCreated` method. Attributes are properties of each vertex, and when we allocate buffers for them, they must all be arrays of equal length. Other attributes that you will encounter are vertex normals, texture coordinates, and vertex colors. Uniforms will be used to specify information that applies to the whole material, such as in this case, the solid color applied to the whole surface.

Also, note that the `gl_FragColor` and `gl_Position` variables are built-in variable names that OpenGL is looking for you to set. Think of them as the returns on your shader function. There are other built-in output variables, which we will see later.

The compileShaders method

We're now ready to implement the `compileShaders` method that `onSurfaceCreated` calls.

Add the following variables on top of `MainActivity`:

```
// Rendering variables
private int simpleVertexShader;
private int simpleFragmentShader;
```

Implement `compileShaders`, as follows:

```
private void compileShaders() {
    simpleVertexShader = loadShader(GLES20.GL_VERTEX_SHADER,
    R.raw.simple_vertex);
    simpleFragmentShader =
    loadShader(GLES20.GL_FRAGMENT_SHADER,
    R.raw.simple_fragment);
}
```

The prepareRenderingTriangle method

The `onSurfaceCreated` method prepares for rendering by allocating memory for vertex buffers, creating OpenGL programs, and initializing the render pipeline handles. We will do this for our triangle shape now.

Add the following variables on top of `MainActivity`:

```
// Rendering variables
private int triProgram;
private int triPositionParam;
private int triColorParam;
```

Here's a skeleton of the function:

```
private void prepareRenderingTriangle() {
    // Allocate buffers
    // Create GL program
    // Get shader params
}
```

We need to prepare some memory buffers that will be passed to OpenGL when each frame is rendered. This is the first go-round for our triangle and simple shaders; we now only need a vertex buffer:

```
// Allocate buffers
// initialize vertex byte buffer for shape coordinates (4
bytes per float)
ByteBuffer bb = ByteBuffer.allocateDirect(triCoords.length
* 4);
// use the device hardware's native byte order
bb.order(ByteOrder.nativeOrder());

// create a floating point buffer from the ByteBuffer
triVerticesBuffer = bb.asFloatBuffer();
// add the coordinates to the FloatBuffer
triVerticesBuffer.put(triCoords);
// set the buffer to read the first coordinate
triVerticesBuffer.position(0);
```

These five lines of code result in the setting up of the triVerticesBuffer value, which are as follows:

- A ByteBuffer is allocated that is big enough to hold our triangle coordinate values

- The binary data is arranged to match the hardware's native byte order

- The buffer is formatted for a floating point and assigned to our FloatBuffer vertex buffer

- The triangle data is put into it, and then we reset the buffer cursor position to the beginning

Next, we build the OpenGL ES program executable. Create an empty OpenGL ES program using glCreateProgram, and assign its ID as triProgram. This ID will be used in other methods as well. We attach any shaders to the program, and then build the executable with glLinkProgram:

```
// Create GL program
// create empty OpenGL ES Program
triProgram = GLES20.glCreateProgram();
// add the vertex shader to program
GLES20.glAttachShader(triProgram, simpleVertexShader);
// add the fragment shader to program
GLES20.glAttachShader(triProgram, simpleFragmentShader);
// build OpenGL ES program executable
GLES20.glLinkProgram(triProgram);
// set program as current
GLES20.glUseProgram(triProgram);
```

Lastly, we get a handle on the render pipeline. A call to `glGetAttribLocation` on `a_Position` retrieves the location of the vertex buffer parameter, `glEnableVertexAttribArray` gives permission to access it, and a call to `glGetUniformLocation` on `u_Color` retrieves the location of the color components. We'll be happy that we did this once we get to `onDrawEye`:

```
// Get shader params
// get handle to vertex shader's a_Position member
triPositionParam = GLES20.glGetAttribLocation(triProgram,
"a_Position");
// enable a handle to the triangle vertices
GLES20.glEnableVertexAttribArray(triPositionParam);
// get handle to fragment shader's u_Color member
triColorParam = GLES20.glGetUniformLocation(triProgram,
"u_Color");
```

So, we've isolated the code needed to prepare a drawing of the triangle model in this function. First, it sets up buffers for the vertices. Then, it creates a GL program, attaching the shaders it'll use. Then, we get handles to the parameters in the shaders that we'll use to draw.

onDrawEye

Ready, Set, and Go! If you think of what we've written so far as the "Ready Set" part, now we do the "Go" part! That is, the app starts and creates the activity, calling `onCreate`. The surface is created and calls `onSurfaceCreated` to set up the buffers and shaders. Now, as the app runs, for each frame, the display is updated. Go!

The `CardboardView.StereoRenderer` interface delegates these methods. We can handle `onNewFrame` (and will later on). For now, we'll just implement the `onDrawEye` method, which will draw the contents from the point of view of an eye. This method gets called twice, once for each eye.

All that `onDrawEye` needs to do for now is render our lovely triangle. Nonetheless, we'll split it into a separate function (that'll make sense later):

```
@Override
public void onDrawEye(Eye eye) {
    drawTriangle();
}

private void drawTriangle() {
    // Add program to OpenGL ES environment
    GLES20.glUseProgram(triProgram);
```

```
    // Prepare the coordinate data
    GLES20.glVertexAttribPointer(triPositionParam,
    COORDS_PER_VERTEX,
            GLES20.GL_FLOAT, false, 0, triVerticesBuffer);

    // Set color for drawing
    GLES20.glUniform4fv(triColorParam, 1, triColor, 0);

    // Draw the model
    GLES20.glDrawArrays(GLES20.GL_TRIANGLES, 0,
    triVertexCount);
}
```

We need to specify which shader program we are using by calling `glUseProgram`. A call to `glVertexAttribPointer` sets our vertex buffer to the pipeline. We also set the color using `glUniform4fv` (4fv refers to the fact that our uniform is a vector with four floats). Then, we actually draw using `glDrawArrays`.

Building and running

That's it. *Yee haa!* That wasn't so bad, was it? Actually, if you're familiar with Android development and OpenGL, you might have breezed through this.

Let's build and run it. Go to **Run | Run 'app'**, or simply use the green triangle **Run** icon on the toolbar.

Gradle will do its build thing. Select the **Gradle Console** tab at the bottom of the Android Studio window to view the Gradle build messages. Then, assuming that all goes well, the APK file will be installed on your connected phone (it's connected and turned on, right?). Select the **Run** tab at the bottom to view the upload and launch messages.

This is what it displays:

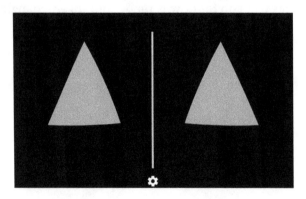

Actually, it kind of looks like a Halloween pumpkin carving! *Spooky*. But in VR you'll see just a single triangle.

Notice that while the triangle vertex coordinates define edges with straight lines, the `CardboardView` renders it with barrel distortion to compensate for the lens optics in the headset. Also, the left image is different from the right, one for each eye. When you insert the phone in a Google Cardboard headset, the left and right stereoscopic views appear as one triangle floating in space with straight edges.

That's great! We just built a simple Cardboard app for Android from scratch. Like any Android app, there are a number of different pieces that need to be defined just to get a basic thing going, including the `AndroidManifest.xml`, `activity_main.xml`, and `MainActivity.java` files.

Hopefully everything went as planned. Like a good programmer, you've probably been building and running the app after making incremental changes to the account for syntax errors and unhandled exceptions. A little bit later, we will call the GLError function to check error information from OpenGL. As always, pay close attention to errors in logcat (try filtering for the running application) and to variable names. You might have a syntax error in your shader, causing its compiling to fail, or you might have a typo in the attribute/uniform name when trying to access the handles. These kind of things will not result in any compile-time errors (shaders are compiled at runtime), and your app will run but may not render anything as a result.

3D camera, perspective, and head rotation

As awesome as this is (*ha ha*), our app is kind of boring and not very Cardboard-like. Specifically, it's stereoscopic (dual views) and has lens distortion, but it's not yet a 3D perspective view and it doesn't move with your head. We're going to fix this now.

Welcome to the matrix

We can't talk about developing for virtual reality without talking about matrix mathematics for 3D computer graphics.

What is a matrix? The answer is out there, Neo, and it's looking for you, and it will find you if you want it to. That's right, it's time to learn about the matrix. Everything will be different now. Your perspective is about to change.

We're building a three-dimensional scene. Each location in space is described by the X, Y, and Z coordinates. Objects in the scene may be constructed from X, Y, and Z vertices. An object can be transformed by moving, scaling, and/or rotating its vertices. This transformation can be represented mathematically with a matrix of 16 floating point values (four rows of four floats each). How it works mathematically is cool, but we won't get into it here.

Matrices can be combined by multiplying them together. For example, if you have a matrix that represents how much to resize an object (scale) and another matrix to reposition (translate), then you could make a third matrix, representing both the resizing and repositioning by multiplying the two together. You can't just use the primitive * operator though. Also, note that unlike a simple scalar multiplication, matrix multiplication is not commutative. In other words, we know that $a * b = b * a$. However, for matrices A and B, $AB \neq BA$! The Matrix Android class library provides functions for doing matrix math. Here's an example:

```
// allocate the matrix arrays
float scale[] = new float[16];
float translate[] = new float[16];
float scaleAndTranslate[] = new float[16];

// initialize to Identity
Matrix.setIdentityM(scale, 0);
Matrix.setIdentityM(translate, 0);

// scale by 2, move by 5 in Z
Matrix.scaleM(scale, 0, 2.0, 2.0, 2.0);
Matrix.translateM(translate, 0, 0, 0.0, 0.0, 5.0);

// combine them with a matrix multiply
Matrix.multipyMM(scaleAndTranslate, 0, translate, 0, scale, 0);
```

Note that due to the way in which matrix multiplication works, multiplying a vector by the result matrix will have the same effect as first multiplying it by the scale matrix (right-hand side), and then multiplying it by the translate matrix (left-hand side). This is the opposite of what you might expect.

 The documentation of the Matrix API can be found at http://developer.android.com/reference/android/opengl/Matrix.html.

This matrix stuff will be used a lot. Something that is worth mentioning here is precision loss. You might get a "drift" from the actual values if you repeatedly scale and translate that combined matrix because floating point calculations lose information due to rounding. It's not just a problem for computer graphics but also for banks and Bitcoin mining! (Remember the movie *Office Space*?)

One fundamental use of this matrix math, which we need immediately, is to transform a scene into a screen image (projection) as viewed from the user's perspective.

In a Cardboard VR app, to render the scene from a particular viewpoint, we think of a camera that is looking in a specific direction. The camera has X, Y, and Z positions like any other object and is rotated to its view direction. In VR, when you turn your head, the Cardboard SDK reads the motion sensors in your phone, determines the current head pose (the view direction and angles), and gives your app the corresponding transformation matrix.

In fact, in VR for each frame, we render two slightly different perspective views: one for each eye, offset by the actual distance between one's eyes (the interpupillary distance).

Also, in VR, we want to render the scene using a perspective projection (versus isometric) so that objects closer to you appear larger than the ones further away. This can be represented with a 4 x 4 matrix as well.

We can combine each of these transformations by multiplying them together to get a `modelViewProjection` matrix:

```
modelViewProjection = modelTransform X camera  X  eyeView  X
perspectiveProjection
```

A complete `modelViewProjection` (MVP) transformation matrix is a combination of any model transforms (for example, scaling or positioning the model in the scene) with the camera eye view and perspective projection.

When OpenGL goes to draw an object, the vertex shader can use this `modelViewProjection` matrix to render the geometry. The whole scene gets drawn from the user's viewpoint, in the direction his head is pointing, with a perspective projection for each eye to appear stereoscopically through your Cardboard viewer. VR MVP FTW!

The MVP vertex shader

The super simple vertex shader that we wrote earlier doesn't transform each vertex; it just passed it through the next step in the pipeline. Now, we want it to be 3D-aware and use our `modelViewProjection` (MVP) transformation matrix. Create a shader to handle it.

In the hierarchy view, right-click on the `app/res/raw` folder, go to **New | File**, enter the name, `mvp_vertex.shader`, and click on **OK**. Write the following code:

```
uniform mat4 u_MVP;
attribute vec4 a_Position;
void main() {
    gl_Position = u_MVP * a_Position;
}
```

This shader is almost the same as `simple_vertex` but transforms each vertex by the `u_MVP` matrix. (Note that while multiplying matrices and vectors with `*` does not work in Java, it does work in the shader code!)

Replace the shader resource in the `compleShaders` function to use `R.raw.mvp_vertex` instead:

```
simpleVertexShader = loadShader(GLES20.GL_VERTEX_SHADER,
R.raw.mvp_vertex)
```

Setting up the perspective viewing matrices

To add the camera and view to our scene, we define a few variables. In the `MainActivity.java` file, add the following code to the beginning of the `MainActivity` class:

```
// Viewing variables
private static final float Z_NEAR = 0.1f;
private static final float Z_FAR = 100.0f;
private static final float CAMERA_Z = 0.01f;

private float[] camera;
private float[] view;
private float[] modelViewProjection;

// Rendering variables
private int triMVPMatrixParam;
```

The `Z_NEAR` and `Z_FAR` constants define the depth planes used later to calculate the perspective projection for the camera eye. `CAMERA_Z` will be the position of the camera (for example, at X=0.0, Y=0.0, and Z=0.01).

The `triMVPMatrixParam` variable will be used to set the model transformation matrix in our improved shader.

The `camera`, `view`, and `modelViewProjection` matrices will be 4 x 4 matrices (an array of 16 floats) used for perspective calculations.

In `onCreate`, we initialize the `camera`, `view`, and `modelViewProjection` matrices:

```
protected void onCreate(Bundle savedInstanceState) {
    //...

    camera = new float[16];
    view = new float[16];
    modelViewProjection = new float[16];
}
```

In `prepareRenderingTriangle`, we initialize the `triMVPMatrixParam` variable:

```
// get handle to shape's transformation matrix
triMVPMatrixParam = GLES20.glGetUniformLocation(triProgram,
"u_MVP");
```

The default camera in OpenGL is at the origin (0,0,0) and looks down at the negative Z axis. In other words, objects in the scene are facing toward the positive Z axis at the camera. To place them in front of the camera, give them a position with some negative Z value.

There is a longstanding (and pointless) debate in the 3D graphics world about which axis is up. We can somehow all agree that the X axis goes left and right, but does the Y axis go up and down, or is it Z? Plenty of software picks Z as the up-and-down direction, and defines Y as pointing in and out of the screen. On the other hand, the Cardboard SDK, Unity, Maya, and many others choose the reverse. If you think of the coordinate plane as drawn on graph paper, it all depends on where you put the paper. If you think of the graph as you look down from above, or draw it on a whiteboard, then Y is the vertical axis. If the graph is sitting on the table in front of you, then the *missing* Z axis is vertical, pointing up and down. In any case, the Cardboard SDK, and therefore the projects in this book, treat Z as the *forward and backward* axis.

Render in perspective

With things set up, we can now handle redrawing the screen for each frame.

First, set the camera position. It can be defined once, like in `onCreate`. But, often in a VR application, the camera position in the scene can change, so we'll reset it for each frame.

The first thing to do is reset the camera matrix at the start of a new frame to a generic front-facing direction. Define the onNewFrame method, as follows:

```
@Override
public void onNewFrame(HeadTransform headTransform) {
    // Build the camera matrix and apply it to the ModelView.
    Matrix.setLookAtM(camera, 0, 0.0f, 0.0f, CAMERA_Z, 0.0f,
    0.0f, 0.0f, 0.0f, 1.0f, 0.0f);
}
```

Note, as you write Matrix, Android Studio will want to auto-import the package. Ensure that the import you choose is android.opengl.Matrix, and not some other matrix library, such as android.graphic.Matrix.

Now, when it's time to draw the scene from the viewpoint of each eye, we calculate the perspective view matrix. Modify onDrawEye as follows:

```
public void onDrawEye(Eye eye) {
    GLES20.glEnable(GLES20.GL_DEPTH_TEST);
    GLES20.glClear(GLES20.GL_COLOR_BUFFER_BIT |
    GLES20.GL_DEPTH_BUFFER_BIT);

    // Apply the eye transformation to the camera
    Matrix.multiplyMM(view, 0, eye.getEyeView(), 0, camera,
    0);

    // Get the perspective transformation
    float[] perspective = eye.getPerspective(Z_NEAR, Z_FAR);

    // Apply perspective transformation to the view, and draw
    Matrix.multiplyMM(modelViewProjection, 0, perspective, 0,
    view, 0);

    drawTriangle();
}
```

The first two lines that we added reset the OpenGL depth buffer. When 3D scenes are rendered, in addition to the color of each pixel, OpenGL keeps track of the distance the object occupying that pixel is from the eye. If the same pixel is rendered for another object, the depth buffer will know whether it should be visible (closer) or ignored (further away). (Or, perhaps the colors get combined in some way, for example, transparency). We clear the buffer before rendering any geometry for each eye. The color buffer, which is the one you actually see on screen, is also cleared. Otherwise, in this case, you would end up filling the entire screen with a solid color.

Now, let's move on to the viewing transformations. onDrawEye receives the current Eye object, which describes the stereoscopic rendering details of the eye. In particular, the eye.getEyeView() method returns a transformation matrix that includes head tracking rotation, position shift, and interpupillary distance shift. In other words, where the eye is located in the scene and what direction it's looking. Though Cardboard does not offer positional tracking, the positions of the eyes do change in order to simulate a virtual head. Your eyes don't rotate on a central axis, but rather your head pivots around your neck, which is a certain distance from the eyes. As a result, when the Cardboard SDK detects a change in orientation, the two virtual cameras move around the scene as though they were actual eyes in an actual head.

We need a transformation that represents the perspective view of the camera at this eye's position. As mentioned earlier, this is calculated as follows:

```
modelViewProjection = modelTransform  X  camera  X  eyeView  X
perspectiveProjection
```

We multiply the camera by the eye view transform (getEyeView), then multiply the result by the perspective projection transform (getPerspective). Presently, we do not transform the triangle model itself and leave the modelTransform matrix out.

The result (modelViewProjection) is passed to OpenGL to be used by the shaders in the rendering pipeline (via glUniformMatrix4fv). Then, we draw our stuff (via glDrawArrays as written earlier).

Now, we need to pass the view matrix to the shader program. In the drawTriangle method, add it as follows:

```
private void drawTriangle() {
    // Add program to OpenGL ES environment
    GLES20.glUseProgram(triProgram);

    // Pass the MVP transformation to the shader
    GLES20.glUniformMatrix4fv(triMVPMatrixParam, 1, false,
    modelViewProjection, 0);

    // . . .
```

Building and running

Let's build and run it. Go to **Run** | **Run 'app'**, or simply use the green triangle **Run** icon on the toolbar. Now, moving the phone will change the display synchronized with your view direction. Insert the phone in a Google Cardboard viewer and it's like VR (*kinda sorta*).

Note that if your phone is lying flat on the table when the app starts, the camera in our scene will be facing straight down rather than forward at our triangle. What's worse, when you pick up the phone, the neutral direction may not be facing straight in front of you. So, each time you run apps in this book, pick up the phone first, so you look forward in VR, or keep the phone propped up in position (personally, I use a Gekkopod, which is available at http://gekkopod.com/).

Also, in general, make sure that your phone is not set to **Lock Portrait** in the **Settings** dialog box.

Repositioning the triangle

Our matrix-fu has really gotten us places. Let's go further.

I want to move the triangle out of the way. We'll do this by setting up another transformation matrix and then using it on the model when it's time to draw.

Add two new matrices named `triTransform` and `triView`:

```
// Model variables
private float[] triTransform;

// Viewing variables
private float[] triView;
```

Initialize them in `onCreate` as well:

```
triTransform = new float[16];
triView = new float[16];
```

Let's set the model matrix that positions the triangle in the `initializeScene` method (called by `onSurfaceCreated`). We'll offset it by 5 units in X and backwards 5 units in Z. Add the following code to `initializeScene`:

```
// Position the triangle
Matrix.setIdentityM(triTransform, 0);
Matrix.translateM(triTransform, 0, 5, 0, -5);
```

Lastly, we use the model matrix to build the `modelViewProjection` matrix in `onDrawEye`. Modify `onDrawEye`, as follows:

```
public void onDrawEye(Eye eye) {
    ...
    // Apply perspective transformation to the view, and draw
    Matrix.multiplyMM(triView, 0, view, 0, triTransform, 0);
```

```
    Matrix.multiplyMM(modelViewProjection, 0, perspective, 0,
    triView, 0);
    drawTriangle();
}
```

Build and run it. You will now see the triangle further away and off to the side.

> To summarize one more time: the modelViewProjection matrix is a combination of the triangle's position transform (triTransform), the camera's location and orientation (camera), the current eye's viewpoint from CardboardView based on the phone's motion sensors (eye.getEyeView), and the perspective projection. This MVP matrix is handed to the vertex shader to determine its actual location when drawing the triangle on the screen.

Hello, cube!

A flat triangle floating in 3D space may be amazing, but it's nothing compared to what we're going to do next: a 3D cube!

The cube model data

The triangle, with just three vertices, was declared in the MainActivity class to keep the example simple. Now, we will introduce more complex geometry. We'll put it in a class named Cube.

Okay, it's just a cube that is composed of eight distinct vertices, forming six faces, right?

Well, GPUs prefer to render triangles rather than quads, so subdivide each face into two triangles; that's 12 triangles in total. To define each triangle separately, that's a total of 36 vertices, with proper winding directions, defining our model, as shown in CUBE_COORDS. Why not just define eight vertices and reuse them? We'll show you how to do this later.

> Remember that we always need to be careful of the winding order of the vertices (counter-clockwise) so that the visible side of each triangle is facing outward.

In Android Studio, in the Android project hierarchy pane on the left-hand side, find your Java code folder (such as com.cardbookvr.cardboardbox). Right-click on it, and go to **New | Java Class**. Then, set **Name: Cube**, and click on **OK**. Then, edit the file, as follows (remember that the code for the projects in this book are available for download from the publisher's website and from the book's public GitHub repositories):

```java
package com.cardbookvr.cardboardbox;

public class Cube {

    public static final float[] CUBE_COORDS = new float[] {
        // Front face
        -1.0f, 1.0f, 1.0f,
        -1.0f, -1.0f, 1.0f,
        1.0f, 1.0f, 1.0f,
        -1.0f, -1.0f, 1.0f,
        1.0f, -1.0f, 1.0f,
        1.0f, 1.0f, 1.0f,

        // Right face
        1.0f, 1.0f, 1.0f,
        1.0f, -1.0f, 1.0f,
        1.0f, 1.0f, -1.0f,
        1.0f, -1.0f, 1.0f,
        1.0f, -1.0f, -1.0f,
        1.0f, 1.0f, -1.0f,

        // Back face
        1.0f, 1.0f, -1.0f,
        1.0f, -1.0f, -1.0f,
        -1.0f, 1.0f, -1.0f,
        1.0f, -1.0f, -1.0f,
        -1.0f, -1.0f, -1.0f,
        -1.0f, 1.0f, -1.0f,

        // Left face
        -1.0f, 1.0f, -1.0f,
        -1.0f, -1.0f, -1.0f,
        -1.0f, 1.0f, 1.0f,
        -1.0f, -1.0f, -1.0f,
        -1.0f, -1.0f, 1.0f,
        -1.0f, 1.0f, 1.0f,
```

```
        // Top face
        -1.0f,  1.0f, -1.0f,
        -1.0f,  1.0f,  1.0f,
         1.0f,  1.0f, -1.0f,
        -1.0f,  1.0f,  1.0f,
         1.0f,  1.0f,  1.0f,
         1.0f,  1.0f, -1.0f,

        // Bottom face
         1.0f, -1.0f, -1.0f,
         1.0f, -1.0f,  1.0f,
        -1.0f, -1.0f, -1.0f,
         1.0f, -1.0f,  1.0f,
        -1.0f, -1.0f,  1.0f,
        -1.0f, -1.0f, -1.0f,
    };
}
```

Cube code

Returning to the `MainActivity` file, we'll just copy/paste/edit the triangle code and reuse it for the cube. Obviously, this isn't ideal, and once we see a good pattern, we can abstract out some of this into reusable methods. Also, we'll use the same shaders as those of the triangle, and then in the next section, we'll replace them with a better lighting model. That is to say, we'll implement lighting or what a 2D artist might call **shading**, which we haven't done so far.

Like the triangle, we declare a bunch of variables that we are going to need. The vertex count, obviously, should come from the new `Cube.CUBE_COORDS` array:

```
// Model variables
private static float cubeCoords[] = Cube.CUBE_COORDS;
private final int cubeVertexCount = cubeCoords.length /
COORDS_PER_VERTEX;
private float cubeColor[] = { 0.8f, 0.6f, 0.2f, 0.0f }; //
yellow-ish
private float[] cubeTransform;
private float cubeDistance = 5f;

// Viewing variables
private float[] cubeView;

// Rendering variables
private FloatBuffer cubeVerticesBuffer;
```

```
        private int cubeProgram;
        private int cubePositionParam;
        private int cubeColorParam;
        private int cubeMVPMatrixParam;
```

Add the following code to onCreate:

```
        cubeTransform = new float[16];
        cubeView = new float[16];
```

Add the following code to onSurfaceCreated:

```
        prepareRenderingCube();
```

Write the prepareRenderingCube method, as follows:

```
    private void prepareRenderingCube() {
        // Allocate buffers
        ByteBuffer bb =
        ByteBuffer.allocateDirect(cubeCoords.length * 4);
        bb.order(ByteOrder.nativeOrder());
        cubeVerticesBuffer = bb.asFloatBuffer();
        cubeVerticesBuffer.put(cubeCoords);
        cubeVerticesBuffer.position(0);

        // Create GL program
        cubeProgram = GLES20.glCreateProgram();
        GLES20.glAttachShader(cubeProgram, simpleVertexShader);
        GLES20.glAttachShader(cubeProgram, simpleFragmentShader);
        GLES20.glLinkProgram(cubeProgram);
        GLES20.glUseProgram(cubeProgram);

        // Get shader params
        cubePositionParam =
        GLES20.glGetAttribLocation(cubeProgram, "a_Position");
        cubeColorParam = GLES20.glGetUniformLocation(cubeProgram,
        "u_Color");
        cubeMVPMatrixParam =
        GLES20.glGetUniformLocation(cubeProgram, "u_MVP");

        // Enable arrays
        GLES20.glEnableVertexAttribArray(cubePositionParam);
    }
```

We will position the cube 5 units away and rotate it 30 degrees on a diagonal axis of (1, 1, 0). Without the rotation, we'll just see the square of the front face. Add the following code to `initializeScene`:

```
// Rotate and position the cube
Matrix.setIdentityM(cubeTransform, 0);
Matrix.translateM(cubeTransform, 0, 0, 0, -cubeDistance);
Matrix.rotateM(cubeTransform, 0, 30, 1, 1, 0);
```

Add the following code to `onDrawEye` to calculate the MVP matrix, including the `cubeTransform` matrix, and then draw the cube:

```
Matrix.multiplyMM(cubeView, 0, view, 0, cubeTransform, 0);
Matrix.multiplyMM(modelViewProjection, 0, perspective, 0,
cubeView, 0);
drawCube();
```

Write the `drawCube` method, which is very similar to the `drawTri` method, as follows:

```
private void drawCube() {
    GLES20.glUseProgram(cubeProgram);
    GLES20.glUniformMatrix4fv(cubeMVPMatrixParam, 1, false,
    modelViewProjection, 0);
    GLES20.glVertexAttribPointer(cubePositionParam,
    COORDS_PER_VERTEX,
            GLES20.GL_FLOAT, false, 0, cubeVerticesBuffer);
    GLES20.glUniform4fv(cubeColorParam, 1, cubeColor, 0);
    GLES20.glDrawArrays(GLES20.GL_TRIANGLES, 0,
    cubeVertexCount);
}
```

Build and run it. You will now see a 3D view of the cube, as shown in the following screenshot. It needs shading.

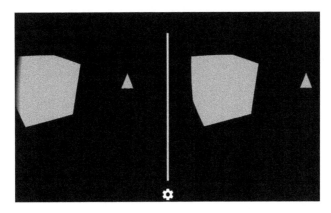

Lighting and shading

We need to introduce a light source into the scene and provide a shader that will use it. For this, the cube needs additional data, defining normal vectors and colors at each vertex.

> Vertex colors aren't always required for shading, but in our case, the gradient is very subtle, and the different color faces will help you distinguish the edges of the cube. We will also be doing shading calculations in the vertex shader, which is a faster way to do it (there are fewer vertices than raster pixels), but works less well for smooth objects, such as spheres. To do vertex lighting, you need vertex colors in the pipeline, so it also makes sense to do something with those colors. In this case, we choose a different color per face of the cube. Later in this book, you will see an example of per-pixel lighting and the difference it makes.

We'll now build the app to handle our lighted cube. We'll do this by performing the following steps:

- Write and compile a new shader for lighting
- Generate and define cube vertex normal vectors and colors
- Allocate and set up data buffers for rendering
- Define and set up a light source for rendering
- Generate and set up transformation matrices for rendering

Adding shaders

Let's write an enhanced vertex shader that can use a light source and vertex normals from a model.

Right-click on the `app/res/raw` folder in the project hierarchy, go to **New | File**, and name it `light_vertex.shader`. Add the following code:

```
uniform mat4 u_MVP;
uniform mat4 u_MVMatrix;
uniform vec3 u_LightPos;

attribute vec4 a_Position;
attribute vec4 a_Color;
attribute vec3 a_Normal;
```

```
const float ONE = 1.0;
const float COEFF = 0.00001;

varying vec4 v_Color;

void main() {
    vec3 modelViewVertex = vec3(u_MVMatrix * a_Position);
    vec3 modelViewNormal = vec3(u_MVMatrix * vec4(a_Normal, 0.0));

    float distance = length(u_LightPos - modelViewVertex);
    vec3 lightVector = normalize(u_LightPos - modelViewVertex);
    float diffuse = max(dot(modelViewNormal, lightVector), 0.5);

    diffuse = diffuse * (ONE / (ONE + (COEFF * distance * distance)));
    v_Color = a_Color * diffuse;
    gl_Position = u_MVP * a_Position;
}
```

Without going through the details of writing a lighting shader, you can see that the vertex color is calculated based on a formula related to the angle between the light ray and the surface and how far the light source is from the vertex. Note that we are also bringing in the ModelView matrix as well as the MVP matrix. This means that you will need to have access to both steps of the process, and you can't overwrite/throw away the MV matrix after you're done with it.

Notice that we used a small optimization. Numeric literals (for example, 1.0) use uniform space, and on certain hardware, this can cause problems, so we declare constants instead (refer to http://stackoverflow.com/questions/13963765/declaring-constants-instead-of-literals-in-vertex-shader-standard-practice-or).

There are more variables to be set in this shader, as compared to the earlier simple one, for the lighting calculations. We'll send these over to the draw methods.

We also need a slightly different fragment shader. Right-click on the raw folder in the project hierarchy, go to **New** | **File**, and name it passthrough_fragment.shader. Add the following code:

```
precision mediump float;
varying vec4 v_Color;

void main() {
    gl_FragColor = v_Color;
}
```

The only difference in the fragment shader from the simple one is that we replace uniform vec4 u_Color with varying vec4 v_Color because colors are now passed in from the vertex shader in the pipeline. And the vertex shader now gets an array buffer of colors. This is a new issue that we'll need to address in our setup/draw code.

Then, in MainActivity, add these variables:

```
// Rendering variables
private int lightVertexShader;
private int passthroughFragmentShader;
```

Compile the shader in the compileShaders method:

```
lightVertexShader = loadShader(GLES20.GL_VERTEX_SHADER,
        R.raw.light_vertex);
passthroughFragmentShader =
loadShader(GLES20.GL_FRAGMENT_SHADER,
        R.raw.passthrough_fragment);
```

Cube normals and colors

Each face of a cube faces outwards in a different direction that's perpendicular to the face. A vector is an XYZ coordinate. One that is normalized to a length of 1 can be used to indicate this direction, and is called a **normal vector**.

The geometry we pass to OpenGL is defined as vertices, not faces. Therefore, we need to provide a normal vector for each vertex of the face, as shown in the following diagram. Strictly speaking, not all vertices on a given face have to face the same direction. This is used in a technique called **smooth shading**, where the lighting calculations give the illusion of a curved face instead of a flat one. We will be using the same normal for each face (**hard edges**), which also saves us time while specifying the normal data. Our array only needs to specify six vectors, which can be expanded into a buffer of 36 normal vectors. The same applies to color values.

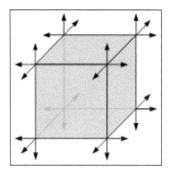

Each vertex also has a color. Assuming that each face of the cube is a solid color, we can assign each vertex of that face the same color. In the Cube.java file, add the following code:

```
public static final float[] CUBE_COLORS_FACES = new float[] {
    // Front, green
    0f, 0.53f, 0.27f, 1.0f,
    // Right, blue
    0.0f, 0.34f, 0.90f, 1.0f,
    // Back, also green
    0f, 0.53f, 0.27f, 1.0f,
    // Left, also blue
    0.0f, 0.34f, 0.90f, 1.0f,
    // Top, red
    0.84f,  0.18f,  0.13f, 1.0f,
    // Bottom, also red
    0.84f,  0.18f,  0.13f, 1.0f,
};

public static final float[] CUBE_NORMALS_FACES = new float[] {
    // Front face
    0.0f, 0.0f, 1.0f,
    // Right face
    1.0f, 0.0f, 0.0f,
    // Back face
    0.0f, 0.0f, -1.0f,
    // Left face
    -1.0f, 0.0f, 0.0f,
    // Top face
    0.0f, 1.0f, 0.0f,
    // Bottom face
    0.0f, -1.0f, 0.0f,
};
```

For each face of the cube, we defined a solid color (CUBE_COLORS_FACES) and a normal vector (CUBE_NORMALS_FACES).

Now, write a reusable method, cubeFacesToArray, to generate the float arrays actually needed in MainActivity. Add the following code to your Cube class:

```
/**
 * Utility method for generating float arrays for cube faces
 *
 * @param model - float[] array of values per face.
```

```
 * @param coords_per_vertex - int number of coordinates per
 vertex.
 * @return - Returns float array of coordinates for
 triangulated cube faces.
 *                    6 faces X 6 points X coords_per_vertex
 */
public static float[] cubeFacesToArray(float[] model, int
coords_per_vertex) {
    float coords[] = new float[6 * 6 * coords_per_vertex];
    int index = 0;
    for (int iFace=0; iFace < 6; iFace++) {
        for (int iVertex=0; iVertex < 6; iVertex++) {
            for (int iCoord=0; iCoord < coords_per_vertex;
            iCoord++) {
                coords[index] = model[iFace*coords_per_vertex
                + iCoord];
                index++;
            }
        }
    }
    return coords;
}
```

Add this data to `MainActivity` with the other variables, as follows:

```
// Model variables
private static float cubeCoords[] = Cube.CUBE_COORDS;
private static float cubeColors[] =
Cube.cubeFacesToArray(Cube.CUBE_COLORS_FACES, 4);
private static float cubeNormals[] =
Cube.cubeFacesToArray(Cube.CUBE_NORMALS_FACES, 3);
```

You can also delete the declaration of `private float cubeColor[]`, as it's not needed now.

Armed with a normal and color, the shader can calculate the values of each pixel occupied by the object.

Preparing the vertex buffers

The rendering pipeline requires that we set up memory buffers for the vertices, normals, and colors. We already have vertex buffers from before, we now need to add the others.

Add the variables, as follows:

```
// Rendering variables
private FloatBuffer cubeVerticesBuffer;
private FloatBuffer cubeColorsBuffer;
private FloatBuffer cubeNormalsBuffer;
```

Prepare the buffers, and add the following code to the prepareRenderingCube method (called from onSurfaceCreated). (This is the first half of the full prepareRenderingCube method):

```
private void prepareRenderingCube() {
    // Allocate buffers
    ByteBuffer bb =
    ByteBuffer.allocateDirect(cubeCoords.length * 4);
    bb.order(ByteOrder.nativeOrder());
    cubeVerticesBuffer = bb.asFloatBuffer();
    cubeVerticesBuffer.put(cubeCoords);
    cubeVerticesBuffer.position(0);

    ByteBuffer bbColors =
    ByteBuffer.allocateDirect(cubeColors.length * 4);
    bbColors.order(ByteOrder.nativeOrder());
    cubeColorsBuffer = bbColors.asFloatBuffer();
    cubeColorsBuffer.put(cubeColors);
    cubeColorsBuffer.position(0);

    ByteBuffer bbNormals =
    ByteBuffer.allocateDirect(cubeNormals.length * 4);
    bbNormals.order(ByteOrder.nativeOrder());
    cubeNormalsBuffer = bbNormals.asFloatBuffer();
    cubeNormalsBuffer.put(cubeNormalParam);
    cubeNormalsBuffer.position(0);

    // Create GL program
```

Preparing the shaders

Having defined the lighting_vertex shader, we need to add the param handles to use it. At the top of the MainActivity class, add four more variables to the lighting shader params:

```
// Rendering variables
private int cubeNormalParam;
private int cubeModelViewParam;
private int cubeLightPosParam;
```

In the `prepareRenderingCube` method (which is called by `onSurfaceCreated`), attach the `lightVertexShader` and `passthroughFragmentShader` shaders instead of the simple ones, get the shader params, and enable the arrays so that they now read as follows. (This is the second half of `prepareRenderingCube`, continuing from the preceding section):

```
// Create GL program
cubeProgram = GLES20.glCreateProgram();
GLES20.glAttachShader(cubeProgram, lightVertexShader);
GLES20.glAttachShader(cubeProgram,
passthroughFragmentShader);
GLES20.glLinkProgram(cubeProgram);
GLES20.glUseProgram(cubeProgram);

// Get shader params
cubeModelViewParam =
GLES20.glGetUniformLocation(cubeProgram, "u_MVMatrix");
cubeMVPMatrixParam =
GLES20.glGetUniformLocation(cubeProgram, "u_MVP");
cubeLightPosParam =
GLES20.glGetUniformLocation(cubeProgram, "u_LightPos");

cubePositionParam =
GLES20.glGetAttribLocation(cubeProgram, "a_Position");
cubeNormalParam = GLES20.glGetAttribLocation(cubeProgram,
"a_Normal");
cubeColorParam = GLES20.glGetAttribLocation(cubeProgram,
"a_Color");

// Enable arrays
GLES20.glEnableVertexAttribArray(cubePositionParam);
GLES20.glEnableVertexAttribArray(cubeNormalParam);
GLES20.glEnableVertexAttribArray(cubeColorParam);
```

If you refer to the shader code that we wrote earlier, you'll notice that these calls to `glGetUniformLocation` and `glGetAttribLocation` correspond to the `uniform` and `attribute` parameters declared in those scripts, including the change of `cubeColorParam` from `u_Color` to now `a_Color`. This renaming is not required by OpenGL, but it helps us distinguish between vertex attributes and uniforms.

Shader attributes that reference array buffers must be enabled.

Adding a light source

Next, we'll add a light source to our scene and tell the shader its position when we draw. The light will be positioned just above the user.

At the top of `MainActivity`, add variables to the light position:

```
// Scene variables
// light positioned just above the user
private static final float[] LIGHT_POS_IN_WORLD_SPACE = new
float[] { 0.0f, 2.0f, 0.0f, 1.0f };
private final float[] lightPosInEyeSpace = new float[4];
```

Calculate the position of the light by adding the following code to `onDrawEye`:

```
// Apply the eye transformation to the camera
Matrix.multiplyMM(view, 0, eye.getEyeView(), 0, camera,
0);

// Calculate position of the light
Matrix.multiplyMV(lightPosInEyeSpace, 0, view, 0,
LIGHT_POS_IN_WORLD_SPACE, 0);
```

Note that we're using the `view` matrix (the eye `view` * `camera`) to transform the light position into the current view space using the `Matrix.multiplyMV` function.

Now, we just tell the shader about the light position and the viewing matrices it needs. Modify the `drawCube` method (called by `onDrawEye`), as follows:

```
private void drawCube() {
    GLES20.glUseProgram(cubeProgram);

    // Set the light position in the shader
    GLES20.glUniform3fv(cubeLightPosParam, 1,
    lightPosInEyeSpace, 0);

    // Set the ModelView in the shader, used to calculate
    lighting
    GLES20.glUniformMatrix4fv(cubeModelViewParam, 1, false,
    cubeView, 0);

    GLES20.glUniformMatrix4fv(cubeMVPMatrixParam, 1, false,
    modelViewProjection, 0);

    GLES20.glVertexAttribPointer(cubePositionParam,
    COORDS_PER_VERTEX,
        GLES20.GL_FLOAT, false, 0, cubeVerticesBuffer);
```

```
GLES20.glVertexAttribPointer(cubeNormalParam, 3,
GLES20.GL_FLOAT, false, 0,
        cubeNormalsBuffer);
GLES20.glVertexAttribPointer(cubeColorParam, 4,
GLES20.GL_FLOAT, false, 0,
        cubeColorsBuffer);

GLES20.glDrawArrays(GLES20.GL_TRIANGLES, 0,
cubeVertexCount);
}
```

Building and running the app

We are now ready to go. When you build and run the app, you will see a screen similar to the following screenshot:

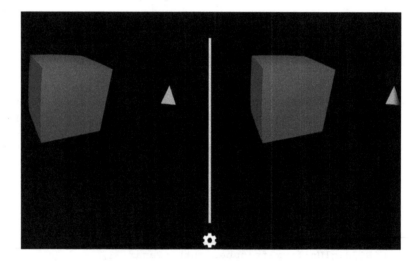

Spinning the cube

The next step is a quick one. Let's make the cube spin. This is achieved by rotating the cubeTransform matrix a little bit for each frame. We can define a TIME_DELTA value for this. Add the static variable, as follows:

```
// Viewing variables
private static final float TIME_DELTA = 0.3f;
```

Then, modify cubeTransform for each frame, and add the following line of code to the onNewFrame method:

```
Matrix.rotateM(cubeTransform, 0, TIME_DELTA, 0.5f, 0.5f, 1.0f);
```

The `Matrix.rotateM` function applies a rotation to a transformation matrix based on an angle and an axis. In this case, we are rotating by an angle of `TIME_DELTA` around the axis vector (0.5, 0.5, 1). Strictly speaking, you should provide a normalized axis, but all that matters is the direction of the vector and not the magnitude.

Build and run it. Now the cube is spinning. *Animazing!*

Hello, floor!

Having a sense of being grounded can be important in virtual reality. It can be much more comfortable to feel like you're standing (or sitting) than to be floating in space like a bodyless eyeball. So, let's add a floor to our scene.

This should be much more familiar now. We'll have a shader, model, and rendering pipeline similar to the cube. So, we'll just do it without much explanation.

Shaders

The floor will use our `light_shader` with a small modification and a new fragment shader.

Modify the `light_vertex.shader` by adding a `v_Grid` variable, as follows:

```
uniform mat4 u_Model;
uniform mat4 u_MVP;
uniform mat4 u_MVMatrix;
uniform vec3 u_LightPos;

attribute vec4 a_Position;
attribute vec4 a_Color;
attribute vec3 a_Normal;

varying vec4 v_Color;
varying vec3 v_Grid;

const float ONE = 1.0;
const float COEFF = 0.00001;

void main() {
    v_Grid = vec3(u_Model * a_Position);

    vec3 modelViewVertex = vec3(u_MVMatrix * a_Position);
    vec3 modelViewNormal = vec3(u_MVMatrix * vec4(a_Normal, 0.0));
```

```
    float distance = length(u_LightPos - modelViewVertex);
    vec3 lightVector = normalize(u_LightPos - modelViewVertex);
    float diffuse = max(dot(modelViewNormal, lightVector), 0.5);

    diffuse = diffuse * (ONE / (ONE + (COEFF * distance *
    distance))));
    v_Color = a_Color * diffuse;
    gl_Position = u_MVP * a_Position;
}
```

Create a new shader in `app/res/raw` named `grid_fragment.shader`, as follows:

```
precision mediump float;
varying vec4 v_Color;
varying vec3 v_Grid;

void main() {
    float depth = gl_FragCoord.z / gl_FragCoord.w; // Calculate
    world-space distance.

    if ((mod(abs(v_Grid.x), 10.0) < 0.1) || (mod(abs(v_Grid.z),
    10.0) < 0.1)) {
        gl_FragColor = max(0.0, (90.0-depth) / 90.0) * vec4(1.0,
    1.0, 1.0, 1.0)
                    + min(1.0, depth / 90.0) * v_Color;
    } else {
        gl_FragColor = v_Color;
    }
}
```

It may seem complicated, but all that we are doing is drawing some grid lines on a solid color shader. The `if` statement will detect whether we are within 0.1 units of a multiple of 10. If so, we draw a color that is somewhere between white (1, 1, 1, 1) and `v_Color`, based on the depth of that pixel, or its distance from the camera. `gl_FragCoord` is a built-in value that gives us the position of the pixel that we are rendering in window space as well as the value in the depth buffer (z), which will be within the range [0, 1]. The fourth parameter, `w`, is essentially the inverse of the camera's draw distance and, when combined with the depth value, gives the world-space depth of the pixel. The `v_Grid` variable has actually given us access to the world-space position of the current pixel, based on the local vertex position and the model matrix that we introduced in the vertex shader.

In `MainActivity`, add a variable for the new fragment shader:

```
    // Rendering variables
    private int gridFragmentShader;
```

Compile the shader in the `compileShaders` method, as follows:

```
gridFragmentShader = loadShader(GLES20.GL_FRAGMENT_SHADER,
        R.raw.grid_fragment);
```

Floor model data

Create a new Java file named `Floor` in the project. Add the floor plane coordinates, normals, and colors:

```
public static final float[] FLOOR_COORDS = new float[] {
    200f, 0, -200f,
    -200f, 0, -200f,
    -200f, 0, 200f,
    200f, 0, -200f,
    -200f, 0, 200f,
    200f, 0, 200f,
};

public static final float[] FLOOR_NORMALS = new float[] {
    0.0f, 1.0f, 0.0f,
    0.0f, 1.0f, 0.0f,
    0.0f, 1.0f, 0.0f,
    0.0f, 1.0f, 0.0f,
    0.0f, 1.0f, 0.0f,
    0.0f, 1.0f, 0.0f,
};

public static final float[] FLOOR_COLORS = new float[] {
        0.0f, 0.34f, 0.90f, 1.0f,
        0.0f, 0.34f, 0.90f, 1.0f,
        0.0f, 0.34f, 0.90f, 1.0f,
        0.0f, 0.34f, 0.90f, 1.0f,
        0.0f, 0.34f, 0.90f, 1.0f,
        0.0f, 0.34f, 0.90f, 1.0f,
};
```

Variables

Add all the variables that we need to `MainActivity`:

```
// Model variables
private static float floorCoords[] = Floor.FLOOR_COORDS;
private static float floorColors[] = Floor.FLOOR_COLORS;
```

```
private static float floorNormals[] = Floor.FLOOR_NORMALS;
private final int floorVertexCount = floorCoords.length /
COORDS_PER_VERTEX;
private float[] floorTransform;
private float floorDepth = 20f;

// Viewing variables
private float[] floorView;

// Rendering variables
private int gridFragmentShader;

private FloatBuffer floorVerticesBuffer;
private FloatBuffer floorColorsBuffer;
private FloatBuffer floorNormalsBuffer;
private int floorProgram;
private int floorPositionParam;
private int floorColorParam;
private int floorMVPMatrixParam;
private int floorNormalParam;
private int floorModelParam;
private int floorModelViewParam;
private int floorLightPosParam;
```

onCreate

Allocate the matrices in `onCreate`:

```
floorTransform = new float[16];
floorView = new float[16];
```

onSurfaceCreated

Add a call to `prepareRenderingFloor` in `onSufraceCreated`, which we'll write as follows:

```
prepareRenderingFloor();
```

initializeScene

Set up the `floorTransform` matrix in the `initializeScene` method:

```
// Position the floor
Matrix.setIdentityM(floorTransform, 0);
Matrix.translateM(floorTransform, 0, 0, -floorDepth, 0);
```

prepareRenderingFloor

Here's the complete `prepareRenderingFloor` method:

```java
private void prepareRenderingFloor() {
    // Allocate buffers
    ByteBuffer bb =
    ByteBuffer.allocateDirect(floorCoords.length * 4);
    bb.order(ByteOrder.nativeOrder());
    floorVerticesBuffer = bb.asFloatBuffer();
    floorVerticesBuffer.put(floorCoords);
    floorVerticesBuffer.position(0);

    ByteBuffer bbColors =
    ByteBuffer.allocateDirect(floorColors.length * 4);
    bbColors.order(ByteOrder.nativeOrder());
    floorColorsBuffer = bbColors.asFloatBuffer();
    floorColorsBuffer.put(floorColors);
    floorColorsBuffer.position(0);

    ByteBuffer bbNormals =
    ByteBuffer.allocateDirect(floorNormals.length * 4);
    bbNormals.order(ByteOrder.nativeOrder());
    floorNormalsBuffer = bbNormals.asFloatBuffer();
    floorNormalsBuffer.put(floorNormals);
    floorNormalsBuffer.position(0);

    // Create GL program
    floorProgram = GLES20.glCreateProgram();
    GLES20.glAttachShader(floorProgram, lightVertexShader);
    GLES20.glAttachShader(floorProgram, gridFragmentShader);
    GLES20.glLinkProgram(floorProgram);
    GLES20.glUseProgram(floorProgram);

    // Get shader params
    floorPositionParam =
    GLES20.glGetAttribLocation(floorProgram, "a_Position");
    floorNormalParam =
    GLES20.glGetAttribLocation(floorProgram, "a_Normal");
    floorColorParam = GLES20.glGetAttribLocation(floorProgram,
    "a_Color");

    floorModelParam =
    GLES20.glGetUniformLocation(floorProgram, "u_Model");
    floorModelViewParam =
    GLES20.glGetUniformLocation(floorProgram, "u_MVMatrix");
```

```
floorMVPMatrixParam =
GLES20.glGetUniformLocation(floorProgram, "u_MVP");
floorLightPosParam =
GLES20.glGetUniformLocation(floorProgram, "u_LightPos");

// Enable arrays
GLES20.glEnableVertexAttribArray(floorPositionParam);
GLES20.glEnableVertexAttribArray(floorNormalParam);
GLES20.glEnableVertexAttribArray(floorColorParam);
}
```

onDrawEye

Calculate MVP and draw the floor in `onDrawEye`:

```
Matrix.multiplyMM(floorView, 0, view, 0, floorTransform,
0);
Matrix.multiplyMM(modelViewProjection, 0, perspective, 0,
floorView, 0);
drawFloor();
```

drawFloor

Define a `drawFloor` method, as follows:

```
private void drawFloor() {
    GLES20.glUseProgram(floorProgram);
    GLES20.glUniform3fv(floorLightPosParam, 1,
    lightPosInEyeSpace, 0);
    GLES20.glUniformMatrix4fv(floorModelParam, 1, false,
    floorTransform, 0);
    GLES20.glUniformMatrix4fv(floorModelViewParam, 1, false,
    floorView, 0);
    GLES20.glUniformMatrix4fv(floorMVPMatrixParam, 1, false,
    modelViewProjection, 0);
    GLES20.glVertexAttribPointer(floorPositionParam,
    COORDS_PER_VERTEX,
            GLES20.GL_FLOAT, false, 0, floorVerticesBuffer);
    GLES20.glVertexAttribPointer(floorNormalParam, 3,
    GLES20.GL_FLOAT, false, 0,
            floorNormalsBuffer);
    GLES20.glVertexAttribPointer(floorColorParam, 4,
    GLES20.GL_FLOAT, false, 0,
            floorColorsBuffer);
    GLES20.glDrawArrays(GLES20.GL_TRIANGLES, 0,
    floorVertexCount);
}
```

Build and run it. It will now look like the following screenshot:

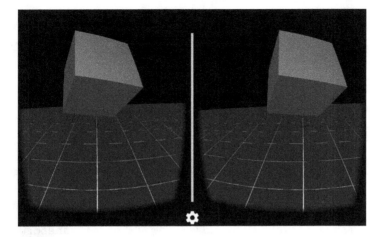

Woot!

Hey, look at this!

In the last part of the project, we add a feature that detects when you're looking at an object (the cube) and highlights it with a different color.

This is accomplished with the help of the CardboardView interface method, onNewFrame, which passes the current head transformation information.

The isLookingAtObject method

Let's start with the most interesting part. We'll borrow the isLookingAtObject method from Google's Treasure Hunt demo. It checks whether the user is looking at an object by calculating where the object is in the eye space and returns true if the user is looking at the object. Add the following code to MainActivity:

```
/**
    * Check if user is looking at object by calculating where the
  object is in eye-space.
    *
    * @return true if the user is looking at the object.
    */
  private boolean isLookingAtObject(float[] modelView, float[]
  modelTransform) {
      float[] initVec = { 0, 0, 0, 1.0f };
      float[] objPositionVec = new float[4];
```

```
// Convert object space to camera space. Use the headView
from onNewFrame.
Matrix.multiplyMM(modelView, 0, headView, 0,
modelTransform, 0);
Matrix.multiplyMV(objPositionVec, 0, modelView, 0,
initVec, 0);

float pitch = (float) Math.atan2(objPositionVec[1], -
objPositionVec[2]);
float yaw = (float) Math.atan2(objPositionVec[0], -
objPositionVec[2]);

return Math.abs(pitch) < PITCH_LIMIT && Math.abs(yaw) <
YAW_LIMIT;
}
```

The method takes two arguments: the `modelView` and `modelTransform` transformation matrices of the object we want to test. It also references the `headView` class variable, which we'll set in `onNewFrame`.

A more precise way to do this might be to cast a ray from the camera into the scene in the direction in which the camera is looking and determines whether it intersects any geometry in the scene. This will be very effective but also very computationally expensive.

Instead, this function takes a simpler approach and doesn't even use the geometry of the object. It rather uses the object's view transform to determine how far the object is from the center of the screen and tests whether the angle of that vector is within a narrow range (`PITCH_LIMIT` and `YAW_LIMIT`). *Yeah I know, people get PhDs to come up with this stuff!*

Let's define the variables that we need as follows:

```
// Viewing variables
private static final float YAW_LIMIT = 0.12f;
private static final float PITCH_LIMIT = 0.12f;

private float[] headView;
```

Allocate `headView` in `onCreate`:

```
headView = new float[16];
```

Get the current `headView` value on each new frame. Add the following code to `onNewFrame`:

```
headTransform.getHeadView(headView, 0);
```

Then, modify `drawCube` to check whether the user is looking at the cube and decide which colors to use:

```
if (isLookingAtObject(cubeView, cubeTransform)) {
    GLES20.glVertexAttribPointer(cubeColorParam, 4,
    GLES20.GL_FLOAT, false, 0,
            cubeFoundColorsBuffer);
} else {
    GLES20.glVertexAttribPointer(cubeColorParam, 4,
    GLES20.GL_FLOAT, false, 0,
            cubeColorsBuffer);
}
```

That's it! Except for one (minor) detail: we need a second set of vertex colors for the highlight mode. We'll highlight the cube by drawing all the faces with the same yellow color. There are a few changes to be made in order to make this happen.

In `Cube`, add the following RGBA values:

```
public static final float[] CUBE_FOUND_COLORS_FACES = new
float[] {
    // Same yellow for front, right, back, left, top, bottom
    faces
    1.0f,   0.65f, 0.0f, 1.0f,
    1.0f,   0.65f, 0.0f, 1.0f,
    1.0f,   0.65f, 0.0f, 1.0f,
    1.0f,   0.65f, 0.0f, 1.0f,
    1.0f,   0.65f, 0.0f, 1.0f,
    1.0f,   0.65f, 0.0f, 1.0f,
};
```

In `MainActivity,` add these variables:

```
// Model variables
private static float cubeFoundColors[] =
Cube.cubeFacesToArray(Cube.CUBE_FOUND_COLORS_FACES, 4);

// Rendering variables
private FloatBuffer cubeFoundColorsBuffer;
```

Add the following code to the `prepareRenderingCube` method:

```
ByteBuffer bbFoundColors =
ByteBuffer.allocateDirect(cubeFoundColors.length * 4);
bbFoundColors.order(ByteOrder.nativeOrder());
cubeFoundColorsBuffer = bbFoundColors.asFloatBuffer();
cubeFoundColorsBuffer.put(cubeFoundColors);
cubeFoundColorsBuffer.position(0);
```

Build and run it. When you look directly at the cube, it gets highlighted.

> It may be more fun and challenging if the cubes weren't so close. Try setting `cubeDistance` to something like *12f*.
>
> Like the Treasure Hunt demo, try setting a new set of random values for the cube position every time you look at it. Now, you have a game!

Summary

In this chapter, we built a Cardboard Android app from scratch, starting with a new project and adding Java code a little bit at a time. In our first build, we had a stereoscopic view of a triangle that you can see in a Google Cardboard headset.

We then added the model transformation, 3D camera views, perspective and head rotation transformations, and discussed a bit about matrix mathematics. We built a 3D model of a cube, and then created shader programs to use a light source to render the cube with shading. We also animated the cube and added a floor grid. Lastly, we added a feature that highlights the cube when the user is looking at it.

Along the way, we enjoyed good discussions of 3D geometry, OpenGL, shaders, matrix math for 3D perspective viewing, geometric normals, and data buffers for the rendering pipeline. We also started thinking about the ways in which you can abstract common patterns in the code into reusable methods.

In the next chapter, we will take a different approach to stereoscopic rendering using Android layout views to build a useful "virtual lobby" that can be used as a 3D menu system or portal into other worlds.

4
Launcher Lobby

This project creates a Cardboard VR app that can be used to launch the other Cardboard apps installed on your device. We'll call it **LauncherLobby**. When you open LauncherLobby, you will see up to 24 icons arranged horizontally. As you turn your head to the right or left, the icons scroll as if they are inside a cylinder. You can open an app by gazing at its icon and pulling the Cardboard trigger.

For this project, we take a minimal approach to creating stereoscopic views. The project simulates parallax using standard Android ViewGroup layouts and simply shifts the images to the left or right in each eye, creating the parallax visual effect. We do not use 3D graphics. We do not use OpenGL directly, though most modern versions of Android render views with OpenGL. In fact, we hardly use the Cardboard SDK at all; we only use it to paint the split screen overlay and get the head orientation. The view layout and image shifting logic, however, is derived from Google's Treasure Hunt sample (where it is used to draw a text overlay).

The advantages of this approach are multifold. It illustrates how it's possible to build Cardboard apps even without high-level graphics, matrix math, render engines, and physics. Of course, these are often required, but in this case, they're not. If you have experience with Android development, the classes and patterns used here may be especially familiar. This project demonstrates how Cardboard VR, at a minimum, only needs a Cardboard SDK head transform and a split-screen layout to produce a stereoscopic application.

Practically speaking, we chose this approach so that we can use Android's TextView. Rendering arbitrary text in 3D is actually pretty complicated (though certainly possible), so for the sake of simplicity, we are constraining this project to 2D views and Android layouts.

To build the project, we'll first walk you through some basics of putting a text string and icon image on the screen and viewing them stereoscopically. Then, we'll design a virtual screen that works like the inside of a cylinder unraveled. Turning your head horizontally will be like panning across this virtual screen. The screen will be divided into slots, each containing the icon and the name of a Cardboard app. Gazing at and clicking on one of the slots will launch the corresponding application. If you've used the Cardboard Samples app (so called at the time of writing), this interface will be familiar.

In this chapter, we will cover the following topics:

- Creating a new Cardboard project
- Adding a *Hello Virtual World* text overlay
- Using virtual screen space
- Responding to head look
- Adding an icon to the view
- Listing installed Cardboard apps
- Highlighting the current app shortcut
- Using the trigger to pick and launch an app

The source code for this project can be found on the Packt Publishing website and on GitHub at `https://github.com/cardbookvr/launcherlobby` (with each topic as a separate commit).

Creating a new project

If you'd like more details and an explanation of these steps, refer to the *Creating a new Cardboard project* section of *Chapter 2, The Skeleton Cardboard Project*, and follow along there:

1. With Android Studio opened, create a new project. Let's name it `LauncherLobby` and target **Android 4.4 KitKat (API 19)** with an **Empty Activity**.

2. Add the Cardboard SDK `common.aar` and `core.aar` library files to your project as new modules, using **File | New | New Module...**.

3. Set the library modules as dependencies to the project app, using **File | Project Structure**.

4. Edit the `AndroidManifest.xml` file as explained in *Chapter 2, The Skeleton Cardboard Project*, being careful to preserve the `package` name for this project.

5. Edit the `build.gradle` file as explained in *Chapter 2, The Skeleton Cardboard Project*, to compile against SDK 22.

6. Edit the `activity_main.xml` layout file as explained in *Chapter 2, The Skeleton Cardboard Project*.

7. Edit the `MainActivity` Java class so that it extends `CardboardActivity` and implements `CardboardView.StereoRenderer`. Modify the class declaration line as follows:

```
public class MainActivity extends CardboardActivity
implements CardboardView.StereoRenderer {
```

8. Add the stub method overrides for the interface (using intellisense **Implement Methods** or pressing *Ctrl + I*).

9. Lastly, edit `onCreate()` by adding the `CardboadView` instance as follows:

```
@Override
protected void onCreate(Bundle savedInstanceState) {
    super.onCreate(savedInstanceState);
    setContentView(R.layout.activity_main);

    CardboardView cardboardView = (CardboardView)
    findViewById(R.id.cardboard_view);
    cardboardView.setRenderer(this);
    setCardboardView(cardboardView);
}
```

Adding Hello Virtual World text overlay

For starters, we're just going to put some text on the screen that you might use for a toast message to the user, or a **heads-up display** (HUD) with informative content. We're going to implement this incrementally in small steps:

1. Create a simple overlay view with some text.

2. Center it on the screen.

3. Add parallax for stereoscopic viewing.

A simple text overlay

First, we'll add some overlay text in a simple way, not stereoscopically, just text on the screen. This will be our initial implementation of the `OverlayView` class.

Open the `activity_main.xml` file, and add the following lines to add an `OverlayView` to your layout:

```
<.OverlayView
    android:id="@+id/overlay"
    android:layout_width="fill_parent"
    android:layout_height="fill_parent"
    android:layout_alignParentLeft="true"
    android:layout_alignParentTop="true" />
```

Note that we reference the `OverlayView` class with just `.OverlayView`. You may do this if your view class is in the same package as your `MainActivity` class. We did the same earlier for `.MainActivity`.

Next, we write the Java class. Right-click on the `app/java` folder (`app/src/main/java/com.cardbookvr.launcherlobby/`), and navigate to **New | Java Class**. Name it `OverlayView`.

Define the class so that it extends `LinearLayout`, and add a constructor method, as follows:

```java
public class OverlayView extends LinearLayout{

    public OverlayView(Context context, AttributeSet attrs) {
        super(context, attrs);

        TextView textView = new TextView(context, attrs);
        addView(textView);

        textView.setTextColor(Color.rgb(150, 255, 180));
        textView.setText("Hello Virtual World!");
        setVisibility(View.VISIBLE);
    }
}
```

The `OverlayView()` constructor method creates a new `TextView` instance with a pleasant greenish color and the text **Hello Virtual World!**.

Run the app, and you will notice our text in the top-left corner of the screen, as shown in the following screenshot:

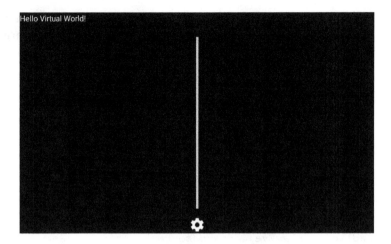

Center the text using a child view

Next, we create a separate view group and use it to control the text object. Specifically, to center it in the view.

In the `OverlayView` constructor, replace the `TextView` with an instance of a different `ViewGroup` helper class that we're going to write called `EyeView`. Presently, it's monoscopic but soon we'll use this class to create two views: one for each eye:

```java
public OverlayView(Context context, AttributeSet attrs) {
    super(context, attrs);

    LayoutParams params = new LayoutParams(
        LayoutParams.MATCH_PARENT,
        LayoutParams.MATCH_PARENT, 1.0f);
    params.setMargins(0, 0, 0, 0);

    OverlayEye eye = new OverlayEye(context, attrs);
    eye.setLayoutParams(params);
    addView(eye);

    eye.setColor(Color.rgb(150, 255, 180));
    eye.addContent("Hello Virtual World!");
    setVisibility(View.VISIBLE);
}
```

We create a new instance of OverlayEye named eye, set its color, and add the text string.

When using a ViewGroup class, you need to specify LayoutParams to tell the parent how to lay out the view, which we want to be full screen size with no margins (refer to http://developer.android.com/reference/android/view/ViewGroup.LayoutParams.html).

In the same OverlayView.java file, we're going to add the private class named OverlayEye, as follows:

```java
private class OverlayEye extends ViewGroup {
    private Context context;
    private AttributeSet attrs;
    private TextView textView;
    private int textColor;

    public OverlayEye(Context context, AttributeSet attrs) {
        super(context, attrs);
        this.context = context;
        this.attrs = attrs;
    }

    public void setColor(int color) {
        this.textColor = color;
    }

    public void addContent(String text) {
        textView = new TextView(context, attrs);
        textView.setGravity(Gravity.CENTER);
        textView.setTextColor(textColor);
        textView.setText(text);
        addView(textView);
    }
}
```

We have separated the TextView creation from the OverlayEye constructor. The reason for this will soon become clear.

The OverlayEye constructor registers the context and attributes needed to add new content views to the group.

Then, addContent creates the TextView instance and adds it to the layout.

Now we define `onLayout` for `OverlayEye`, which sets the margins of textview, specifically the top margin, as a mechanism to force the text to be vertically centered:

```
@Override
protected void onLayout(boolean changed, int left, int
top, int right, int bottom) {
    final int width = right - left;
    final int height = bottom - top;

    final float verticalTextPos = 0.52f;

    float topMargin = height * verticalTextPos;
    textView.layout(0, (int) topMargin, width, bottom);
}
```

To center the text vertically, we push it down from the top of the screen using a top margin. The text will be positioned vertically just below the center of the screen, as specified by `verticalTextPos`, a percentage value where 1.0 is the full height of the screen. We picked a value of 0.52 to push the top of the text down to an extra 2% just below the middle of the screen.

Run the app, and you will notice that our text is now centered on the screen:

Create stereoscopic views for each eye

Now, we get real. Virtually, that is. For VR, we need stereoscopic left and right eye views. Fortunately, we have this handy `OverlayEye` class that we can reuse for each eye.

Your eyes are separated by a measurable distance, which is referred to as your **interpupillary distance (IPD)**. When you view a stereoscopic image in a Cardboard headset, there are separate views for each eye, offset (horizontally) by a corresponding distance.

Let's assume that our text is on a plane perpendicular to the view direction. That is, we're looking straight at the text plane. Given a numeric value corresponding to the distance of the text from your eyes, we can shift the views for the left and right eyes horizontally by a fixed number of pixels to create the parallax effect. We'll call this the depthOffset value. A larger depth offset will cause the text to appear closer; a smaller depth offset will cause the text to appear further away. A depth offset of zero will indicate no parallax, as if the text is very far away (greater than 20 feet).

For our application, we're going to choose a depth offset factor of 0.01, or 1% measured in screen coordinates (a fraction of screen size). The icons will appear to be about 2 meters away (6 feet), which is a comfortable distance for VR, although this value is an ad hoc approximation. Using percentages of screen size instead of actual pixel amounts, we can ensure that our application will adapt to any screen/device size.

Let's implement this now.

To begin, declare variables for the leftEye and rightEye values at the top of the OverlayView class:

```
public class OverlayView extends LinearLayout{
    private final OverlayEye leftEye;
    private final OverlayEye rightEye;
```

Initialize them in the OverlayView constructor method:

```
public CardboardOverlayView(Context context, AttributeSet
attrs) {
    super(context, attrs);

    LayoutParams params = new LayoutParams(
            LayoutParams.MATCH_PARENT,
            LayoutParams.MATCH_PARENT, 1.0f);
    params.setMargins(0, 0, 0, 0);

    leftEye = new OverlayEye(context, attrs);
    leftEye.setLayoutParams(params);
    addView(leftEye);

    rightEye = new OverlayEye(context, attrs);
    rightEye.setLayoutParams(params);
```

```
addView(rightEye);

setDepthFactor(0.01f);
setColor(Color.rgb(150, 255, 180));
addContent("Hello Virtual World!");
setVisibility(View.VISIBLE);
}
```

Notice the six lines in the middle where we define `leftView` and `rightView` and call `addView` for them. The `setDepthFactor` call will set that value in the views.

Add the setter methods for the depth, color, and text content:

```
public void setDepthFactor(float factor) {
    leftEye.setDepthFactor(factor);
    rightEye.setDepthFactor(-factor);
}

public void setColor(int color) {
    leftEye.setColor(color);
    rightEye.setColor(color);
}

public void addContent(String text) {
    leftEye.addContent(text);
    rightEye.addContent(text);
}
```

 Important: notice that for the `rightEye` value we use a negative of the offset value. To create the parallax effect, it needs to be shifted to the opposite direction of the left eye view. We can still achieve parallax by only shifting one eye, but then all of the content will appear to be slightly off center.

The `OverlayEye` class needs the depth factor setter, which we convert to pixels as `depthOffset`. Also, declare a variable for the physical view width (in pixels):

```
private int depthOffset;
private int viewWidth;
```

In `onLayout`, set the view width in pixels after it's been calculated:

```
viewWidth = width;
```

Define the setter method, which converts the depth factor to a pixel offset:

```
public void setDepthFactor(float factor) {
    this.depthOffset = (int)(factor * viewWidth);
}
```

Now, when we create `textView` in `addContent`, we can shift it by the `depthOffset` value in pixels:

```
textView.setX(depthOffset);
addView(textView);
```

When you run the app, your screen will look like this:

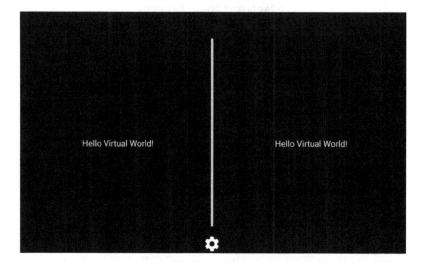

The text is now in stereo views, although it's "stuck to your face" as it doesn't move when your head moves. It's attached to a visor or HUD.

Controlling the overlay view from MainActivity

The next step is to remove some of the hardcoded properties and control them from the `MainActivity` class.

In `MainActivity.java`, add an `overlayView` variable at the top of the class:

```
public class MainActivity extends CardboardActivity implements
CardboardView.StereoRenderer {
    private OverlayView overlayView;
```

Initialize its value in `onCreate`. We'll display the text using the `addContent()` method:

```
...
setCardboardView(cardboardView);
overlayView = (OverlayView) findViewById(R.id.overlay);
overlayView.addContent("Hello Virtual World");
```

Don't forget to remove the call to `addContent` from the `OverlayView` method:

```
setDepthOffset(0.01f);
setColor(Color.rgb(150, 255, 180));
addContent("Hello Virtual World!");
setVisibility(View.VISIBLE);
}
```

Run the app one more time. It should look the same as shown earlier.

You can use code like this to create a 3D toast, such as a text notification message. Or, it can be used to construct a HUD panel to share in-game status or report the current device attributes. For example, to show the current screen parameters you can put them into `MainActivity`:

```
ScreenParams sp =
cardboardView.getHeadMountedDisplay().getScreenParams();
overlayView.setText(sp.toString());
```

This will show the phone's physical width and height in pixels.

Using a virtual screen

In virtual reality, the space you are looking into is bigger than what is on the screen at a given time. The screen is like a viewport into the virtual space. In this project, we're not calculating 3D views and clipping planes, and we're constraining the head motion to left/right yaw rotation.

You can think of the visible space as the inside surface of a cylinder, with your head at the center. As you rotate your head, a portion of the unraveled cylinder is displayed on the screen.

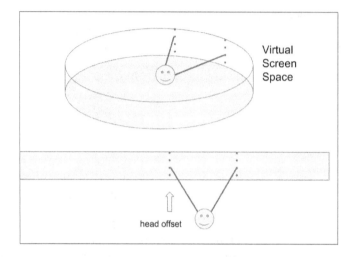

The height of the virtual screen in pixels is the same as the physical device.

We need to calculate the virtual width. One way to do this, for example, would be to figure out the number of pixels in one degree of head rotation. Then, the width of a full rotation would be *pixels per degree * 360*.

We can easily find the physical width of the display in pixels. In fact, we already found it in onLayout as the viewWidth variable. Alternatively, it can be retrieved from the Cardboard SDK call:

```
ScreenParams sp =
cardboardView.getHeadMountedDisplay().getScreenParams();
Log.d(TAG, "screen width: " + sp.getWidth());
```

From the SDK, we can also get the **field of view** (**FOV**) angle of the Cardboard headset (in degrees). This value will vary from one device to the next and is part of the Cardboard device configuration parameters:

```
FieldOfView fov =
cardboardView.getHeadMountedDisplay().
getCardboardDeviceParams().getLeftEyeMaxFov();
Log.d(TAG, "FOV: " + fov.getLeft());
```

Given this, we can calculate the number of pixels per degree and the total width in pixels of the virtual screen. For example, on my Nexus 4, the device width (landscape mode) is 1,280, and using a Homido viewer, the FOV is 40.0 degrees. Thus, the split screen view is 640 pixels, giving us 16.0 pixels per degree and a virtual screen width of 5,760 pixels.

While we're at it, we can also calculate and remember the `pixelsPerRadian` value, which will be useful to determine the head offset based on the current user's `HeadTransform` (given in radians).

Let's add it. At the top of the `OverlayView` class, add these variables:

```
private int virtualWidth;
private float pixelsPerRadian;
```

Then, add the following method:

```
public void calcVirtualWidth(CardboardView cardboard) {
    int screenWidth =
    cardboard.getHeadMountedDisplay().
    getScreenParams().getWidth() / 2;
    float fov = cardboard.getCardboardDeviceParams().
    getLeftEyeMaxFov().getLeft();
    float pixelsPerDegree = screenWidth / fov;
    pixelsPerRadian = (float) (pixelsPerDegree * 180.0 /
    Math.PI);
    virtualWidth = (int) (pixelsPerDegree * 360.0);
}
```

In the `onCreate` method of `MainActivity`, add the following call:

```
overlayView.calcVirtualWidth(cardboardView);
```

Note that the FOV value reported from the device parameters is a rough approximation defined by the headset manufacturer, and, in some devices, may be overestimated and padded. The actual FOV can be retrieved from the eye object passed to `onDrawEye()`, since that represents the actual frustum that should be rendered. Once the project is working, you might consider making this change to your own code.

Now, we can use these values to respond to the user's head look rotation.

Responding to head look

Let's make the text move with our head, so it doesn't appear to be stuck to your face! As you look left or right, we'll move the text in the opposite direction, so it appears to be stationary in space.

To do this, we'll start in `MainActivity`. In the `onNewFrame` method, we'll determine the horizontal head rotation angle and pass that to the `overlayView` object.

In `MainActivity`, define `onNewFrame`:

```
public void onNewFrame(HeadTransform headTransform) {
    final float[] angles = new float[3];
    headTransform.getEulerAngles(angles, 0);
    runOnUiThread(new Runnable() {
        @Override
        public void run() {
            overlayView.setHeadYaw(angles[1]);
        }
    });
}
```

The `onNewFrame` method receives the current `HeadTransform` instance as an argument, which is an object that provides the current head pose.

There are various ways to mathematically represent the head pose, such as a forward XYZ direction vector, or a combination of angles. The `getEulerAngles` method gets the pose as three angles called **Euler angles** (pronounced *oiler*), about the three axes for pitch, yaw, and roll:

- **Pitch** turns your head as if nodding "yes"
- **Yaw** turns your head to the left/right (as if shaking "no")
- **Roll** turns your head from ear to shoulders ("Do a barrel roll!")

These axes correspond to the X, Y, and Z coordinate axes, respectively. We're going to constrain this experience to yaw, as you look left or right to select from a row of menu items. Therefore, we send just the second Euler angle, `angles[1]`, to the `overlayView` class.

Note the use of `runOnUiThread`, which ensures that the `overlayView` update is run on the UI thread. Otherwise, we'll cause all sorts of exceptions and break the UI (you can refer to `http://developer.android.com/reference/android/app/Activity.html#runOnUiThread(java.lang.Runnable)`).

So, back in `OverlayView`, add a variable to `headOffset` and a method to set it, `setHeadYaw`:

```
private int headOffset;

public void setHeadYaw(float angle) {
    headOffset = (int)( angle * pixelsPerRadian );
```

```
        leftEye.setHeadOffset(headOffset);
        rightEye.setHeadOffset(headOffset);
    }
```

The idea here is to convert the head rotation into a positional offset for the text object on the screen. When your head turns to the left, move the objects to the right. When your head turns to the right, move the objects to the left. Thus, the objects scroll on the screen as you turn your head.

The yaw angle (rotation about the vertical *Y* axis) that we get from the Cardboard SDK is in radians. We calculate the number of pixels to offset the view, in the opposite direction from the head. Thus, we take the angle and multiply that by `pixelsPerRadian`. Why don't we negate the angle? It just turns out that the clockwise rotation is registered as a negative rotation in the *Y* axis. Go figure.

Lastly, in `OverlayEye`, define the `setHeadOffset` method to change the X position of the view objects. Make sure that you include the `depthOffset` variable as well:

```
public void setHeadOffset(int headOffset) {
    textView.setX( headOffset + depthOffset );
}
```

Run the app. When you move your head, the text should scroll in the opposite direction.

Adding an icon to the view

Next, we'll add an icon image to the view.

For now, let's just use a generic icon, such as `android_robot.png`. A copy of this can be found on the Internet, and there's a copy included with the files for this chapter. Paste the `android_robot.png` file into your project's `app/res/drawable/` folder. Don't worry, we'll be using the actual app icons later.

We want to display both the text and an icon together, so we can add the code in order to add the image views to the `addContent` method.

In the `onCreate` method of `MainActivity`, modify the `addContent` call to pass the icon as a second parameter:

```
Drawable icon = getResources()
    .getDrawable(R.drawable.android_robot, null);
overlayView.addContent("Hello Virtual World!", icon);
```

In `addContent` of `OverlayView`, add the icon parameter and pass it to the `OverlayEye` views:

```
public void addContent(String text, Drawable icon) {
    leftEye.addContent(text, icon);
    rightEye.addContent(text, icon);
}
```

Now for the `OverlayEye` class. At the top of `OverlayEye`, add a variable to the `ImageView` instance:

```
private class OverlayEye extends ViewGroup {
    private TextView textView;
    private ImageView imageView;
```

Modify `addContent` of `OverlayEye` in order to also take a `Drawable` icon and create the `ImageView` instance for it. The modified method now looks like this:

```
public void addContent(String text, Drawable icon) {
    textView = new TextView(context, attrs);
    textView.setGravity(Gravity.CENTER);
    textView.setTextColor(textColor);
    textView.setText(text);
    addView(textView);

    imageView = new ImageView(context, attrs);
    imageView.setScaleType
    (ImageView.ScaleType.CENTER_INSIDE);
    imageView.setAdjustViewBounds(true);
    // preserve aspect ratio
    imageView.setImageDrawable(icon);
    addView(imageView);
}
```

Using `imageView.setScaleType.CENTER_INSIDE` tells the view to scale the image from its center. Setting `setAdjustViewBounds` to `true` tells the view to preserve the image's aspect ratio.

Set the layout parameters of `ImageView` in the `onLayout` method of `OverlayEye`. Add the following code to the bottom of the `onLayout` method:

```
final float imageSize = 0.1f;
final float verticalImageOffset = -0.07f;
float imageMargin = (1.0f - imageSize) / 2.0f;
topMargin = (height * (imageMargin +
verticalImageOffset));
float botMargin = topMargin + (height * imageSize);
imageView.layout(0, (int) topMargin, width, (int)
botMargin);
```

When the image is drawn, it will fit within the top and bottom margins, scaled automatically. In other words, given a desired image size (such as 10% of the screen height, or 0.1f), the image margin factor is *(1 - size)/2*, multiplied by the pixel height of the screen to get the margin in pixels. We also add a small vertical offset (negative, to move it up) for spacing between the icon and the text below it.

Finally, add the `imageView` offset to the `setHeadOffset` method:

```
public void setHeadOffset(int headOffset) {
    textView.setX( headOffset + depthOffset );
    imageView.setX( headOffset + depthOffset );
}
```

Run the app. Your screen will look like this. When you move your head, both the icon and text will scroll.

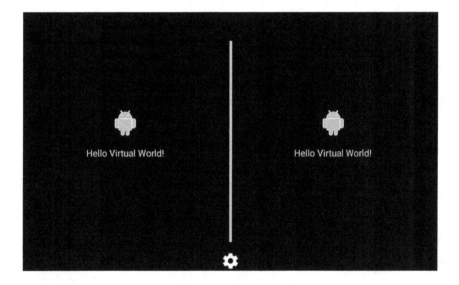

Listing installed Cardboard apps

If you haven't forgotten, the purpose of this LauncherLobby app is to show a list of Cardboard apps on the device and let the user pick one to launch it.

If you like what we've built so far, you may want to save a copy for future reference. The changes we're going to make next will significantly modify the code to support a list of views as shortcuts to your apps.

We're going to replace the `addContent` method with `addShortcut` and the `imageView` and `textView` variables with a list of shortcuts. Each shortcut consists of an `ImageView` and a `TextView` to display the shortcut, as well as an `ActivityInfo` object for the purpose of launching the app. The shortcut images and text will appear on top of each other, as shown earlier, and will be arranged horizontally in a line, a fixed distance apart.

Queries for Cardboard apps

First, let's get the list of Cardboard apps installed on the device. At the end of the `onCreate` method of `MainActivity`, add a call to a new method, `getAppList`:

```
getAppList();
```

Then, define this method in `MainActivity`, as follows:

```
private void getAppList() {
    final Intent mainIntent = new Intent(Intent.ACTION_MAIN,
    null);
    mainIntent.addCategory
    ("com.google.intent.category.CARDBOARD");
    mainIntent.addFlags(PackageManager.GET_INTENT_FILTERS);

    final List<ResolveInfo> pkgAppsList =
    getPackageManager().queryIntentActivities( mainIntent,
    PackageManager.GET_INTENT_FILTERS);

    for (ResolveInfo info : pkgAppsList) {
        Log.d("getAppList",
        info.loadLabel(getPackageManager()).toString());
    }
}
```

Run it, and review the `logcat` window in Android Studio. The code gets the list of Cardboard apps on the current device (`pkgAppsList`) and prints their label (`name`) to the debug console.

Cardboard apps are identified by having the `CARDBOARD` intent category, so we filter by that. The call to `addFlags` and specifying the flag in `queryIntentActivities` are important, because otherwise we won't get the list of intent filters and note of the apps will match the `CARDBOARD` category. Also, note that we're using the `Activity` class's `getPackageManager()` function. If you need to put this method in another class, it will need a reference to the activity. We will be using intents again later on in this book. For more information on the package manager and Intents, refer to http://developer.android.com/reference/android/content/pm/PackageManager.html and http://developer.android.com/reference/android/content/Intent.html.

Create the Shortcut class for apps

Next, we'll define a Shortcut class that holds the details we require of each Cardboard app in a convenient object.

Create a new Java class named Shortcut. Define it as follows:

```
public class Shortcut {
    private static final String TAG = "Shortcut";
    public String name;
    public Drawable icon;
    ActivityInfo info;

    public Shortcut(ResolveInfo info, PackageManager
    packageManager){
        name = info.loadLabel(packageManager).toString();
        icon = info.loadIcon(packageManager);
        this.info = info.activityInfo;
    }
}
```

In MainActivity, modify getAppList() to build shortcuts from pkgAppsList and add them to overlayView:

```
    . . .
    int count = 0;
    for (ResolveInfo info : pkgAppsList) {
        overlayView.addShortcut( new Shortcut(info,
        getPackageManager()));
        if (++count == 24)
            break;
    }
```

We need to limit the number of shortcuts that will fit within our view cylinder. In this case, I chose 24 as a reasonable number.

Add shortcuts to OverlayView

Now, we modify OverlayView to support a list of shortcuts that will be rendered. First, declare a list variable, shortcuts, to hold them:

```
public class OverlayView extends LinearLayout {
    private List<Shortcut> shortcuts = new ArrayList<Shortcut>();
    private final int maxShortcuts = 24;
    private int shortcutWidth;
```

The `addShortcut` method is as follows:

```
public void addShortcut(Shortcut shortcut){
    shortcuts.add(shortcut);
    leftEye.addShortcut(shortcut);
    rightEye.addShortcut(shortcut);
}
```

As you can see, this calls the `addShortcut` method in the `OverlayEye` class. This builds a list of `TextView` and `ImageView` instances for the layout.

Note the `maxShortcuts` and `shortcutWidth` variables. `maxShortcuts` defines the maximum number of shortcuts we want to fit on the virtual screen, and `shortcutWidth` will be the width of each shortcut slot on the screen. Initialize `shortcutWidth` in `calcVirtualWidth()`, adding the following line of code at the end of `calcVirtualWidth`:

```
shortcutWidth = virtualWidth / maxShortcuts;
```

Using view lists in OverlayEye

At the top of `OverlayEye`, replace the `textView` and `imageView` variables with lists:

```
private class OverlayEye extends LinearLayout {
    private final List<TextView> textViews = new
    ArrayList<TextView>();
    private final List<ImageView> imageViews = new
    ArrayList<ImageView>();
```

Now we're ready to write the `addShortcut` method in `OverlayEye`. It looks very much like the `addContent` method we're replacing. It creates `textView` and `imageView` (as mentioned earlier) but then stuffs them into a list:

```
public void addShortcut(Shortcut shortcut) {
    TextView textView = new TextView(context, attrs);
    textView.setTextSize(TypedValue.COMPLEX_UNIT_DIP,
    12.0f);
    textView.setGravity(Gravity.CENTER);
    textView.setTextColor(textColor);
    textView.setText(shortcut.name);
    addView(textView);
    textViews.add(textView);

    ImageView imageView = new ImageView(context, attrs);
    imageView.setScaleType
      (ImageView.ScaleType.CENTER_INSIDE);
```

```
imageView.setAdjustViewBounds(true);
imageView.setImageDrawable(shortcut.icon);
addView(imageView);
imageViews.add(imageView);
}
```

Setting `setAdjustViewBounds` to `true` preserves the image aspect ratio.

Delete the obsolete `addContent` method definitions in both the `OverlayView` and `OverlayEye` classes.

In `onLayout`, we now iterate over the list of `textViews`, as follows:

```
for(TextView textView : textViews) {
    textView.layout(0, (int) topMargin, width,
    bottom);
}
```

We also iterate over the list of `imageViews`, as follows:

```
for(ImageView imageView : imageViews) {
    imageView.layout(0, (int) topMargin, width, (int)
    botMargin);
}
```

Lastly, we also need to iterate over the list in `setHeadOffset`:

```
public void setHeadOffset(int headOffset) {
    int slot = 0;
    for(TextView textView : textViews) {
        textView.setX(headOffset + depthOffset +
        (shortcutWidth * slot));
        slot++;
    }
    slot = 0;
    for(ImageView imageView : imageViews) {
        imageView.setX(headOffset + depthOffset +
        (shortcutWidth * slot));
        slot++;
    }
}
```

Run the app. You will now see your Cardboard shortcuts neatly arranged in a horizontal menu that you can scroll by turning your head.

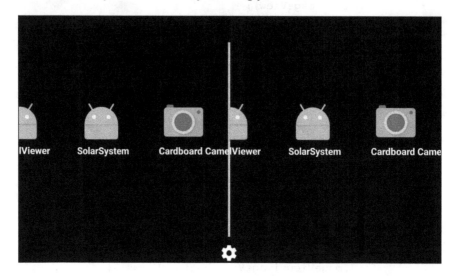

Note that some Java programmers out there might point out that the list of shortcuts and the list of views in each OverlayEye class are redundant. They are, indeed, but it turns out to be quite complicated to refactor the draw functionality per-eye into the Shortcut class. We found that this way was the simplest and easiest to understand.

Highlighting the current shortcut

When the user gazes at a shortcut, it should be able to indicate that it is selectable. In the next section, we'll wire it up to highlight the selected item and to actually launch the corresponding app.

The trick here is to determine which slot is in front of the user. To highlight it, we'll brighten the text color.

Let's write a helper method to determine which slot is currently in the gaze, based on the headOffset variable (which was calculated from the head yaw angle). Add the getSlot method to the OverlayView class:

```
public int getSlot() {
    int slotOffset = shortcutWidth/2 - headOffset;
    slotOffset /= shortcutWidth;
    if(slotOffset < 0)
```

```
        slotOffset = 0;
    if(slotOffset >= shortcuts.size())
        slotOffset = shortcuts.size() - 1;
    return slotOffset;
}
```

One half of the shortcutWidth value is added to the headOffset value, so we detect gazing at the center of the shortcut. Then, we add the negative of headOffset since that was originally calculated as the positional offset, which is opposite of the view direction. Negative values of headOffset actually correspond to slot numbers greater than zero.

getSlot should return a number between 0 and the number of slots in our virtual layout; in this case, its 24. Since it is possible to look to the right and set a positive headOffset variable, getSlot can return negative numbers, so we check the boundary conditions.

Now, we can highlight the currently selected slot. We'll do it by changing the text label color. Modify setHeadOffset as follows:

```
public void setHeadOffset(int headOffset) {
    int currentSlot = getSlot();
    int slot = 0;
    for(TextView textView : textViews) {
        textView.setX(headOffset + depthOffset +
        (shortcutWidth * slot));
        if (slot==currentSlot) {
            textView.setTextColor(Color.WHITE);
        } else {
            textView.setTextColor(textColor);
        }
        slot++;
    }
    slot = 0;
    for(ImageView imageView : imageViews) {
        imageView.setX(headOffset + depthOffset +
        (shortcutWidth * slot));
        slot++;
    }
}
```

Run the app and the item in front of your gaze will become highlighted. Of course, there may be other interesting ways to highlight the selected app, but this is good enough for now.

Using the trigger to pick and launch the app

The final piece is to detect which shortcut the user is gazing at and respond to a trigger (click) by launching the app.

When we launch a new app from this one, we need to reference the `MainActivity` object. One way to do it is to make it a singleton object. Let's do that now. Note that you can get into trouble defining activities as singletons. Android can launch multiple instances of a single `Activity` class, but even across apps, static variables are shared.

At the top of the `MainActivity` class, add an `instance` variable:

```
public static MainActivity instance;
```

Initialize it in `onCreate`:

```
protected void onCreate(Bundle savedInstanceState) {
    super.onCreate(savedInstanceState);
    instance = this;
```

Now in `MainActivity`, add a handler to the Cardboard trigger:

```
@Override
public void onCardboardTrigger(){
    overlayView.onTrigger();
}
```

Then, in `OverlayView`, add the following method:

```
public void onTrigger() {
    shortcuts.get( getSlot() ).launch();
}
```

We're using `getSlot` to index into our shortcuts list. Because we checked the boundary conditions in `getSlot` itself, we don't need to worry about `ArrayIndexOutOfBounds` exceptions.

Finally, add a `launch()` method to `Shortcut`:

```
public void launch() {
    ComponentName name = new
    ComponentName(info.applicationInfo.packageName,
            info.name);
    Intent i = new Intent(Intent.ACTION_MAIN);
```

```
        i.addCategory(Intent.CATEGORY_LAUNCHER);
        i.setFlags(Intent.FLAG_ACTIVITY_NEW_TASK |
                Intent.FLAG_ACTIVITY_RESET_TASK_IF_NEEDED);
        i.setComponent(name);

        if(MainActivity.instance != null) {
            MainActivity.instance.startActivity(i);
        } else {
            Log.e(TAG, "Cannot find activity singleton");
        }
    }
}
```

We use the `ActivityInfo` object that we stored in the `Shortcut` class to create a new `Intent` instance, and then call `MainActivity.instance.startActivity` with it as an argument to launch the app.

Note that once you've launched a new app, there's no system-wide way to get back to LauncherLobby from within VR. The user will have to remove the phone from the Cardboard Viewer, and then click on the back button. However, the SDK does support `CardboardView.setOnCardboardBackButtonListener` which can be added to your Cardboard apps if you want to present a back or exit button.

There you have it! LauncherLobby is ready to rock and roll.

Further enhancements

Some ideas for how to improve and enhance this project include the following:

- Support more than 24 shortcuts, perhaps adding multiple rows or an infinite scrolling mechanic

- Reuse images and text view objects; you only ever see a few at a time

- Currently, really long app labels will overlap, tweak your view code to make the text wrap, or introduce an ellipsis (...) when the label is too long

- Add a cylindrical background image (skybox)

- Alternative ways to highlight the current shortcut, perhaps with a glow, or move it closer by adjusting its parallax offset

- Add sounds and/or vibrations to enhance the experience and reinforce the selection feedback

Summary

In this chapter, we built the LauncherLobby app, which can be used to launch other Cardboard apps on your device. Rather than using 3D graphics and OpenGL, we implemented this using Android GUI and a virtual cylindrical screen.

The first part of the implementation was largely instructional: how to add a `TextView` overlay, center it in the view group, and then display it stereoscopically with left/right eye parallax views. Then, we determined the size of the virtual screen, an unraveled cylinder, based on the current physical device size and the current Cardboard device field of view parameters. Objects are scrolled on the virtual screen as the user moves his head left and right (yaw rotation). Finally, we queried the Android device for installed Cardboard apps, displayed their icons and titles in a horizontal menu, and allowed you to pick one to launch by gazing at it and clicking on the trigger.

In the next chapter, we go back to 3D graphics and OpenGL. This time, we're building a software abstraction layer that helps encapsulate much of the lower level details and housekeeping. This engine will be reusable for other projects in this book as well.

5
RenderBox Engine

While the Cardboard Java SDK and OpenGL ES are powerful and robust libraries for mobile VR applications, they're pretty low level. Software development best practices expect that we abstract common programming patterns into new classes and data structures. In *Chapter 3, Cardboard Box*, we got some hands-on experience with the nitty gritty details. This time, we're revisiting those details while abstracting them into a reusable library that we'll call **RenderBox**. There'll be vector math, materials, lighting, and more, all rolled up into a neat little package.

In this chapter, you will learn to:

- Create a new Cardboard project
- Write a `Material` class with shaders
- Explore our `Math` package
- Write a `Transform` class
- Write a `Component` class with `RenderObject` `Cube`, `Camera`, and `Light` components
- Add a `Material` class for rendering cubes with vertex colors and lighting
- Write a `Time` animation class
- Export all this into a `RenderBox` library for reuse

The source code for this project can be found on the Packt Publishing website, and on GitHub at `https://github.com/cardbookvr/renderboxdemo` (with each topic as a separate commit). The final `RenderBoxLib` project, which will continue to be maintained and reused in other projects in this book, can also be found on the Packt Publishing website and on GitHub at `https://github.com/cardbookvr/renderboxlib`.

Introducing RenderBox – a graphics engine

In a virtual reality app, you are creating a three-dimensional space with a bunch of objects. The user's viewpoint, or camera, is also located in this space. With the help of the Cardboard SDK, the scene is rendered twice, once for the left and right eye, to create the side-by-side stereoscopic views. The second and equally important feature translates the sensor data into a head look direction, tracking the real-life user's head. The pixels are drawn on the screen, or rendered, using the OpenGL ES library, which talks to the hardware **graphics processor** (**GPU**) on your device.

We're going to organize the graphics rendering code into separate Java classes, which we'll be able to extract into a reusable graphics engine library. We'll call this library **RenderBox**.

As you'll see, the `RenderBox` class implements the `CardboardView.StereoRender` interface. But it's more than that. Virtual reality needs 3D graphics rendering, and to do all this in low-level OpenGL ES calls (and other supporting APIs) can be tedious, to say the least, especially as your application grows. Furthermore, these APIs require you to think like a semiconductor chip! Buffers, shaders, and matrix math, oh my! I mean seriously, who wants to think like that all the time? I'd rather think like a 3D artist and VR developer.

There are many distinct pieces to track and manage, and they can get complicated. As software developers, it's our role to identify common patterns and implement layers of abstraction, which serve to reduce this complexity, avoid duplicated code, and express the program as objects (software classes) closer to the problem domain. In our case, this domain makes 3D scenes that can be rendered on Cardboard VR devices.

`RenderBox` starts to abstract away details into a nice clean layer of code. It is designed to take care of OpenGL calls and complex arithmetic, while still letting us set up our app-specific code the way we want. It also creates a common pattern known as the **entity component pattern** (`https://en.wikipedia.org/wiki/Entity_component_system`) for new materials and component types if our projects demand any special cases. Here's an illustration of the major classes in our library:

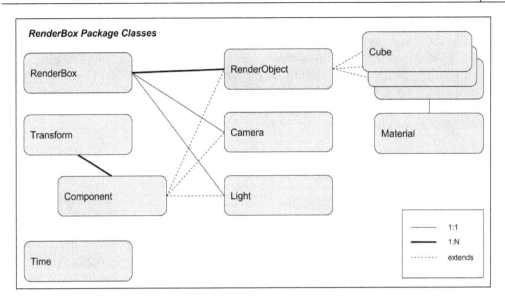

The `RenderBox` class implements `CardboardView.StereoRenderer`, relieving that responsibility from the app's `MainActivity` class. As we'll see, `MainActivity` communicates with `RenderBox` through the `IRenderBox` interface (with the setup, `preDraw`, and `postDraw` hooks) so that `MainActivity` implements `IRenderBox`.

Let's consider the kinds of `Component` that can participate in a 3D VR scene:

- `RenderObject`: These are drawable models in the scene, such as cubes and spheres
- `Camera`: This is the viewpoint of the user, which is used to render the scene
- `Light`: These are sources of illumination used for shading and shadows

Every object in our scene has an X, Y, and Z location in space, a rotation, and three scale dimensions. These properties are defined by the `Transform` class. Transforms can be arranged in a hierarchy, letting you build more complex objects that are assembled from simpler ones.

Each `Transform` class can be associated with one or more `Component` classes. Different kinds of components (for example, `Camera`, `Light`, and `RenderObject`) extend the `Component` class. A component should not exist without being attached to a `Transform` class but the reverse (a transform with no components) is perfectly fine.

Internally, `RenderBox` maintains a list of `RenderObjects`. These are the geometric models in the scene. Types of `RenderObjects` include `Cube` and `Sphere`, for example. These objects are associated with a `Material`, which defines their color, texture, and/or shading properties. Materials, in turn, reference, compile, and execute low-level shader programs. Maintaining a flat list of components to render each frame is more efficient than traversing the transform hierarchy every frame. It is a perfect example of why we use the entity component pattern.

Other things in the `RenderBox` package include a `Time` class used to implement animations, and a library of `Math` functions used for vector and matrix operations.

Now, let's start putting this together.

What's the game plan? The end goal is to create our `RenderBox` graphics engine library. It will be handy to maintain it in its own project (and repository if you're using source control, such as Git), so it can be improved and maintained independently. However, to kick this off, we need a simple app to build it, show you how to use it, and verify (if not test) that it is working properly. This will be called `RenderBoxDemo`. At the end of the chapter, we will extract the `RenderBox` code into an Android library module and then export it.

Creating a new project

If you'd like more details and explanation about these steps, refer to the *Creating a new Cardboard project* section *Chapter 2, The Skeleton Cardboard Project*, and follow along there:

1. With Android Studio opened, create a new project. Let's name it `RenderBoxDemo` and target **Android 4.4 KitKat (API 19)** with an **Empty Activity**.

2. Add the Cardboard SDK `common.aar` and `core.aar` library files to your project as new modules, using **File | New | New Module....**

3. Set the library modules as dependencies to the project app, using **File | Project Structure**.

4. Edit the `AndroidManifest.xml` file as explained in *Chapter 2, The Skeleton Cardboard Project*, being careful to preserve the `package` name for this project.

5. Edit the `build.gradle` file as explained in *Chapter 2, The Skeleton Cardboard Project*, to compile against SDK 22.

6. Edit the `activity_main.xml` layout file as explained in *Chapter 2, The Skeleton Cardboard Project*.

Now, open the `MainActivity.java` file and edit the `MainActivity` Java class to extend `CardboardActivity`:

```
public class MainActivity extends CardboardActivity {
    private static final String TAG = "RenderBoxDemo";
```

> Note that unlike the previous chapters, we do not implement `CardboardView.StereoRender`. Instead, we will implement that interface in the `RenderBox` class (in the next topic).

Creating the RenderBox package folder

Since our plan is to export the `RenderBox` code as a library, let's put it all into its own package.

In the Android hierarchy panel, use the `Gear` icon and uncheck **Compact Empty Middle Packages** so that we can insert the new package under **com.cardbookvr**.

Right-click on the `app/java/com/carbookvr/` folder in the project view, navigate to **New | Package**, and name it `renderbox`. You may now wish to enable **Compact Empty Middle Packages** again.

Within the `renderbox` folder, create three package subfolders named `components`, `materials`, and `math`. The project should now have the same folders as shown in the following screenshot:

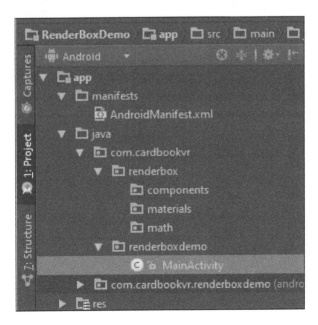

Creating an empty RenderBox class

Let's begin by creating a skeleton of the RenderBox class Java code. Right-click on the renderbox/ folder, navigate to **New | Java Class**, and name it RenderBox.

Now, open the RenderBox.java file and edit it to implement the CardboardView. StereoRenderer interfaces. Add the following code:

```
public class RenderBox implements CardboardView.StereoRenderer {
    private static final String TAG = "RenderBox";

    public static RenderBox instance;
    public Activity mainActivity;
    IRenderBox callbacks;

    public RenderBox(Activity mainActivity, IRenderBox callbacks){
        instance = this;
        this.mainActivity = mainActivity;
        this.callbacks = callbacks;
    }
}
```

It's primarily housekeeping at this point. The RenderBox class is defined as implements CardboardView.StereoRenderer. Its constructor will receive a reference to the MainActivity instance and the IRenderBox implementer (in this case, also the MainActivity) class. MainActivity will now have to implement the IRenderBox methods (to be defined next). In this way, we instantiate the framework and implement the critical methods.

Note that we also make RenderBox a singleton by registering the this instance in the class constructor.

We must also add the method overrides for the StereoRenderer class. From the intellisense menu, select **Implement Methods...** (or *Ctrl + I*) to add the stub method overrides for the interface, as follows:

```
@Override
public void onNewFrame(HeadTransform headTransform) {
}

@Override
public void onDrawEye(Eye eye) {
}

@Override
public void onFinishFrame(Viewport viewport) {
}
```

```
@Override
public void onSurfaceChanged(int i, int i1) {
}

@Override
public void onSurfaceCreated(EGLConfig eglConfig) {
}

@Override
public void onRendererShutdown() {
}
```

It is now a good time to add an error reporting method, `checkGLError`, to `RenderBox` to log OpenGL rendering errors, as illustrated in the following code:

```
/**
 * Checks if we've had an error inside of OpenGL ES, and if so
   what that error is.
 * @param label Label to report in case of error.
 */
public static void checkGLError(String label) {
    int error;
    while ((error = GLES20.glGetError()) !=
    GLES20.GL_NO_ERROR) {
        String errorText = String.format("%s: glError %d, %s",
        label, error, GLU.gluErrorString(error));
        Log.e(TAG, errorText);
        throw new RuntimeException(errorText);
    }
}
```

In the previous chapter projects, we defined `MainActivity` so that it implements `CardboardView.StereoRenderer`. Now this is delegated to our new `RenderBox` object. Let's tell `MainActivity` to use it.

In `MainActivity.java`, modify the `onCreate` method to create a new instance of `RenderBox` and set it as the view renderer, as follows:

```
protected void onCreate(Bundle savedInstanceState) {
    super.onCreate(savedInstanceState);
    setContentView(R.layout.activity_main);

    CardboardView cardboardView = (CardboardView)
    findViewById(R.id.cardboard_view);
    cardboardView.setRenderer(new RenderBox(this,this));
    setCardboardView(cardboardView);
}
```

Note that `cardboardView.setRender` is passed new `RenderBox`, which takes the `MainActivity` instance as both the `Activity` and `IRenderBox` arguments. Voila, we've taken control of the Cardboard SDK integration entirely, and now it's all about implementing `IRenderbox`. In this way, we have wrapped the Cardboard SDK, OpenGL, and a variety of other external dependencies in our own library. Now, if these specifications change, all we have to do is keep `RenderBox` up to date, and our app can tell `RenderBox` what to do, the same way as always.

Adding the IRenderBox interface

Once we've put all this together, the `MainActivity` class will implement the `IRenderBox` interface. The interface provides callbacks for the `setup`, `preDraw`, and `postDraw` functions that the activity may implement.

The setup method will be called after doing some generic work in `onSurfaceCreated`. The `preDraw` and `postDraw` methods will be called during `onDrawEye`. We'll get to see this later in the chapter.

We can set that up now. Right-click on `renderbox` in the hierarchy panel, navigate to **New | Java Class**, select **Kind: "Interface"**, and name it `IRenderBox`. It's only a few lines and should include just the following code:

```
public interface IRenderBox {
    public void setup();
    public void preDraw();
    public void postDraw();
}
```

Then, modify `MainActivity` so that it implements `IRenderBox`:

```
public class MainActivity extends CardboardActivity implements
IRenderBox {
```

Select intellisense **Implement Methods** (or *Ctrl + I*), to add the interface methods overrides. Android Studio will automatically fill in the following:

```
@Override
public void setup() {

}

@Override
public void preDraw() {

}
```

```
@Override
public void postDraw() {

}
```

If you run the empty app now, you will not get any build errors, and it'll display the empty Cardboard split view:

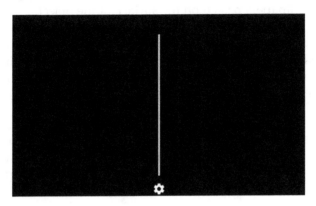

Now we have created a skeleton app, ready to implement the RenderBox package and utilities, which we can use to help build new Cardboard VR applications.

In the next few topics, we will build some of the classes needed in RenderBox. Unfortunately, we can't display anything interesting on your Cardboard device until we get these coded up. This also limits our ability to test and verify that the coding is correct. This could be an appropriate time to introduce unit testing, such as JUnit. Refer to the *Unit testing support* docs for details (http://tools.android.com/tech-docs/unit-testing-support). Unfortunately, space does not allow us to introduce this subject and use it for the projects in this book. But we encourage you to pursue this on your own. (And I'll remind you that the GitHub repository for this project has separate commits for each topic, incrementally adding code as we go along).

Materials, textures, and shaders

In *Chapter 3, Cardboard Box*, we introduced the OpenGL ES 2.0 graphics pipeline and simple shaders. We will now extract that code into a separate Material class.

In computer graphics, materials refer to the visual surface characteristics of geometric models. When rendering an object in the scene, materials are used together with lighting and other scene information required by the shader code and the OpenGL graphics pipeline.

A solid colored material is the simplest; the entire surface of the object is a single color. Any color variation in the final rendering will be due to lighting, shadows, and other features in a different shader variant. It is quite possible to produce solid color materials with lighting and shadows, but the simplest possible example just fills raster segments with the same color, such as our very first shader.

A textured material may have surface details defined in an image file (such as a JPG). Textures are like wallpapers pasted on the surface of the object. They can be used to a great extent and are responsible for most of the details that the user perceives on an object. A solid colored sphere may look like a ping pong ball. A textured sphere may look like the Earth. More texture channels can be added to define variations in shading or even to emit light when the surface is in shadow. You will see this kind of effect at the end of *Chapter 6, Solar System*, when we add an artificial light to the dark side of the Earth.

More realistic physically-based shading goes beyond texture maps to include simulated height maps, metallic shininess, and other imperfections, such as rust or dirt. We won't be going into that in this book, but it's common in graphics engines such as Unity 3D and the Unreal Engine. Our `RenderBox` library could be extended to support it.

Presently, we'll build the infrastructure for a basic solid colored material and associated shaders. Later in the chapter, we'll expand it with lighting.

Abstract material

In the `renderbox/materials/` folder, create a new Java class named `Material` and begin to write it as follows:

```
public abstract class Material {
    private static final String TAG = "RenderBox.Material";

    protected static final float[] modelView = new float[16];
    protected static final float[] modelViewProjection = new
    float[16];

    public static int createProgram(int vertexShaderResource, int
    fragmentShaderResource) {
        int vertexShader = loadGLShader(GLES20.GL_VERTEX_SHADER,
        vertexShaderResource);
        int passthroughShader =
        loadGLShader(GLES20.GL_FRAGMENT_SHADER,
        fragmentShaderResource);

        int program = GLES20.glCreateProgram();
        GLES20.glAttachShader(program, vertexShader);
```

```
        GLES20.glAttachShader(program, passthroughShader);
        GLES20.glLinkProgram(program);
        GLES20.glUseProgram(program);

        RenderBox.checkGLError("Material.createProgram");
        return program;
    }

    public abstract void draw(float[] view, float[] perspective);
}
```

This defines an abstract class that will be used to extend the various types of materials we define. The `createProgram` method loads the designated shader scripts and builds an OpenGL ES program with the shaders attached.

We also define an abstract `draw()` method that will be implemented in each shader separately. Among other things, it requires the `modelView` and `modelViewProjection` transformation matrices be declared at the top of the class. At this point, we will actually only use `modelViewProjection`, but a separate reference to the `modelView` matrix will be needed when we add lighting.

Next, add the following utility methods to the `Material` class to load the shaders:

```
/**
 * Converts a raw text file, saved as a resource, into an
 OpenGL ES shader.
 *
 * @param type The type of shader we will be creating.
 * @param resId The resource ID of the raw text file about to
 be turned into a shader.
 * @return The shader object handler.
 */
public static int loadGLShader(int type, int resId) {
    String code = readRawTextFile(resId);
    int shader = GLES20.glCreateShader(type);
    GLES20.glShaderSource(shader, code);
    GLES20.glCompileShader(shader);

    // Get the compilation status.
    final int[] compileStatus = new int[1];
    GLES20.glGetShaderiv(shader, GLES20.GL_COMPILE_STATUS,
    compileStatus, 0);

    // If the compilation failed, delete the shader.
    if (compileStatus[0] == 0) {
```

```
            Log.e(TAG, "Error compiling shader: " +
            GLES20.glGetShaderInfoLog(shader));
            GLES20.glDeleteShader(shader);
            shader = 0;
        }

        if (shader == 0) {
            throw new RuntimeException("Error creating shader.");
        }

        return shader;
    }

    /**
     * Converts a raw text file into a string.
     *
     * @param resId The resource ID of the raw text file about to
       be turned into a shader.
     * @return The context of the text file, or null in case of
       error.
     */
    private static String readRawTextFile(int resId) {
        InputStream inputStream = RenderBox.instance.
        mainActivity.getResources().openRawResource(resId);
        try {
            BufferedReader reader = new BufferedReader(new
            InputStreamReader(inputStream));
            StringBuilder sb = new StringBuilder();
            String line;
            while ((line = reader.readLine()) != null) {
                sb.append(line).append("\n");
            }
            reader.close();
            return sb.toString();
        } catch (IOException e) {
            e.printStackTrace();
        }
        return null;
    }
```

As discussed in *Chapter 3*, *Cardboard Box*, these methods will load a shader script and compile it.

Later on, we'll derive specific materials from this class, and define specific shaders that each one will use.

The Math package

In *Chapter 3, Cardboard Box*, we introduced 3D geometry and matrix math calculations. We will wrap these up into even more useful functions.

Much of this math code that we've put together is from existing open source projects (attributions are given in comments in the source code). After all, we might as well take advantage of the math geniuses who like this stuff and have open sourced excellent true and tested code. The code list is included with the file downloads for this book.

 The following list documents our math API. The actual code is included with the file downloads for this book and the GitHub repository.

Generally speaking, the mathematics falls within the subject of linear algebra, but most of it is specific to graphics programming and works within the constraints of fast floating point math on modern CPUs.

We encourage you to browse the source code included with the book, which you will obviously need access to in order to complete the project. Suffice it to say that everything included is pretty standard fare for a 3D game engine and was, in fact, largely sourced from (or checked against) an open source engine called **LibGDX**. The math library for LibGDX is pretty vast, optimized for mobile CPUs, and could make a great drop-in replacement for our simpler math package. We will also use the Android `Matrix` class extensively, which, in most cases, runs in native code and avoids the overhead of the **Java Virtual Machine** (**JVM** or Dalvik VM in the case of Android).

Here's a summary of our math API.

MathUtils

The `MathUtils` variables and methods are mostly self-explanatory: `PI`, `sin`, `cos`, and so on, defined to use `floats` as an alternative to Java's `Math` class, which contains doubles. In computer graphics, we speak floats. The math takes less power and fewer transistors and the precision loss is acceptable. Your `MathUtils` class should look like the following code:

```
// File: renderbox/math/MathUtils.java
public class MathUtils {
    static public final float PI = 3.1415927f;
    static public final float PI2 = PI * 2;
    static public final float degreesToRadians = PI / 180;
    static public final float radiansToDegrees = 180f / PI;
}
```

Matrix4

The `Matrix4` class manages 4 x 4 transformation matrices and is used to translate (position), rotate, and scale points in three-dimensional space. We'll make good use of these soon. Here is an abridged version of the `Matrix4` class with function bodies removed:

```
// File: renderbox/math/Matrix4.java
public class Matrix4{
    public final float[] val = new float[16];
    public Matrix4()
    public Matrix4 toIdentity()

    public static Matrix4 TRS(Vector3 position, Vector3 rotation,
    Vector3 scale)
    public Matrix4 translate(Vector3 position)
    public Matrix4 rotate(Vector3 rotation)
    public Matrix4 scale(Vector3 scale)
    public Vector3 multiplyPoint3x4(Vector3 v)
    public Matrix4 multiply(Matrix4 matrix)
    public Matrix4 multiply(float[] matrix)
```

Make a special note of the TRS function. It is used by the `Transform` class to combine the position, rotation, and scale information into a useful matrix, which represents all three. The order in which this matrix is created is important. First, we generate a translation matrix, and then we rotate and scale it. The resulting matrix can be multiplied by any 3D point (our vertices) to apply these three operations hierarchically.

Quaternion

A **quaternion** represents a rotational orientation in three-dimensional space in such a way that, when two quaternions are combined, no information is lost.

From a human point of view, it's easier to think of rotational orientation as three Euler (pronounced "oiler") angles since we think of three dimensions of rotation: pitch, yaw, and roll. The reason we use quaternions as opposed to a more straightforward vector representation of rotations is that depending on the order in which you apply the three Euler rotations to an object, the resulting 3D orientation will be different.

For more information on quaternions and Euler angles, refer to the
following links:
- https://en.wikipedia.org/wiki/Quaternions_
  and_spatial_rotation
- https://en.wikipedia.org/wiki/Euler_angles
- http://mathworld.wolfram.com/EulerAngles.html
- https://en.wikipedia.org/wiki/Conversion_
  between_quaternions_and_Euler_angles

Even though quaternions are a four-dimensional construct, we treat each quaternion
as a single value, which represents a 3D orientation. Thus, when we apply multiple
rotation operations in a row, we don't run into issues where one axis' rotation
influences the effect of another. If none of this makes any sense, don't worry. This is
one of the trickiest concepts in 3D graphics. Here is the abridged Quaternion class:

```java
// File: renderbox/math/Quaternion.java
public class Quaternion {
    public float x,y,z,w;
    public Quaternion()
    public Quaternion(Quaternion quat)

    public Quaternion setEulerAngles (float pitch, float yaw,
    float roll) public Quaternion setEulerAnglesRad (float
    pitch, float yaw, float roll)
    public Quaternion conjugate ()
    public Quaternion multiply(final Quaternion other)
    public float[] toMatrix4()
    public String toString()
```

Vector2

A **Vector2** is a two-dimensional point or direction vector defined by (X,Y)
coordinates. With the Vector2 class, you can transform and manipulate
vectors. Here is the abridged Vector2 class:

```java
// File: renderbox/math/Vector2.java
public class Vector2 {
    public float x;
    public float y;

    public static final Vector2 zero = new Vector2(0, 0);
    public static final Vector2 up = new Vector2(0, 1);
    public static final Vector2 down = new Vector2(0, -1);
    public static final Vector2 left = new Vector2(-1, 0);
```

```
public static final Vector2 right = new Vector2(1, 0);

public Vector2()

public Vector2(float xValue, float yValue)
public Vector2(Vector2 other)
public Vector2(float[] vec)

public final Vector2 add(Vector2 other)
public final Vector2 add(float otherX, float otherY, float
otherZ)
public final Vector2 subtract(Vector2 other)
public final Vector2 multiply(float magnitude)
public final Vector2 multiply(Vector2 other)
public final Vector2 divide(float magnitude)
public final Vector2 set(Vector2 other)
public final Vector2 set(float xValue, float yValue)
public final Vector2 scale(float xValue, float yValue)
public final Vector2 scale(Vector2 scale)
public final float dot(Vector2 other)
public final float length2()
public final float distance2(Vector2 other)
public Vector2 normalize()
public final Vector2 zero()
public float[] toFloat3()
public float[] toFloat4()
public float[] toFloat4(float w)
public String toString()
```

Vector3

A **Vector3** is a three-dimensional point or direction vector defined by X, Y, and Z coordinates. With the Vector3 class, you can transform and manipulate vectors. Here is the abridged Vector3 class:

```
// File: renderbox/math/Vector3.java
public final class Vector3 {
    public float x;
    public float y;
    public float z;

    public static final Vector3 zero = new Vector3(0, 0, 0);
    public static final Vector3 up = new Vector3(0, 1, 0);
    public static final Vector3 down = new Vector3(0, -1, 0);
```

```
public static final Vector3 left = new Vector3(-1, 0, 0);
public static final Vector3 right = new Vector3(1, 0, 0);
public static final Vector3 forward = new Vector3(0, 0, 1);
public static final Vector3 backward = new Vector3(0, 0, -1);

public Vector3()
public Vector3(float xValue, float yValue, float zValue)
public Vector3(Vector3 other)
public Vector3(float[] vec)

public final Vector3 add(Vector3 other)
public final Vector3 add(float otherX, float otherY, float
otherZ)
public final Vector3 subtract(Vector3 other)
public final Vector3 multiply(float magnitude)
public final Vector3 multiply(Vector3 other)
public final Vector3 divide(float magnitude)
public final Vector3 set(Vector3 other)
public final Vector3 set(float xValue, float yValue, float
zValue)
public final Vector3 scale(float xValue, float yValue, float
zValue)
public final Vector3 scale(Vector3 scale)
public final float dot(Vector3 other)
public final float length()
public final float length2()
public final float distance2(Vector3 other)
public Vector3 normalize()
public final Vector3 zero()
public float[] toFloat3()
public float[] toFloat4()
public float[] toFloat4(float w)
public String toString()
```

Vector2 and Vector3 share a lot of the same functionality, but pay special attention to the functions that exist in 3D, and that do not exist in 2D. Next, we'll see how the math library gets used when we implement the Transform class.

The Transform class

A 3D virtual reality scene will be constructed from various objects, each with a position, rotation, and scale in 3D dimensional space defined by a Transform.

It will also be naturally useful to permit transforms to be grouped hierarchically. This grouping also creates a distinction between local space and world space, where children only keep track of the difference between their **translation, rotation, and scale (TRS)** and that of their parent (local space). The actual data that we are storing is the local position (we'll use the words position and translation interchangeably), rotation, and scale. Global position, rotation, and scale are computed by combining the local TRS all the way up the chain of parents.

First, let's define the `Transform` class. In the Android Studio hierarchy panel, right-click on `renderbox/`, go to **New** | **Java Class**, and name it `Transform`.

Each `Transform` may have one or more associated components. Typically there is just one, but it is possible to add as many as you want (as we'll see in the other projects in this book). We'll maintain a list of components in the transform, as follows:

```
public class Transform {
    private static final String TAG = "RenderBox.Transform";

    List<Component> components = new ArrayList<Component>();

     public Transform()  {}

    public Transform addComponent(Component component){
        component.transform = this;
        return this;
    }
    public List<Component> getComponents(){
        return components;
    }
}
```

We will define the `Component` class in the next topic. If it really bothers you to reference it now before it's defined, you can start with an empty Component Java class in the `renderbox/components` folder.

Now back to the `Transform` class. A `Transform` object has a location, orientation, and scale in space, defined by its `localPosition`, `localRotation`, and `localScale` variables. Let's define these private variables, and then add the methods to manipulate them.

Also, as transforms can be arranged in a hierarchy, we'll include a reference to a possible `parent` transform, as follows:

```
private Vector3 localPosition = new Vector3(0,0,0);
private Quaternion localRotation = new Quaternion();
private Vector3 localScale = new Vector3(1,1,1);

private Transform parent = null;
```

The position, rotation, and scale values are initialized to identity values, that is, no positional offset, rotation, or resizing until they are explicitly set elsewhere. Note that the identity scale is (1, 1, 1).

The `parent` transform variable allows each transform to have a single parent in the hierarchy. You can keep the list of children in the transform, but you might be surprised to know how far you can get without having to move down the hierarchy. If you can avoid it, as we have, you can save a good deal of branching when setting/unsetting a parent reference. Maintaining the list of children means an $O(n)$ operation every time you unparent an object, and an extra $O(1)$ insertion cost on setting a parent. It is also not very efficient to hunt through children looking for a particular object.

Parent methods

The transform can be added or removed from its position in the hierarchy with the `setParent` and `unParent` methods, respectively. Let's define them now:

```
public Transform setParent(Transform Parent){
    setParent(parent, true);
    return this;
}

public Transform setParent(Transform parent, boolean
updatePosition){
    if(this.parent == parent)
    //Early-out if setting same parent--don't do anything
        return this;
    if(parent == null){
        unParent(updatePosition);
        return this;
    }

    if(updatePosition){
        Vector3 tmp_position = getPosition();
        this.parent = parent;
        setPosition(tmp_position);
    } else {
        this.parent = parent;
    }
    return this;
}

public Transform upParent(){
    unParent(true);
    return this;
```

```
    }

    public Transform unParent(boolean updatePosition){
        if(parent == null)
        //Early out--we already have no parent
            return this;
        if(updatePosition){
            localPosition = getPosition();
        }
        parent = null;
        return this;
    }
}
```

Simply, the setParent method sets this.parent to the given parent transform. Optionally, you can specify that the position is updated relative to the parent. We added an optimization to skip this procedure if the parent is already set. Setting the parent to null is equivalent to calling unParent.

The unParent method removes the transform from the hierarchy. Optionally, you can specify that the position is updated relative to the (previous) parents, so that the transform is now disconnected from the hierarchy but remains in the same position in world space.

Note that the rotation and scale can, and should, also be updated when parenting and unparenting. We don't need that in the projects in this book, so they have been left as an exercise for the reader. Also, note that our setParent methods include an argument for whether to update the position. If it is false, the operation runs a little faster, but the global state of the object will change if the parent transform was not set to identity (no translation, rotation, or scale). For convenience, you may set updatePosition to true, which will apply the current global transformation to the local variables, keeping the object fixed in space, with its current rotation and scale.

Position methods

The setPosition methods set the transform position relative to the parent, or apply absolute world position to the local variable if there is no parent. Two overloads are provided if you want to use a vector or individual component values. getPosition will compute the world space position based on parent transforms, if they exist. Note that this will have a CPU cost related to the depth of the transform hierarchy. As an optimization, you may want to include a system to cache world space positions within the Transform class, invalidating the cache whenever a parent transform is modified. A simpler alternative would be to make sure that you store the position in a local variable right after calling getPosition. The same optimization applies for rotation and scale.

Define the position getters and setters as follows:

```
public Transform setPosition(float x, float y, float z){
    if(parent != null){
        localPosition = new
        Vector3(x,y,z).subtract(parent.getPosition());
    } else {
        localPosition = new Vector3(x, y, z);
    }
    return this;
}

public Transform setPosition(Vector3 position){
    if(parent != null){
        localPosition = new
        Vector3(position).subtract(parent.getPosition());
    } else {
        localPosition = position;
    }
    return this;
}

public Vector3 getPosition(){
    if(parent != null){
        return Matrix4.TRS(parent.getPosition(),
        parent.getRotation(),
        parent.getScale()).multiplyPoint3x4(localPosition);
    }
    return localPosition;
}

public Transform setLocalPosition(float x, float y, float z){
    localPosition = new Vector3(x, y, z);
    return this;
}

public Transform setLocalPosition(Vector3 position){
    localPosition = position;
    return this;
}

public Vector3 getLocalPosition(){
    return localPosition;
}
```

Rotation methods

The `setRotation` methods set the transform rotation relative to the parent, or the absolute world rotation is applied to the local variable if there is no parent. Again, multiple overloads provide options for different input data. Define the rotation getters and setters as follows:

```
public Transform setRotation(float pitch, float yaw,
float roll){
    if(parent != null){
        localRotation = new Quaternion(parent.getRotation()).
        multiply(new Quaternion().setEulerAngles(pitch, yaw,
        roll).conjugate()).conjugate();
    } else {
        localRotation = new Quaternion().setEulerAngles(pitch,
        yaw, roll);
    }
    return this;
}


/**
 * Set the rotation of the object in global space
 * Note: if this object has a parent, setRoation modifies the
 input rotation!
 * @param rotation
 */
public Transform setRotation(Quaternion rotation){
    if(parent != null){
        localRotation = new Quaternion(parent.getRotation()).
        multiply(rotation.conjugate()).conjugate();
    } else {
        localRotation = rotation;
    }
    return this;
}

public Quaternion getRotation(){
    if(parent != null){
        return new Quaternion(parent.getRotation()).
        multiply(localRotation);
    }
    return localRotation;
}
```

```
public Transform setLocalRotation(float pitch, float yaw,
float roll){
    localRotation = new Quaternion().setEulerAngles(pitch,
    yaw, roll);
    return this;
}

public Transform setLocalRotation(Quaternion rotation){
    localRotation = rotation;
    return this;
}

public Quaternion getLocalRotation(){
    return localRotation;
}

public Transform rotate(float pitch, float yaw, float roll){
    localRotation.multiply(new Quaternion().
    setEulerAngles(pitch, yaw, roll));
    return this;
}
```

Scale methods

The setScale methods set the transform scale relative to the parent, or apply the absolute scale to the local variable if there is no parent. Define getters and setters for the scale as follows:

```
public Vector3 getScale(){
    if(parent != null){
        Matrix4 result = new Matrix4();
        result.setRotate(localRotation);
        return new Vector3(parent.getScale())
            .scale(localScale);
    }
    return localScale;
}

public Transform setLocalScale(float x, float y, float z){
    localScale = new Vector3(x,y,z);
    return this;
}

public Transform setLocalScale(Vector3 scale){
```

```
        localScale = scale;
        return this;
    }

    public Vector3 getLocalScale(){
        return localScale;
    }

    public Transform scale(float x, float y, float z){
        localScale.scale(x, y, z);
        return this;
    }
```

Transform to matrix and draw

The last thing we need to do with the `Transform` class is transform an identity matrix into one that will tell OpenGL how to draw the object correctly. To do this, we translate, rotate, and scale the matrix, in that order. Technically, we can also do cool things with matrices, such as shearing and skewing models, but the math is complicated enough as it is. If you want to learn more, type `transformation matrix`, `quaternion to matrix`, and some of the other terms that we have been throwing around into a search engine. The actual math behind all of this is fascinating and way too detailed to explain in a single paragraph.

We also provide the `drawMatrix()` function that sets up the lighting and model matrices for a draw call. Since the lighting model is an intermediate step, it makes sense to combine this call;

```
    public float[] toFloatMatrix(){
        return Matrix4.TRS(getPosition(), getRotation(),
        getScale()).val;
    }

    public float[] toLightMatrix(){
        return Matrix4.TR(getPosition(), getRotation()).val;
    }

    /**
     * Set up the lighting model and model matrices for a draw
     call
     * Since the lighting model is an intermediate step, it makes
     sense to combine this call
     */
    public void drawMatrices() {
```

```
    Matrix4 modelMatrix = Matrix4.TR(getPosition(),
    getRotation());
    RenderObject.lightingModel = modelMatrix.val;
    modelMatrix = new Matrix4(modelMatrix);
    RenderObject.model = modelMatrix.scale(getScale()).val;
}
```

The `drawMatrices` method uses variables from the `RenderObject` class, which will be defined later. It might seem very anti-Java that we are just setting our matrices to static variables in the `RenderObject` class. As you will see, there is actually no need for multiple instances of the `lightingModel` object and model to exist. They are always calculated just in time for each object as they are drawn. If we were to introduce optimizations that avoid recomputing this matrix all the time, it would make sense to keep the information around. For the sake of simplicity, we just recalculate the matrix every time each object is drawn, since it might have changed since the last frame.

Next, we'll see how the `Transform` class gets used when we implement the `Component` class, which will be extended by a number of classes that define objects in the 3D scene.

The Component class

Our 3D virtual reality scenes consist of various kinds of components. Components may include geometric objects, lights, and cameras. Components can be positioned, rotated, and scaled in 3D space, according to their associated transform. Let's create a `Component` class that will serve as the basis for other object classes in the scene.

If you haven't created `Component.java` yet, create one now in the `renderbox/ components` folder. Define it as follows:

```
public class Component {
    public Transform transform;

    public boolean enabled = true;
}
```

We've included an `enabled` flag, which will come in handy to easily hide/show objects when we draw our scene.

That's it. Next, we'll define our first component, `RenderObject`, to represent geometric objects in the scene.

The RenderObject component

`RenderObject` will serve as the parent class of geometric objects that can be rendered in the scene. `RenderObject` extends `Component`, so it has a `Transform`.

In the `renderbox/components` folder, create a new Java class, `RenderObject`. Define it as an abstract class that extends `Component`:

```
public abstract class RenderObject extends Component {
    private static final String TAG = "RenderObject";

    public RenderObject(){
        super();
        RenderBox.instance.renderObjects.add(this);
    }
}
```

The first thing we do is have each instance add itself to the list of `renderObjects` maintained by the `RenderBox` instance. Let's jump over to the `RenderBox` class now and add support for this list.

Open the `RenderBox.java` file and add a `renderObjects` list:

```
public class RenderBox implements CardboardView.StereoRenderer {

    public List<RenderObject> renderObjects = new
    ArrayList<RenderObject>();
```

Now, back to the `RenderObject` class; we'll implement three methods: `allocateFloatBuffer`, `allocateShortBuffer`, and `draw`.

OpenGL ES requires us to allocate a number of different memory buffers for various data, including model vertices, normal vectors, and index lists. The `allocateFloatBuffer` and `allocateShortBuffer` methods are utility methods that objects can use for floats and integers, respectively. Indexes are integers (specifically, shorts); everything else will be floats. These will be available to derived object classes:

```
public abstract class RenderObject extends Component {
        . . .
    protected static FloatBuffer allocateFloatBuffer(float[]
    data){
        ByteBuffer bbVertices =
        ByteBuffer.allocateDirect(data.length * 4);
        bbVertices.order(ByteOrder.nativeOrder());
        FloatBuffer buffer = bbVertices.asFloatBuffer();
        buffer.put(data);
        buffer.position(0);
```

```
        return buffer;
    }

    protected static ShortBuffer allocateShortBuffer(short[]
    data){
        ByteBuffer bbVertices =
        ByteBuffer.allocateDirect(data.length * 2);
        bbVertices.order(ByteOrder.nativeOrder());
        ShortBuffer buffer = bbVertices.asShortBuffer();
        buffer.put(data);
        buffer.position(0);
        return buffer;
    }
}
```

Clever readers might have noticed that we're using `ByteBuffer` first, and then converting it to `FloatBuffer` or `ShortBuffer`. While the conversion from a byte to float might make sense — raw memory is not often represented as floats — some might wonder why we don't allocate the `ShortBuffer` as a `ShortBuffer` from the start. The reason is actually the same in both cases. We want to take advantage of the `allocateDirect` method, which is more efficient and only exists within the `ByteBuffer` class.

Ultimately, the purpose of a `RenderObject` component is to draw geometry on the screen. This is done by transforming the 3D view and rendering through a `Material` class. Let's define variables for the material, some setter and getter methods, and the `draw` method:

```
    protected Material material;
    public static float[] model;
    public static float[] lightingModel;

    public Material getMaterial(){
        return material;
    }
    public RenderObject setMaterial(Material material){
        this.material = material;
        return this;
    }

    public void draw(float[] view, float[] perspective){
        if(!enabled)
            return;
        //Compute position every frame in case it changed
        transform.drawMatrices();
        material.draw(view, perspective);
    }
```

The `draw` method prepares the model transform for this object, and most of the draw action happens in materials. The `draw` method will be called from the current `Camera` component as it responds to the pose from the Cardboard SDK's `onDrawEye` hook. If the component isn't enabled, it's skipped.

The `RenderObject` class is abstract; we will not be working with `RenderObjects` directly. Instead, we'll derive object classes, such as `Cube` and `Sphere`. Let's create the `Cube` class from the `RenderObject` component next.

The Cube RenderObject component

For demonstration purposes, we'll start with a simple cube. Later on, we'll improve it with lighting. In *Chapter 3, Cardboard Box*, we defined a `Cube` model. We'll start by using the same class and data structure here. You can even copy the code, but it's shown in the following text. Create a `Cube` Java class in the `renderbox/components/` folder:

```java
// File: renderbox/components/Cube.java
public class Cube {
    public static final float[] CUBE_COORDS = new float[] {
            // Front face
            -1.0f, 1.0f, 1.0f,
            -1.0f, -1.0f, 1.0f,
            1.0f, 1.0f, 1.0f,
            -1.0f, -1.0f, 1.0f,
            1.0f, -1.0f, 1.0f,
            1.0f, 1.0f, 1.0f,

            // Right face
            1.0f, 1.0f, 1.0f,
            1.0f, -1.0f, 1.0f,
            1.0f, 1.0f, -1.0f,
            1.0f, -1.0f, 1.0f,
            1.0f, -1.0f, -1.0f,
            1.0f, 1.0f, -1.0f,

            // Back face
            1.0f, 1.0f, -1.0f,
            1.0f, -1.0f, -1.0f,
            -1.0f, 1.0f, -1.0f,
            1.0f, -1.0f, -1.0f,
            -1.0f, -1.0f, -1.0f,
            -1.0f, 1.0f, -1.0f,

            // Left face
```

```
            -1.0f,  1.0f, -1.0f,
            -1.0f, -1.0f, -1.0f,
            -1.0f,  1.0f,  1.0f,
            -1.0f, -1.0f, -1.0f,
            -1.0f, -1.0f,  1.0f,
            -1.0f,  1.0f,  1.0f,

            // Top face
            -1.0f,  1.0f, -1.0f,
            -1.0f,  1.0f,  1.0f,
             1.0f,  1.0f, -1.0f,
            -1.0f,  1.0f,  1.0f,
             1.0f,  1.0f,  1.0f,
             1.0f,  1.0f, -1.0f,

            // Bottom face
             1.0f, -1.0f, -1.0f,
             1.0f, -1.0f,  1.0f,
            -1.0f, -1.0f, -1.0f,
             1.0f, -1.0f,  1.0f,
            -1.0f, -1.0f,  1.0f,
            -1.0f, -1.0f, -1.0f,
    };

    public static final float[] CUBE_COLORS_FACES = new float[] {
            // Front, green
            0f, 0.53f, 0.27f, 1.0f,
            // Right, blue
            0.0f, 0.34f, 0.90f, 1.0f,
            // Back, also green
            0f, 0.53f, 0.27f, 1.0f,
            // Left, also blue
            0.0f, 0.34f, 0.90f, 1.0f,
            // Top, red
            0.84f,  0.18f,  0.13f, 1.0f,
            // Bottom, also red
            0.84f,  0.18f,  0.13f, 1.0f
    };

    /**
     * Utility method for generating float arrays for cube faces
     *
     * @param model - float[] array of values per face.
     * @param coords_per_vertex - int number of coordinates per
     vertex.
     * @return - Returns float array of coordinates for
     triangulated cube faces.
```

```
         *                    6 faces X 6 points X coords_per_vertex
         */
    public static float[] cubeFacesToArray(float[] model, int
    coords_per_vertex) {
        float coords[] = new float[6 * 6 * coords_per_vertex];
        int index = 0;
        for (int iFace=0; iFace < 6; iFace++) {
            for (int iVertex=0; iVertex < 6; iVertex++) {
                for (int iCoord=0; iCoord < coords_per_vertex;
                iCoord++) {
                    coords[index] = model[iFace*coords_per_vertex
                    + iCoord];
                    index++;
                }
            }
        }
        return coords;
    }
}
```

We list the coordinates for each face of the cube. Each face is made up of two triangles, resulting in 12 triangles, or a total of 36 sets of coordinates to define the cube.

We also list the different colors for each face of the cube. Rather than duplicating the colors 36 times, there's the cubeFacesToArray method to generate them.

Now, we need to upgrade Cube for RenderBox.

First, add the words extends RenderObject. This will provide the super() method in the constructor and allow you to call the draw() method:

```
public class Cube extends RenderObject {
```

Allocate buffers for its vertices and colors, and create the Material class that'll be used for rendering:

```
        public static FloatBuffer vertexBuffer;
        public static FloatBuffer colorBuffer;
        public static final int numIndices = 36;

        public Cube(){
            super();
            allocateBuffers();
            createMaterial();
        }

        public static void allocateBuffers(){
            //Already setup?
```

```
        if (vertexBuffer != null) return;
        vertexBuffer = allocateFloatBuffer(CUBE_COORDS);
        colorBuffer = allocateFloatBuffer
          (cubeFacesToArray(CUBE_COLORS_FACES, 4));
    }

    public void createMaterial(){
        VertexColorMaterial mat = new VertexColorMaterial();
        mat.setBuffers(vertexBuffer, colorBuffer, numIndices);
        material = mat;
    }
```

We ensure that `allocateBuffers` is run only once by checking whether `vertexBuffer` is `null`.

We plan to use the `VertexColorMaterial` class for rendering most cubes. That will be defined next.

A `Camera` component will call the `draw` method of the `Cube` class (inherited from `RenderObject`), which, in turn, calls the `Material` class's `draw` method. The `draw` method will be called from the main `Camera` component as it responds to the Cardboard SDK's `onDrawEye` hook.

Vertex color material and shaders

The `Cube` component needs a `Material` to render it on the display. Our `Cube` has separate colors for each face, defined as separate vertex colors. We'll define a `VertexColorMaterial` instance and the corresponding shaders.

Vertex color shaders

At a minimum, the OpenGL pipeline requires that we define a vertex shader, which transforms vertices from 3D space to 2D, and a fragment shader, which calculates the pixel color values for a raster segment. Similar to the simple shaders that we created in *Chapter 3, Cardboard Box*, we'll create two files, `vertex_color_vertex.shader` and `vertex_color_fragment.shader`. Unless you have done so already, create a new Android resource directory with the `raw` type and name it `raw`. Then, for each file, right-click on the directory, and go to **New** | **File**. Use the following code for each of the two files. The code for the vertex shader is as follows:

```
// File:res/raw/vertex_color_vertex.shader
uniform mat4 u_Model;
uniform mat4 u_MVP;

attribute vec4 a_Position;
```

```
attribute vec4 a_Color;

varying vec4 v_Color;

void main() {
   v_Color = a_Color;
   gl_Position = u_MVP * a_Position;
}
```

The code for the fragment shader is as follows:

```
//File: res/raw/vertex_color_fragment.shader
precision mediump float;
varying vec4 v_Color;

void main() {
    gl_FragColor = v_Color;
}
```

The vertex shader transforms each vertex by the u_MVP matrix, which will be supplied by the Material class's draw function. The fragment shader simply passes through the color specified by the vertex shader.

VertexColorMaterial

Now, we're ready to implement our first material, the VertexColorMaterial class. Create a new Java class named VertexColorMaterial in the renderbox/materials/ directory. Define the class as extends Material:

```
public class VertexColorMaterial extends Material {
```

The methods we're going to implement are as follows:

- VertexColorMaterial: These are constructors
- setupProgram: This creates the shader program and gets its OpenGL variable locations
- setBuffers: This sets the allocated buffer used in rendering
- draw: This draws a model from a view perspective

Here's the complete code:

```
public class VertexColorMaterial extends Material {
    static int program = -1;

    static int positionParam;
```

```
static int colorParam;
static int modelParam;
static int MVPParam;

FloatBuffer vertexBuffer;
FloatBuffer colorBuffer;
int numIndices;

public VertexColorMaterial(){
    super();
    setupProgram();
}

public static void setupProgram(){
    //Already setup?
    if (program != -1) return;
    //Create shader program
    program = createProgram(R.raw.vertex_color_vertex,
    R.raw.vertex_color_fragment);

    //Get vertex attribute parameters
    positionParam = GLES20.glGetAttribLocation(program,
    "a_Position");
    colorParam = GLES20.glGetAttribLocation(program,
    "a_Color");

    //Enable vertex attribute parameters
    GLES20.glEnableVertexAttribArray(positionParam);
    GLES20.glEnableVertexAttribArray(colorParam);

    //Shader-specific parameters
    modelParam = GLES20.glGetUniformLocation(program,
    "u_Model");
    MVPParam = GLES20.glGetUniformLocation(program, "u_MVP");

    RenderBox.checkGLError("Solid Color Lighting params");
}

public void setBuffers(FloatBuffer vertexBuffer,  FloatBuffer
colorBuffer, int numIndices){
    this.vertexBuffer = vertexBuffer;
    this.colorBuffer = colorBuffer;
    this.numIndices = numIndices;
}
```

```
    @Override
    public void draw(float[] view, float[] perspective) {
        Matrix.multiplyMM(modelView, 0, view, 0,
        RenderObject.model, 0);
        Matrix.multiplyMM(modelViewProjection, 0, perspective, 0,
        modelView, 0);

        GLES20.glUseProgram(program);

        // Set the Model in the shader, used to calculate lighting
        GLES20.glUniformMatrix4fv(modelParam, 1, false,
        RenderObject.model, 0);

        // Set the position of the cube
        GLES20.glVertexAttribPointer(positionParam, 3,
        GLES20.GL_FLOAT, false, 0, vertexBuffer);

        // Set the ModelViewProjection matrix in the shader.
        GLES20.glUniformMatrix4fv(MVPParam, 1, false,
        modelViewProjection, 0);

        // Set the normal positions of the cube, again for shading
        GLES20.glVertexAttribPointer(colorParam, 4,
        GLES20.GL_FLOAT, false, 0, colorBuffer);

        // Set the ModelViewProjection matrix in the shader.
        GLES20.glUniformMatrix4fv(MVPParam, 1, false,
        modelViewProjection, 0);

        GLES20.glDrawArrays(GLES20.GL_TRIANGLES, 0, numIndices);
    }

    public static void destroy(){
        program = -1;
    }
}
```

The setupProgram method creates an OpenGL ES program for the two shaders that we created in res/raw/ directory—vertex_color_vertex and vertex_color_ fragment. It then gets references to the positionParam, colorParam, and MVPParm shader variables using the GetAttribLocation and GetUniformLocation calls that provide memory locations within the shader program, which are used later for drawing.

The `setBuffers` method sets the memory buffers for vertices that define an object that will be drawn using this material. The method assumes that an object model consists of a set of 3D vertices (X, Y, and Z coordinates).

The `draw()` method renders the object specified in the buffers with a given set of **model-view-perspective (MVP)** transformation matrices. (Refer to the *3D camera, perspective, and head rotation* section of *Chapter 3, Cardboard Box*, for detailed explanations.)

You may have noticed that we aren't using that `ShortBuffer` function mentioned earlier. Later on, materials will use the `glDrawElements` call along with an index buffer. `glDrawArrays` is essentially a degenerate form of `glDrawElements`, which assumes a sequential index buffer (that is, 0, 1, 2, 3, and so on). It is more efficient with complex models to reuse vertices between triangles, which necessitates an index buffer.

For completeness, we will also provide a `destroy()` method for each of the `Material` classes. We will come to know exactly why the material must be destroyed a little later.

As you can see, `Material` encapsulates much of the lower level OpenGL ES 2.0 calls to compile the shader script, create a render program, set the model-view-perspective matrices in the shader, and draw the 3D graphic elements.

We can now implement the `Camera` component.

The Camera component

A `Camera` class is another type of `Component`, positioned in space like other component objects. The camera is special because through the camera's eyes, we render the scene. For VR, we render it twice, once for each eye.

Let's create the `Camera` class, and then see how it works. Create it in the `renderbox/components` folder and define it as follows:

```
public class Camera extends Component {
    private static final String TAG = "renderbox.Camera";

    private static final float Z_NEAR = .1f;
    public static final float Z_FAR = 1000f;

    private final float[] camera = new float[16];
    private final float[] view = new float[16];
    public Transform getTransform(){return transform;}
```

```java
    public Camera(){
        //The camera breaks pattern and creates its own Transform
        transform = new Transform();
    }

    public void onNewFrame(){
        // Build the camera matrix and apply it to the ModelView.
        Vector3 position = transform.getPosition();
        Matrix.setLookAtM(camera, 0, position.x, position.y,
        position.z + Z_NEAR, position.x, position.y, position.z,
        0.0f, 1.0f, 0.0f);

        RenderBox.checkGLError("onNewFrame");
    }

    public void onDrawEye(Eye eye) {
        GLES20.glEnable(GLES20.GL_DEPTH_TEST);
        GLES20.glClear(GLES20.GL_COLOR_BUFFER_BIT |
        GLES20.GL_DEPTH_BUFFER_BIT);

        RenderBox.checkGLError("glClear");

        // Apply the eye transformation to the camera.
        Matrix.multiplyMM(view, 0, eye.getEyeView(), 0,
        camera, 0);

        // Build the ModelView and ModelViewProjection matrices
        float[] perspective = eye.getPerspective(Z_NEAR, Z_FAR);

        for(RenderObject obj : RenderBox.instance.renderObjects) {
            obj.draw(view, perspective);
        }
        RenderBox.checkGLError("Drawing complete");
    }
}
```

The `Camera` class implements two methods: `onNewFrame` and `onDrawEye`, which will be delegated from the `RenderBox` class (which, in turn, is delegated from `MainActivity`).

As the name implies, `onNewFrame` is called on each new frame update. It is passed the current Cardboard SDK's `HeadTransform`, which describes the user's head orientation. Our camera actually doesn't need the `headTransform` value, because `Eye.getEyeView()`, which is combined with the camera matrix, also contains rotation information. Instead, we just need to define its position and initial direction using `Matrix.setLookAtM` (refer to http://developer.android.com/reference/android/opengl/Matrix.html).

The `onDrawEye` method is called by the Cardboard SDK once for each eye view. Given a Cardboard SDK eye view, the method begins to render the scene. It clears the surface, including the depth buffer (used to determine visible pixels), applies the eye transformation to the camera (including perspective), and then draws each `RenderObject` object in the scene.

RenderBox methods

Alright! We're getting closer. We're now ready to build a little scene in `RenderBox` using the code we created earlier. To start, the scene will simply consist of a colored cube and, of course, a camera.

At the beginning of this project, we created the skeleton `RenderBox` class, which implements `CardboardView.StereoRenderer`.

To this, we now add a `Camera` instance. At the top of the `RenderBox` class, declare `mainCamera`, which will get initialized in `onSurfaceCreated`:

```
public static Camera mainCamera;
```

Note that Android Studio may find other `Camera` classes; ensure that it uses the one that we created in this package.

Shortly after your app starts and the `MainActivity` class is instantiated, the `onSurfaceCreated` callback is called. This is where we can clear the screen, allocate buffers, and build shader programs. Let's add that now:

```
public void onSurfaceCreated(EGLConfig eglConfig) {
    RenderBox.reset();
    GLES20.glClearColor(0.1f, 0.1f, 0.1f, 0.5f);

    mainCamera = new Camera();

    checkGLError("onSurfaceCreated");
    callbacks.setup();
}
```

To be safe, the first thing it does is call reset, which will destroy any materials that might have already been compiled by resetting their program handles, before possibly compiling others. The need for this will become clear in the later projects where we will implement the intent feature to launch/relaunch the apps:

```
/**
 * Used to "clean up" compiled shaders, which have to be
 recompiled for a "fresh" activity
 */
```

```
public static void reset(){
    VertexColorMaterial.destroy();
}
```

The last thing `onSurfaceCreated` does is invoke the `setup` callback. This will be implemented in the interface implementer, which in our case is `MainActivity`.

In each new frame, we will call the camera's `onNewFrame` method to build the camera matrix and apply it to its model-view.

Let's also capture the current head pose (`headView` and `headAngles` as transformation matrices and angles, respectively) if we want to reference it in the later projects (refer to `https://developers.google.com/cardboard/android/latest/reference/com/google/vrtoolkit/cardboard/HeadTransform#public-constructors`). Still in `RenderBox`, add the following code:

```
public static final float[] headView = new float[16];
public static final float[] headAngles = new float[3];

public void onNewFrame(HeadTransform headTransform) {
    headTransform.getHeadView(headView, 0);
    headTransform.getEulerAngles(headAngles, 0);
    mainCamera.onNewFrame();
    callbacks.preDraw();
}
```

Then, when the Cardboard SDK goes to draw each eye (for the left and right split screen stereoscopic views), we will call the camera's `onDrawEye` method:

```
public void onDrawEye(Eye eye) {
    mainCamera.onDrawEye(eye);
}
```

While we're at it, we can also enable the `preDraw` and `postDraw` callbacks (in the previous code, in `onNewFrame`, and in `onFinishFrame`, respectively).

```
public void onFinishFrame(Viewport viewport) {
    callbacks.postDraw();
}
```

Should these interface callbacks be implemented in `MainActivity`, they will be called from here.

Now, we can build a scene that uses a `Camera`, a `Cube`, and the `VertexColorMaterial` class.

A simple box scene

Let's rock this riddim! Make a scene with just a cube and, of course, a camera (which has been set up automatically by `RenderBox`). Set up the `MainActivity` class using the `IRenderBox` interface's `setup` callback.

In `setup` of `MainActivity`, we create a `Transform` for the cube and position it so that it's set back and slightly offset in space:

```
Transform cube;

    @Override
public void setup() {
    cube = new Transform();
    cube.addComponent(new Cube());
    cube.setLocalPosition(2.0f, -2.f, -5.0f);
}
```

In Android Studio, click on **Run**. The program should compile, build, and install onto your connected Android phone. If you receive any compile errors, fix them now! As mentioned earlier, with the `Matrix` class, make sure that you are importing the right `Camera` type. There is also a `Camera` class within the SDK, which represents the phone's physical camera.

You will see something like this on your device display. (Remember to start the app while the device is facing you, or you might need to look behind you to find the cube!)

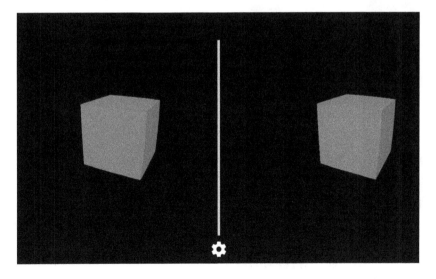

I don't know about you, but I'm excited! Now, let's add some light and shading.

Cube with face normals

Now, let's add a light to the scene and render the cube with it. To do this, we also need to define normal vectors for each face of the cube, which are used in the shader calculations.

If you derive Cube from the one in *Chapter 3, Cardboard Box,* you may already have this code:

```
public static final float[] CUBE_NORMALS_FACES = new float[] {
    // Front face
    0.0f, 0.0f, 1.0f,
    // Right face
    1.0f, 0.0f, 0.0f,
    // Back face
    0.0f, 0.0f, -1.0f,
    // Left face
    -1.0f, 0.0f, 0.0f,
    // Top face
    0.0f, 1.0f, 0.0f,
    // Bottom face
    0.0f, -1.0f, 0.0f,
};
```

Now, add a buffers for the normals, like we have for colors and vertices, and allocate them:

```
public static FloatBuffer normalBuffer;
...

public static void allocateBuffers(){
    ...
    normalBuffer = allocateFloatBuffer(
    cubeFacesToArray(CUBE_NORMALS_FACES, 3) );
}
```

We're going to add a lighting option argument to createMaterial and implement it using VertexColorLightingMaterial if it is set to true:

```
public Cube createMaterial(boolean lighting){
    if(lighting){
        VertexColorLightingMaterial mat = new
        VertexColorLightingMaterial();
        mat.setBuffers(vertexBuffer, colorBuffer,
        normalBuffer, 36);
        material = mat;
```

```
        } else {
            VertexColorMaterial mat = new VertexColorMaterial();
            mat.setBuffers(vertexBuffer, colorBuffer, numIndices);
            material = mat;
        }
        return this;
    }
```

Of course, the VertexColorLightingMaterial class hasn't been written yet. That's coming up soon. However, first we should create a Light component that can also be added to illuminate the scene.

We will refactor the Cube() constructor method with two variations. When no arguments are given, the Cube does not create any Material. When a Boolean lighting argument is given, that gets passed to createMaterial in order to choose the material:

```
    public Cube(){
        super();
        allocateBuffers();
    }

    public Cube(boolean lighting){
        super();
        allocateBuffers();
        createMaterial(lighting);
    }
```

We'll remind you later, but don't forget to modify the call to new Cube(true) in MainActivity to pass the lighting option.

Note that we're creating the material in the constructor out of convenience. There is nothing to stop us from just adding a setMaterial() method to RenderObject or making the material variable public. In fact, as the number of object and material types increases, this becomes the only sane way to proceed. This is a drawback of our simplified Material system, which expects a different class per material type.

The Light component

A light source in our scene is a type of Component with a color and a float array that is used to represent the calculated location in eye space. Let's create the Light class now.

Create a new `Light` Java class in the `renderbox/components` folder. Define it as follows:

```
public class Light extends Component {
    private static final String TAG = "RenderBox.Light";

    public final float[] lightPosInEyeSpace = new float[4];
    public float[] color = new float[]{1,1,1,1};

    public void onDraw(float[] view){
        Matrix.multiplyMV(lightPosInEyeSpace, 0, view, 0,
        transform.getPosition().toFloat4(), 0);
    }
}
```

Our default light is white (color 1,1,1).

The `onDraw` method calculates the actual light position in eye space based on the position of `Transform` multiplied by the current view matrix.

It's possible to extend `RenderBox` to support multiple light sources and other fancy rendering, such as shadows and so on. However, we will limit the scene to a single light source. Thus, we'll keep it as an instance variable in `RenderBox`.

Now, we can add a default light to the scene in `RenderBox`, like how we added the `Camera` component earlier. In `RenderBox.java`, add the following code:

```
public Light mainLight;
```

Modify `onSurfaceCreated` to initialize the light and add it to the scene:

```
public void onSurfaceCreated(EGLConfig eglConfig) {
    ...
    mainLight = new Light();
    new Transform().addComponent(mainLight);
    mainCamera = new Camera();
    ...
}
```

Then, compute its position in the `Camera` class's `onDrawEye` (it might change for every frame). Edit the `Camera` class in `Camera.java`:

```
public void onDrawEye(Eye eye) {
    ...
    // Apply the eye transformation to the camera.
    Matrix.multiplyMM(view, 0, eye.getEyeView(), 0, camera,
    0);

    // Compute lighting position
    RenderBox.instance.mainLight.onDraw(view);
```

Then, we'll also be able to reference the `mainLight` object in our `Material` class's `draw` method. We could have declared the color and position as static variables, since we are only using one light, but it makes more sense to plan for supporting multiple lights in the future.

Vertex color lighting material and shaders

This next topic gets a bit complicated. We're going to write new vertex and fragment shaders that handle lighting and write a corresponding class extending `Material` that makes use of them. Don't worry though, we've already done this once before. We're just going to actually explain it this time.

Let's dive right into it. Locate the `res/raw/` folder. Then, for each file, right-click on it, and go to **New | File** to create new files.

File: `res/raw/vertex_color_lighting_vertex.shader`

```
uniform mat4 u_Model;
uniform mat4 u_MVP;
uniform mat4 u_MVMatrix;
uniform vec3 u_LightPos;

attribute vec4 a_Position;
attribute vec4 a_Color;
attribute vec3 a_Normal;

varying vec4 v_Color;

const float ONE = 1.0;
const float COEFF = 0.00001;

void main() {
    vec3 modelViewVertex = vec3(u_MVMatrix * a_Position);
    vec3 modelViewNormal = vec3(u_MVMatrix * vec4(a_Normal, 0.0));

    float distance = length(u_LightPos - modelViewVertex);
    vec3 lightVector = normalize(u_LightPos - modelViewVertex);
    float diffuse = max(dot(modelViewNormal, lightVector), 0.5);

    diffuse = diffuse * (ONE / (ONE + (COEFF * distance *
    distance)));
    v_Color = a_Color * diffuse;
    gl_Position = u_MVP * a_Position;
}
```

The vertex shader maps a 3D vertex to 2D screen space using a model-view transformation matrix. Then, it finds the light distance and direction to calculate the light color and intensity at that point. These values are passed through the graphics pipeline. The fragment shader then determines the pixel colors in the raster segment.

```
// File: res/raw/vertex_color_lighting_fragment.shader
precision mediump float;
varying vec4 v_Color;

void main() {
    gl_FragColor = v_Color;
}
```

Now, we'll create the Material. In the renderbox/materials/ folder, create a VertexColorLightingMaterial class. Define it so it extends Material, and then declare its buffers and methods for setupProgram and draw. Here's the code in all its gory glory:

```
public class VertexColorLightingMaterial extends Material {
    private static final String TAG = "vertexcollight";
    static int program = -1;
    //Initialize to a totally invalid value for setup state

    static int positionParam;
    static int colorParam;
    static int normalParam;
    static int MVParam;
    static int MVPParam;
    static int lightPosParam;

    FloatBuffer vertexBuffer;
    FloatBuffer normalBuffer;
    FloatBuffer colorBuffer;
    int numIndices;

    public VertexColorLightingMaterial(){
        super();
        setupProgram();
    }

    public static void setupProgram(){
        //Already setup?
        if (program != -1) return;
        //Create shader program
```

```
    program = createProgram(R.raw.
    vertex_color_lighting_vertex,
    R.raw.vertex_color_lighting_fragment);

    //Get vertex attribute parameters
    positionParam = GLES20.glGetAttribLocation(program,
    "a_Position");
    normalParam = GLES20.glGetAttribLocation(program,
    "a_Normal");
    colorParam = GLES20.glGetAttribLocation(program,
    "a_Color");

    //Enable vertex attribute parameters
    GLES20.glEnableVertexAttribArray(positionParam);
    GLES20.glEnableVertexAttribArray(normalParam);
    GLES20.glEnableVertexAttribArray(colorParam);

    //Shader-specific parameteters
    MVParam = GLES20.glGetUniformLocation(program,
    "u_MVMatrix");
    MVPParam = GLES20.glGetUniformLocation(program, "u_MVP");
    lightPosParam = GLES20.glGetUniformLocation(program,
    "u_LightPos");

    RenderBox.checkGLError("Solid Color Lighting params");
}
public void setBuffers(FloatBuffer vertexBuffer, FloatBuffer
colorBuffer, FloatBuffer normalBuffer, int numIndices){
    this.vertexBuffer = vertexBuffer;
    this.normalBuffer = normalBuffer;
    this.colorBuffer = colorBuffer;
    this.numIndices = numIndices;
}

@Override
public void draw(float[] view, float[] perspective) {
    GLES20.glUseProgram(program);

    GLES20.glUniform3fv(lightPosParam, 1,
    RenderBox.instance.mainLight.lightPosInEyeSpace, 0);

    Matrix.multiplyMM(modelView, 0, view, 0,
    RenderObject.lightingModel, 0);
```

```
        // Set the ModelView in the shader, used to calculate
        // lighting
        GLES20.glUniformMatrix4fv(MVParam, 1, false,
        modelView, 0);

        Matrix.multiplyMM(modelView, 0, view, 0,
        RenderObject.model, 0);
        Matrix.multiplyMM(modelViewProjection, 0, perspective, 0,
        modelView, 0);
        // Set the ModelViewProjection matrix in the shader.
        GLES20.glUniformMatrix4fv(MVPParam, 1, false,
        modelViewProjection, 0);

        // Set the normal positions of the cube, again for shading
        GLES20.glVertexAttribPointer(normalParam, 3,
        GLES20.GL_FLOAT, false, 0, normalBuffer);
        GLES20.glVertexAttribPointer(colorParam, 4,
        GLES20.GL_FLOAT, false, 0, colorBuffer);

        // Set the position of the cube
        GLES20.glVertexAttribPointer(positionParam, 3,
        GLES20.GL_FLOAT, false, 0, vertexBuffer);

        GLES20.glDrawArrays(GLES20.GL_TRIANGLES, 0, numIndices);
    }

    public static void destroy(){
        program = -1;
    }
}
}
```

There's a lot going on here, but you can follow along if you read through it carefully. Mostly, the material code sets up the parameters that we wrote in the shader program.

It is especially important that in the draw() method, we obtain the current position transformation matrix, RenderBox.instance.mainLight.lightPosInEyeSpace of mainLight and the light color, and pass them along to the shader program.

Now is a good time to bring up the calls to GLES20.glEnableVertexAttribArray, which is required for each vertex attribute you are using. Vertex attributes are any data which are specified for each vertex, so in this case, we have positions, normals, and colors. Unlike before, we're now using normal and colors.

Having introduced a new `Material`, let's follow our pattern of adding it to
`RenderBox.reset()`:

```
public static void reset(){
    VertexColorMaterial.destroy();
    VertexColorLightingMaterial.destroy();
}
```

Finally, in the `setup()` method of `MainActivity`, make sure that you pass the
lighting parameter to the `Cube` constructor:

```
public void setup() {
    cube = new Transform();
    cube.addComponent(new Cube(true));
    cube.setLocalPosition(2.0f, -2.f, -5.0f);
}
```

Run your app. TAADAA!! There, we have it. The difference from the nonlit material
view may be subtle, but it's more real, virtually.

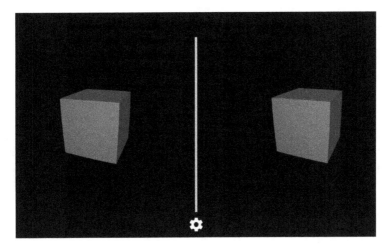

If you'd like to adjust the shading, you might need to play with the attenuation value
used to calculate the diffuse lighting (for example, change COEFF = 0.00001 to
0.001) in `vertex_color_lighting_vertex.shader`, depending on the scale of your
scene. For those still in the dark (pun intended), attenuation is a fancy word for how
light intensity diminishes over distance, and actually refers to the same property of
any physical signal (for example, light, radio, sound, and so on). If you have a very
large scene, you might want a smaller value (so light reaches distant regions) or the
inverse (so not everything is in light). You might also want to make the attenuation a
uniform float parameter, which can be adjusted and set on a per-material or per-light
basis, in order to achieve just the right lighting conditions.

So far, we've been using a single point light to light our scene. A **point light** is a light source with a position in 3D space, which casts light equally in all directions. Just like a standard light bulb placed at a specific location in a room, all that matters is the distance between it and the object, and the angle at which the ray strikes the surface. Rotation doesn't matter for point lights, unless a cookie is used to apply a texture to the light. We do not implement light cookies in the book, but they're super cool.

Other light sources can be directional lights, which will imitate sunlight on earth, where all of the light rays are going essentially in the same direction. Directional lights have a rotation that affects the direction of the light rays, but they do not have a position, as we assume that the theoretical source is infinitely far away along that direction vector. The third type of light source, from a graphics perspective, is a spotlight, where the light takes a cone shape and casts a circle or ellipse on the surface that it hits. The spotlight will end up working in a similar way to the perspective transformation that we do to our MVP matrix. We will only be using a single point light for the examples in this book. Implementation of other light source types is left as an exercise for the reader.

Time for animation

It's time to throw in a little more excitement. Let's animate the cube so that it rotates. This'll help demonstrate the shading as well.

For this, we need a `Time` class. This is a singleton utility class that ticks off frames and makes that information available to the application, for example, via `getDeltaTime`. Note that this is a `final` class, which explicitly means that it cannot be extended. There is no such thing as a static class in Java, but if we make the constructor private, we can ensure that nothing will ever instantiate it.

Create a new `Time` class in the `renderbox/` folder. It won't be getting extended, so we can declare it `final`. Here's the code:

```
public final class Time {
    private Time(){}
    static long startTime;
    static long lastFrame;
    static long deltaTime;
    static int frameCount;

    protected static void start(){
        frameCount = 0;
        startTime = System.currentTimeMillis();
        lastFrame = startTime;
    }
```

```
protected static void update(){
    long current =System.currentTimeMillis();
    frameCount++;
    deltaTime = current - lastFrame;
    lastFrame = current;
}

public static int getFrameCount(){return frameCount;}

public static float getTime(){
    return (float)(System.currentTimeMillis() - startTime) /
    1000;
}

public static float getDeltaTime(){
    return deltaTime * 0.001f;
}
}
```

Start the timer in the `RenderBox` setup:

```
public RenderBox(Activity mainActivity, IRenderBox callbacks){
    . . .
    Time.start();
}
```

Then, in the `onNewFrame` method of `RenderBox`, call `Time.update()`:

```
public void onNewFrame(HeadTransform headTransform) {
    Time.update();
    . . .
}
```

Now, we can use it to modify the cube's transform each frame, via the `preDraw()` interface hook. In `MainActivity`, make the cube rotate 5 degrees per second about the *X* axis, 10 degrees on the *Y* axis, and 7.5 degrees on the *Z* axis:

```
public void preDraw() {
    float dt = Time.getDeltaTime();
    cube.rotate(dt * 5, dt * 10, dt * 7.5f);
}
```

The `getDeltaTime()` method returns the fraction of a second since the previous frame. So, if we want it to rotate 5 degrees around the *X* axis each second, we multiply `deltaTime` by 5 to get the fraction of a degree to turn this particular frame.

Run the app. Rock and roll!!!

Detect looking at objects

Wait, there's more! Just one more thing to add. Building interactive applications require us to be able to determine whether the user is gazing at a specific object. We can put this into `RenderObject`, so any objects in the scene can be gaze detected.

The technique that we'll implement is straightforward. Considering each object we render is projected onto a camera plane, we really only need to determine whether the user is looking at the object's plane. Basically, we check whether the vector between the camera and the plane position is the same as the camera's view direction. But we'll throw in some tolerance, so you don't have to look exactly at the center of the plane (that'd be impractical). We will check a narrow range. A good way to do this is to calculate the angle between the vectors. We calculate the pitch and yaw angles between these vectors (the up/down X axis angle and left/right Y axis angle, respectively). Then, we check whether these angles are within a narrow threshold range, indicating that the user is looking at the plane (more or less).

This method is just like the one used in *Chapter 3, Cardboard Box,* although at that time, we put it in `MainActivity`. Now, we'll move it into the `RenderObject` component.

Note that this can get inefficient. This technique is fine for our projects because there is a limited number of objects, so the calculation isn't expensive. But if we had a large complex scene with many objects, this setup would fall short. In that case, one solution is to add an `isSelectable` flag so that only those objects that should be interactive in a given frame will be interactive.

If we were using a fully-featured game engine, we would have a physics engine capable of doing a `raycast` to precisely determine whether the center of your gaze intersects the object with a high degree of accuracy. While this might be great in the context of a game, it is overkill for our purposes.

At the top of `RenderObject`, add a Boolean variable for an `isLooking` value. Also, add two variables to hold the yaw and pitch range limits to detect the camera viewing angle, and a `modelView` matrix that we'll use for calculations:

```
public boolean isLooking;
private static final float YAW_LIMIT = 0.15f;
private static final float PITCH_LIMIT = 0.15f;
final float[] modelView = new float[16];
```

The implementation of the `isLookingAtObject` method is as follows. We convert the object space to the camera space, using the `headView` value from `onNewFrame`, calculate the pitch and yaw angles, and then check whether they're within the range of tolerance:

```
private boolean isLookingAtObject() {
    float[] initVec = { 0, 0, 0, 1.0f };
    float[] objPositionVec = new float[4];

    // Convert object space to camera space. Use the headView
    // from onNewFrame.
    Matrix.multiplyMM(modelView, 0, RenderBox.headView, 0,
    model, 0);
    Matrix.multiplyMV(objPositionVec, 0, modelView, 0,
    initVec, 0);

    float pitch = (float) Math.atan2(objPositionVec[1], -
    objPositionVec[2]);
    float yaw = (float) Math.atan2(objPositionVec[0], -
    objPositionVec[2]);

    return Math.abs(pitch) < PITCH_LIMIT && Math.abs(yaw) <
    YAW_LIMIT;
}
```

For convenience, we'll set the `isLooking` flag at the same time the object is drawn. Add the call at the end of the `draw` method:

```
public void draw(float[] view, float[] perspective){
    . . .
    isLooking = isLookingAtObject();
}
```

That should do it.

For a simple test, we'll log some text to the console when the user is gazing at the cube. In `MainActivity`, make a separate variable for the `Cube` object:

```
Cube cubeObject;

public void setup() {
    cube = new Transform();
    cubeObject = new Cube(true);
    cube.addComponent(cubeObject);
    cube.setLocalPosition(2.0f, -2.f, -5.0f);
}
```

Then, test it in `postDraw`, as follows:

```
public void postDraw() {
    if (cubeObject.isLooking) {
        Log.d(TAG, "isLooking at Cube");
    }
}
```

Exporting the RenderBox package

Now that we've finished creating this beautiful `RenderBox` library, how do we reuse it in other projects? This is where **modules** and `.aar` files come into play. There are a number of ways to share code between Android projects. The most obvious way is to literally copy pieces of code into the next project as you see fit. While this is perfectly acceptable in certain situations, and in fact should be part of your normal process, it can become quite tedious. What if we have a bunch of files that reference each other and depend on a certain file hierarchy, such as `RenderBox`? If you're familiar with Java development, you might say, "Well, obviously just export the compiled classes in a `.jar` file." You would be right, except that this is Android. We have some generated classes as well as the `/res` folder, which contains, in this case, our shader code. What we actually want is an `.aar` file. Android programmers might be familiar with `.aidl` files, which are used for similar purposes, but specifically to establish interfaces between apps, and not encapsulate feature code.

To generate an `.aar` file, we first need to put our code inside an Android Studio module with a different output than an app. You have a few options from this point onward. We recommend that you create a dedicated Android Studio project, which contains the `RenderBox` module as well a test app, which will build alongside the library and serve as a means to ensure that any changes you make to the library don't break anything. You can also just copy the `renderbox` package and the `/res/raw` folders into a new project and go from there, but eventually, you'll see that a module is much more convenient.

You might think "We're gonna call this new project `RenderBox`," but you might run into a snag. Basically, the build system can't handle a situation where a project and module have the same name (they would be expected to have the same package name, which is a no-no). If you call your project `RenderBox`, (technically, you shouldn't have if you followed the instructions) and include an activity, and then create a module called `RenderBox`, you will see a build error that complains about the project and module sharing a name. If you create an empty project with no activity called `RenderBox` and add a module called `RenderBox`, you happen to get away with it, but as soon as you try to build an app from this project, you'll find that you cannot. Hence, we suggest that your next step from here is to create a new project called `RenderBoxLib`.

Building the RenderBoxLib module

Let's give it a shot. Go to **File | New | New Project**. Name the project `RenderBoxLib`.

We don't need a `MainActivity` class, but we're still going to want one, as discussed, as a test case to ensure that our library works. Adding a test app to the library project not only gives us the convenience of testing changes to the library in a single step, but also ensures that we cannot build a new version of the library without ensuring that an app that uses it can also compile it. Even if your library is free of syntax errors, it might still break compilation when you include it in a new project.

So, go ahead and add an **Empty Activity**, and click on **Finish** in the default options.

All familiar territory so far. However, now we're going to create a new module:

1. Go to **File | New | New Module** and select **Android Library**:

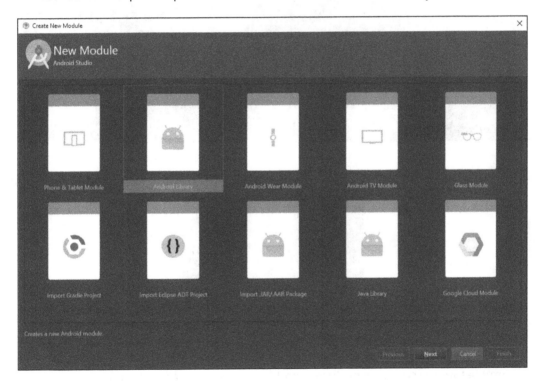

2. Name it `RenderBox`.

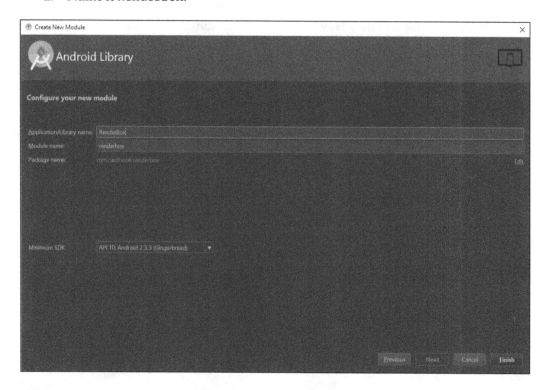

3. Now, we have a new folder in our project view:

Instead of performing the next steps in Android Studio, let's just use our file manager (Windows Explorer or Finder, or the terminal if you're a pro) to copy our `RenderBox` files from the existing project into the new one. If you're using version control, you might consider transferring your repository to the new project, or creating an init commit before the copy; it's up to you and how much you care about preserving your history.

We want to copy all your `RenderBox` code to the new module from the `RenderBoxDemo` project's `/app/src/main/java/com/cardbookvr/renderbox` folder to the `/renderbox/src/main/java/com/cardbookvr/renderbox` folder of `RenderBoxLib`.

The same goes for the resources; copy them from the `RenderBoxDemo` project's `/app/src/main/res/raw` folder to `/renderbox/src/main/res/raw`.

This means that almost every `.java` and `.shader` file that we created in the original project goes into the module of the new project, in their corresponding locations.

We won't be transferring `MainActivity.java`, or any of the XML files, such as `layouts/activity_main.xml` or `AndroidManifest.xml` to the module. These are app-specific files, which are not included in the library.

Once you've copied the files, go back to Android Studio, and click on the **Synchronize** button. This will ensure that Android Studio has noticed the new files.

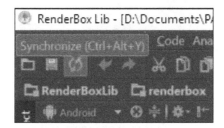

Then, with `renderbox` selected in the hierarchy panel, initiate a build by navigating to **Build | Make Module 'RenderBox'** (or *Ctrl + Shift + F9*). You will see a bunch of errors. Let's take care of them.

`RenderBox` references the Cardboard SDK, and as such, we must include it in the `RenderBox` module as a dependency in a similar way to how we do it for the main app, like at the beginning of this project:

1. Add the Cardboard SDK `common.aar` and `core.aar` library files to your project as new modules, using **File | New | New Module...** and **Import .JAR/.AAR Package**.

2. Set the library modules as dependencies to the `RenderBox` model, using **File | Project Structure**. In the left-side panel, select `RenderBox`, then choose the **Dependencies** tab | **+** | **Module Dependency**, and add common and core modules.

Once you sync the project and trigger a build, you will hopefully see those errors related to `CardboardView` and so on disappear.

Another build. Still, other errors?

This is because of the naming issues mentioned earlier. If the package name of your module doesn't match the package name from the original project (that is, com. cardbookvr.renderbox), you will have to rename it in the copied Java files. Even if these match, we named our original project RenderBoxDemo, which means that the generated R class will be part of the com.cardbookvr.renderboxdemo package. Any import references to this package will need to be changed.

Start by deleting the line that references com.cardbookvr.renderboxdemo (such as the Material Java files). Then, any references to the R class will show up as errors:

```
import com.cardbook.renderbox.materials.UnlitTexMaterial;
import com.cardbook.renderbox.materials.VertexColorLighting
import com.cardbook.renderboxdemo.R;
import c                            CardboardView;
import c   Cannot resolve symbol 'renderboxdemo'  Eye;
```

Delete this line, and Android Studio will generate a new valid import line. Try and build it again. If it's error-free, we're good to go.

You will now see references to R show up as errors with a suggestion:

```
public static void setupProgram(){
    setup = t
    //Create        ? com.cardbook.renderbox.R? Alt+Enter

    program = createProgram(R.raw.vertex_color_

    //Get vertex attribute parameters
    positionParam = GLES20.glGetAttribLocation(
    normalParam = GLES20.glGetAttribLocation(p
```

If you go ahead and press *Alt + Enter*, Android Studio will add the appropriate import line to your code. If you don't see the *Alt + Enter* tooltip, try placing your cursor next to R. Using the feature this way, you'll have to select **Import Class** from the menu you see after pressing *Alt + Enter*. If you still see errors, make sure that you've copied the shader code into the /renderbox/res/raw folder, and that there aren't other errors interfering with this process. Essentially, we are removing any external references from the code and getting RenderBox to build on its own. We can also accomplish this code fix by simply pasting import com.cardbook. renderbox.R; over import com.cardbook.renderboxdemo.R;. That's probably easier than the first method, but then you wouldn't have learned about *Alt + Enter*.

Once this is done, we should be able to build without errors. This might seem like a messy way to work, but it doesn't hurt to get messy once in a while. You might even learn something new about the build pipeline you didn't know earlier.

If everything goes well, you will see a file called `renderbox-debug.aar` in `renderbox/build/outputs/aar/`. If so, you're done. Whew!

One final thought: you should include `renderbox-release.aar` in your final applications, but you will lose useful debugging features in the meantime. We will not discuss how to switch back and forth between debug and release in this book, but understanding build configurations is essential to the publication process.

The RenderBox test app

This new project houses the `renderbox` module, but there's also an `app` folder that we created in the first place. `app` is where we can implement a test application to make sure, at a minimum, that the library is built and basically runs.

We're going to do the same thing to the app module in `RenderBoxLib` that we did in our new projects (like `renderbox`, `app` is a module. It turns out that we've been using modules the whole time!):

1. Right-click on the `app` folder, go to **Open Module Settings**, and add the existing `renderbox` module as a **Module dependency** with **Compile Scope**. Notice that the dependencies cannot be circular. Now that `renderbox` is a dependency of the app, the reverse cannot be true.

2. Update `/res/layout/activity_main.xml` and `AndroidManifest.xml`, as we saw at the top of this chapter. (If you're just copying code, make sure that you change the `package=` value to the current name, for example, `com.cardbookvr.renderboxlib`).

3. Set up `class MainActivity extends CardboardActivity implements IRenderBox`.

4. We now also want our `MainActivity` class to instantiate `RenderBox` and define a `setup()` method, just like `MainActivity` in `RenderBoxDemo`. In fact, just go ahead and copy the entire `MainActivity` class from `RenderBoxDemo`, and make that you do not copy/overwrite the package definition at the top of the new file in your new project.

With any luck, you should be able to click on the green run button, select your target device, and see a running app with our buddy, the vertex color cube. We've officially gone backward in terms of the final result, but our application-specific code is so clean and simple!

Using RenderBox in future projects

Now that we've gone through all of this trouble, let's do a trial run to see how to use our pretty little package all tied up with a bow. One more time. You can perform the following steps to start each of the subsequent projects in this book:

1. Create a new project, called whatever you like, such as `MyCardboardApp`, for API 19 KitKat. Include **Empty Activity**.

2. Now, go to **File | New | New Module…**. It's a little counterintuitive, but even though we are importing an existing module, we're adding a new one to this project. Choose **Import .JAR/.AAR Package**.

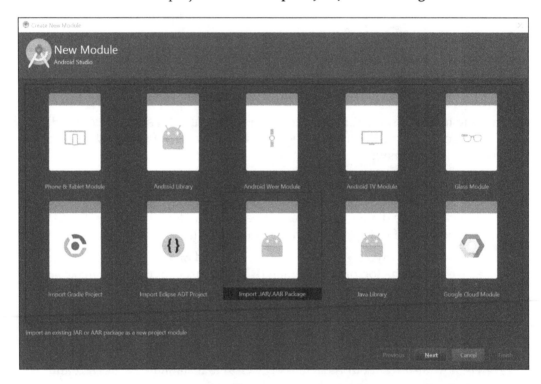

3. You'll need to navigate to the `RenderBoxLib/renderbox/build/outputs` folder of your `RenderBox` lib project, and select the `.aar` file. We recommend that you rename the module to `renderbox`, as opposed to `renderbox-debug`. Click on **Finish**. For a production app, you would want to have two different modules in your project: one for debug and one for release, but we will only be using debug for the projects in this book.

4. Now that we have this new module, we need to add it as a dependency to the default app. Go back to the familiar **Module Settings** screen, and head over to the **Dependencies** tab for app. Click on the plus tab on the right-hand side, and choose **Module dependency**:

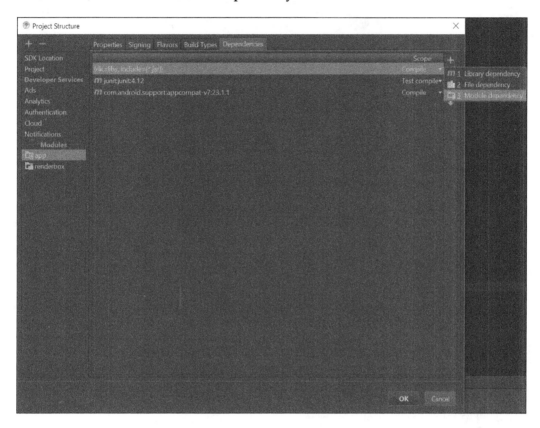

5. Then, you can add `renderbox`:

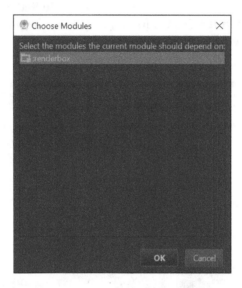

We now have a copy of the `.aar` file in our new project's `/renderbox` module folder. When you've made changes to the `RenderBox` library, you just need to build a new `.aar` file (build menu, `MakeProject`), overwrite the copy in the new project, and trigger a project sync, or clean and rebuild if you want to be sure. The new project does not maintain a link to the build folder of your library output project.

The remaining steps required to setup a new project are as follows:

1. Use **File | New Module** to import the Cardboard SDK `.aar` packages `common` and `core`, and add them as dependencies to the app.
2. Update `/res/layout/activity_main.xml` and `AndroidManifest.xml`, as we've just done for `RenderBoxDemo`.
3. Set up the `MainActivity` class so that it extends `CardboardActivity` and implements `IRenderBox`, using the same code as before.
4. We now also want our `MainActivity` class to instantiate `RenderBox` and define a `setup()` method, just like our `MainActivity` class in `RenderBoxDemo`. In fact, just go ahead and copy the entire `MainActivity` class, and be careful not to copy/overwrite the package definition at the top of the file.

Build and run it yet again. Bagged it! We can now proceed with the cool stuff.

 This will be our new project process from now on, since the rest of the projects in this book make use of the `RenderBox` library module.

A final word on the module process: there's more than one way to peel an orange. You could have just created a new module in the `RenderBox` demo project, grabbed its output, and been off and running. You can also just copy source files around and try using Git submodules or subtrees to synchronize the sources. This page from the IntelliJ docs discusses some of the finer points as well (`https://www.jetbrains. com/idea/help/sharing-android-source-code-and-resources-using- library-projects.html`). We've also made certain decisions in terms of keeping the main activity and layout files completely application-specific, and including most or all of our shaders and materials in the `RenderBox` module, instead of in application code. At any one of these decision points, there are pros and cons, and we recommend that you think carefully about how you structure your own code in future projects.

Summary

In this chapter, we created a short and sweet, lightweight graphics engine to build new Cardboard VR applications. We abstracted the low-level OpenGL ES API calls into a suite of `Material` classes and a `Camera` class. We defined `RenderObject` for geometric entities, a `Camera` and `Light` components which inherit from a `Component` class. We defined a `Transform` class to organize and orient entities (which contain components) hierarchically in 3D space. All of this is integrated under the `RenderBox` class, which is instantiated and controlled in the `MainActivity` class, which, in turn, implements the `IRenderBox` interface. We complete the circle by specifying the `MainActivity` class as the implementer of `IRenderBox` and implementing `setup`, `preDraw`, and `postDraw`.

To develop the library, we followed much of what was covered in *Chapter 3, Cardboard Box*, with less explanation of how to use OpenGL ES and matrix libraries and more focus on implementing our `RenderBox` software architecture.

The resulting `RenderBox` engine library is now in its own project. In subsequent chapters we will reuse this library, and we will expand it, including new Components and Materials. You are encouraged to maintain your `RenderBoxLib` code in a source code repository, such as Git. Of course, the final code is provided with the book assets and in our GitHub repository.

The next chapter is a science project! We're going to build a model of our Solar System, replete with the Sun, planets, moons, and a starscape. Using `RenderBox`, we will add a `Sphere` component, and we will also add textured shaders to our suite of materials.

6
Solar System

When I was 8 years old, for a science project at school, I made a *Solar System* from wires, styrofoam balls, and paint. Today, 8-year olds all around the world will be able to make virtual Solar Systems in VR, especially if they read this chapter! This project creates a Cardboard VR app that simulates our Solar System. Well, maybe not with total scientific accuracy, but good enough for a kid's project and better than styrofoam balls.

In this chapter, you will create a new Solar System project with the `RenderBox` library by performing the following steps:

- Setting up the new project
- Creating a `Sphere` component and a solid color material
- Adding an `Earth` texture material with lighting
- Arranging the Solar System geometry
- Animating the heavenly bodies
- Interactively changing camera locations
- Updating the `RenderBox` library with our new code

As we put these together, we will create planets and moons from a sphere. Much of the code, however, will be in the various materials and shaders for rendering these bodies.

 The source code for this project can be found on the Packt Publishing website, and on GitHub at `https://github.com/cardbookvr/solarsystem` (with each topic as a separate commit).

Setting up a new project

To build this project, we will use our `RenderBox` library created in *Chapter 5, RenderBox Engine*. You can use yours, or grab a copy from the downloadable files provided with this book or our GitHub repository (use the commit tagged `after-ch5` — `https://github.com/cardbookvr/renderboxlib/releases/tag/after-ch5`). For a more detailed description of how to import the `RenderBox` library, refer to the final *Using RenderBox in future projects* section of *Chapter 5, RenderBox Engine*. Perform the following steps to create a new project:

1. With Android Studio opened, create a new project. Let's name it `SolarSystem` and target **Android 4.4 KitKat (API 19)** with an **Empty Activity**.

2. Create new modules for each of `renderbox`, `common` and `core` packages, using **File | New Module | Import .JAR/.AAR Package**.

3. Set the modules as dependencies for the app, using **File | Project Structure**.

4. Edit the `build.gradle` file as explained in *Chapter 2, The Skeleton Cardboard Project*, to compile against SDK 22.

5. Update `/res/layout/activity_main.xml` and `AndroidManifest.xml`, as explained in the previous chapters.

6. Edit `MainActivity` as `class MainActivity extends CardboardActivity implements IRenderBox`, and implement the interface method stubs (*Ctrl + I*).

We can go ahead and define the `onCreate` method in `MainActivity`. The class now has the following code:

```
public class MainActivity extends CardboardActivity implements
IRenderBox {
    private static final String TAG = "SolarSystem";

    @Override
    protected void onCreate(Bundle savedInstanceState) {
        super.onCreate(savedInstanceState);
        setContentView(R.layout.activity_main);

        CardboardView cardboardView = (CardboardView)
        findViewById(R.id.cardboard_view);
        cardboardView.setRenderer(new RenderBox(this, this));
        setCardboardView(cardboardView);
    }
    @Override
    public void setup() {

    }
    @Override
    public void preDraw() {
```

```
    }
    @Override
    public void postDraw() {
    }
}
```

While we build this project, we will be creating new classes that could be good extensions to `RenderBox` lib. We'll make them regular classes in this project at first. Then, at the end of the chapter, we'll help you move them into the `RenderBox` lib project and rebuild the library:

1. Right-click on the `solarsystem` folder (`com.cardbookvr.solarsystem`), select **New | Package**, and name it `RenderBoxExt`.

2. Within `RenderBoxExt`, create package subfolders named `components` and `materials`.

There's no real technical need to make it a separate package, but this helps organize our files, as the ones in `RenderBoxExt` will be moved into our reusable library at the end of this chapter.

You can add a cube to the scene, temporarily, to help ensure that everything is set up properly. Add it to the `setup` method as follows:

```
public void setup() {
    new Transform()
        .setLocalPosition(0,0,-7)
        .setLocalRotation(45,60,0)
        .addComponent(new Cube(true));
}
```

If you remember, a cube is a component that's added to a transform. The cube defines its geometry (for example, vertices). The transform defines its position, rotation, and scale in 3D space.

You should be able to click on **Run 'app'** with no compile errors, and see the cube and Cardboard split screen view on your Android device.

Creating a Sphere component

Our Solar System will be constructed from spheres, representing planets, moons, and the Sun. Let's first create a `Sphere` component. We are going to define a sphere as a triangle mesh of vertices that form the surface of the sphere (For more information on a triangle mesh, refer to `https://en.wikipedia.org/wiki/Triangle_mesh`).

Right-click on the `RenderBoxExt/components` folder, select **New | Java Class**, and name it `Sphere`. Define it as `public class Sphere extends RenderObject`:

```
public class Sphere extends RenderObject{
    private static final String TAG = "RenderBox.Sphere";
    public Sphere() {
        super();
        allocateBuffers();
    }
}
```

The constructor calls a helper method, `allocateBuffers`, which allocates buffers for vertices, normals, textures, and indexes. Let's declare variables for these at the top of the class:

```
public static FloatBuffer vertexBuffer;
public static FloatBuffer normalBuffer;
public static FloatBuffer texCoordBuffer;
public static ShortBuffer indexBuffer;
public static int numIndices;
```

Note that we've decided to declare the buffers `public` to afford future flexibility in creating arbitrary texture materials for objects.

We'll define a sphere with a radius of 1. Its vertices are arranged by 24 longitude sections (as hours of the day) and 16 latitude sections, providing sufficient resolution for our purposes. The top and bottom caps are handled separately. This is a long method, so we'll break it down for you. Here's the first part of the code where we declare and initialize variables, including the vertices array. Similar to our `Material` setup methods, we only need to allocate the `Sphere` buffers once, and in this case, we use the vertex buffer variable to keep track of this state. If it is not null, the buffers have already been allocated. Otherwise, we should continue with the function, which will set this value:

```
public static void allocateBuffers(){
    //Already allocated?
    if (vertexBuffer != null) return;
    //Generate a sphere model
    float radius = 1f;
    // Longitude |||
    int nbLong = 24;
    // Latitude ---
    int nbLat = 16;

    Vector3[] vertices = new Vector3[(nbLong+1) * nbLat +
    nbLong * 2];
    float _pi = MathUtils.PI;
    float _2pi = MathUtils.PI2;
```

Calculate the vertex positions; first, the top and bottom ones and then along the latitude/longitude spherical grid:

```
//Top and bottom vertices are duplicated
for(int i = 0; i < nbLong; i++){
    vertices[i] = new Vector3(Vector3.up).
    multiply(radius);
    vertices[vertices.length - i - 1] = new
    Vector3(Vector3.up).multiply(-radius);
}
for( int lat = 0; lat < nbLat; lat++ )
{
    float a1 = _pi * (float)(lat+1) / (nbLat+1);
    float sin1 = (float)Math.sin(a1);
    float cos1 = (float)Math.cos(a1);

    for( int lon = 0; lon <= nbLong; lon++ )
    {
        float a2 = _2pi * (float)(lon == nbLong ? 0 : lon)
        / nbLong;
        float sin2 = (float)Math.sin(a2);
        float cos2 = (float)Math.cos(a2);

        vertices[lon + lat * (nbLong + 1) + nbLong] =
            new Vector3( sin1 * cos2, cos1, sin1 * sin2 ).
            multiply(radius);
    }
}
```

Next, we calculate the vertex normals and then the UVs for texture mapping:

```
Vector3[] normals = new Vector3[vertices.length];
for( int n = 0; n < vertices.length; n++ )
    normals[n] = new Vector3(vertices[n]).normalize();

Vector2[] uvs = new Vector2[vertices.length];
float uvStart = 1.0f / (nbLong * 2);
float uvStride = 1.0f / nbLong;
for(int i = 0; i < nbLong; i++) {
    uvs[i] = new Vector2(uvStart + i * uvStride, 1f);
    uvs[uvs.length - i - 1] = new Vector2(1 - (uvStart + i
    * uvStride), 0f);
}
for( int lat = 0; lat < nbLat; lat++ )
    for( int lon = 0; lon <= nbLong; lon++ )
```

```
            uvs[lon + lat * (nbLong + 1) + nbLong] = new
            Vector2( (float)lon / nbLong, 1f -
              (float)(lat+1) / (nbLat+1) );
```

This next part of the same `allocateBuffers` method generates the triangular indices, which connect the vertices:

```
int nbFaces = (nbLong+1) * nbLat + 2;
int nbTriangles = nbFaces * 2;
int nbIndexes = nbTriangles * 3;
numIndices = nbIndexes;
short[] triangles = new short[ nbIndexes ];

//Top Cap
int i = 0;
for( short lon = 0; lon < nbLong; lon++ )
{
    triangles[i++] = lon;
    triangles[i++] = (short)(nbLong + lon+1);
    triangles[i++] = (short)(nbLong + lon);
}

//Middle
for( short lat = 0; lat < nbLat - 1; lat++ )
{
    for( short lon = 0; lon < nbLong; lon++ )
    {
        short current = (short)(lon + lat * (nbLong + 1) +
        nbLong);
        short next = (short)(current + nbLong + 1);

        triangles[i++] = current;
        triangles[i++] = (short)(current + 1);
        triangles[i++] = (short)(next + 1);

        triangles[i++] = current;
        triangles[i++] = (short)(next + 1);
        triangles[i++] = next;
    }
}

//Bottom Cap
for( short lon = 0; lon < nbLong; lon++ )
{
    triangles[i++] = (short)(vertices.length - lon - 1);
```

```
            triangles[i++] = (short)(vertices.length - nbLong -
            (lon+1) - 1);
            triangles[i++] = (short)(vertices.length - nbLong -
            (lon) - 1);
    }
```

Finally, apply these calculated values to the corresponding `vertexBuffer`, `normalBuffer`, `texCoordBuffer`, and `indexBuffer` arrays, as follows:

```
        //convert Vector3[] to float[]
        float[] vertexArray = new float[vertices.length * 3];
        for(i = 0; i < vertices.length; i++){
            int step = i * 3;
            vertexArray[step] = vertices[i].x;
            vertexArray[step + 1] = vertices[i].y;
            vertexArray[step + 2] = vertices[i].z;
        }
        float[] normalArray = new float[normals.length * 3];
        for(i = 0; i < normals.length; i++){
            int step = i * 3;
            normalArray[step] = normals[i].x;
            normalArray[step + 1] = normals[i].y;
            normalArray[step + 2] = normals[i].z;
        }
        float[] texCoordArray = new float[uvs.length * 2];
        for(i = 0; i < uvs.length; i++){
            int step = i * 2;
            texCoordArray[step] = uvs[i].x;
            texCoordArray[step + 1] = uvs[i].y;
        }

        vertexBuffer = allocateFloatBuffer(vertexArray);
        normalBuffer = allocateFloatBuffer(normalArray);
        texCoordBuffer = allocateFloatBuffer(texCoordArray);
        indexBuffer = allocateShortBuffer(triangles);
    }
```

This is a lot of code, and might be hard to read on the pages of a book; you can find a copy in the project GitHub repository if you prefer.

Conveniently, since the sphere is centered at the origin (0,0,0), the normal vectors at each vertex correspond to the vertex position itself (radiating from the origin to the vertex). Strictly speaking, since we used a radius of 1, we can avoid the `normalize()` step to generate the array of normals as an optimization. The following image shows the 24 x 16 vertex sphere with its normal vectors:

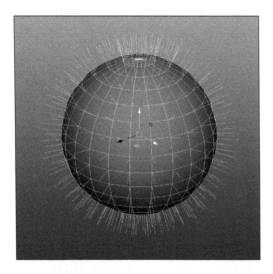

Note that our algorithm includes an interesting fix that avoids a single vertex at the poles (where all the UVs converge at a single point and cause some swirling texture artifacts).

We create *nLon-1* co-located vertices spread across the UV X, offset by *1/(nLon*2)*, drawing teeth at the top and bottom. The following image shows the flattened UV sheet for the sphere illustrating the polar teeth:

A solid color lighted sphere

We are going to start by rendering our sphere in a solid color but with lighted shading. As usual, we start by writing the shader functions that, among other things, define the program variables they will need from the `Material` that uses it. Then, we'll define the `SolidColorLightingMaterial` class and add it to the `Sphere` component.

Solid color lighting shaders

In the previous chapters, where we used shaders with lighting, we did the lighting calculations in the vertex shader. That's simpler (and faster), but transitioning the calculations to the fragment shader yields better results. The reason is that, in the vertex shader, you only have one normal value to compare against the light direction. In the fragment, all vertex attributes are interpolated, meaning that the normal value at a given point between two vertices will be some point in between their two normals. When this is the case, you see a smooth gradient across the triangle face, rather than localized shading artifacts around each vertex. We will be creating a new `Material` class to implement lighting in the fragment shader.

If necessary, create an Android Resource Directory for the shaders (resource type: raw), res/raw/. Then, create the `solid_color_lighting_vertex.shader` and res/raw/solid_color_lighting_fragment.shader files and define them as follows.

File: res/raw/solid_color_lighting_vertex.shader

```
uniform mat4 u_MVP;
uniform mat4 u_MV;

attribute vec4 a_Position;
attribute vec3 a_Normal;

varying vec3 v_Position;
varying vec3 v_Normal;

void main() {
    // vertex in eye space
    v_Position = vec3(u_MV * a_Position);

    // normal's orientation in eye space
    v_Normal = vec3(u_MV * vec4(a_Normal, 0.0));

    // point in normalized screen coordinates
    gl_Position = u_MVP * a_Position;
}
```

Note that we have separate uniform variables for u_MV and u_MVP. Also, if you remember that in the previous chapter, we separated the lighting model from the actual model because we did not want scale to affect lighting calculations. Similarly, the projection matrix is only useful to apply the camera FOV to vertex positions and will interfere with lighting calculations.

File: res/raw/solid_color_lighting_fragment.shader

```
precision mediump float;
// default medium precision in the fragment shader
uniform vec3 u_LightPos;
// light position in eye space
uniform vec4 u_LightCol;
uniform vec4 u_Color;

varying vec3 v_Position;
varying vec3 v_Normal;
varying vec2 v_TexCoordinate;

void main() {
    // distance for attenuation.
    float distance = length(u_LightPos - v_Position);

    // lighting direction vector from the light to the vertex
    vec3 lightVector = normalize(u_LightPos - v_Position);

    // dot product of the light vector and vertex normal.
    // If the normal and light vector are
    // pointing in the same direction then it will get max
    // illumination.
    float diffuse = max(dot(v_Normal, lightVector), 0.01);

    // Add a tiny bit of ambient lighting (this is outerspace)
    diffuse = diffuse + 0.025;

    // Multiply color by the diffuse illumination level and
    // texture value to get final output color
    gl_FragColor = u_Color * u_LightCol * diffuse;
}
```

Solid color lighting material

Next, we define the Material class for the shaders. In the materials folder, create a new Java class named SolidColorLightingMaterial and define it as follows:

```
public class SolidColorLightingMaterial extends Material {
    private static final String TAG = "solidcolorlighting";


}
```

Add the variables for color, program references, and buffers, as shown in the following code:

```
float[] color = new float[4];
static int program = -1;
static int positionParam;
static int colorParam;
static int normalParam;
static int modelParam;
static int MVParam;
static int MVPParam;
static int lightPosParam;
static int lightColParam;

FloatBuffer vertexBuffer;
FloatBuffer normalBuffer;
ShortBuffer indexBuffer;
int numIndices;
```

Now, we can add a constructor, which receives a color (RGBA) value and sets up the shader program, as follows:

```
public SolidColorLightingMaterial(float[] c){
    super();
    setColor(c);
    setupProgram();
}

public void setColor(float[] c){
    color = c;
}
```

As we've seen earlier, the `setupProgram` method creates the shader program and obtains references to its parameters:

```
public static void setupProgram(){
    //Already setup?
    if (program != -1) return;

    //Create shader program
    program = createProgram(R.raw.solid_color_lighting_vertex,
    R.raw.solid_color_lighting_fragment);

    //Get vertex attribute parameters
    positionParam = GLES20.glGetAttribLocation(program,
    "a_Position");
    normalParam = GLES20.glGetAttribLocation(program,
    "a_Normal");

    //Enable them (turns out this is kind of a big deal ;)
    GLES20.glEnableVertexAttribArray(positionParam);
    GLES20.glEnableVertexAttribArray(normalParam);

    //Shader-specific parameters
    colorParam = GLES20.glGetUniformLocation(program,
    "u_Color");
    MVParam = GLES20.glGetUniformLocation(program, "u_MV");
    MVPParam = GLES20.glGetUniformLocation(program, "u_MVP");
    lightPosParam = GLES20.glGetUniformLocation(program,
    "u_LightPos");
    lightColParam = GLES20.glGetUniformLocation(program,
    "u_LightCol");

    RenderBox.checkGLError("Solid Color Lighting params");
}
```

Likewise, we add a `setBuffers` method that is called by the `RenderObject` component (`Sphere`):

```
public void setBuffers(FloatBuffer vertexBuffer, FloatBuffer
normalBuffer, ShortBuffer indexBuffer, int numIndices){
    this.vertexBuffer = vertexBuffer;
    this.normalBuffer = normalBuffer;
    this.indexBuffer = indexBuffer;
    this.numIndices = numIndices;
}
```

Lastly, add the `draw` code, which will be called from the `Camera` component, to render the geometry prepared in the buffers (via `setBuffers`). The `draw` method looks like this:

```
@Override
public void draw(float[] view, float[] perspective) {
    GLES20.glUseProgram(program);

    GLES20.glUniform3fv(lightPosParam, 1,
    RenderBox.instance.mainLight.lightPosInEyeSpace, 0);
    GLES20.glUniform4fv(lightColParam, 1,
    RenderBox.instance.mainLight.color, 0);

    Matrix.multiplyMM(modelView, 0, view, 0,
    RenderObject.lightingModel, 0);
    // Set the ModelView in the shader,
    // used to calculate lighting
    GLES20.glUniformMatrix4fv(MVParam, 1, false,
    modelView, 0);
    Matrix.multiplyMM(modelView, 0, view, 0,
    RenderObject.model, 0);
    Matrix.multiplyMM(modelViewProjection, 0, perspective, 0,
    modelView, 0);
    // Set the ModelViewProjection matrix for eye position.
    GLES20.glUniformMatrix4fv(MVPParam, 1, false,
    modelViewProjection, 0);

    GLES20.glUniform4fv(colorParam, 1, color, 0);

    //Set vertex attributes
    GLES20.glVertexAttribPointer(positionParam, 3,
    GLES20.GL_FLOAT, false, 0, vertexBuffer);
    GLES20.glVertexAttribPointer(normalParam, 3,
    GLES20.GL_FLOAT, false, 0, normalBuffer);

    GLES20.glDrawElements(GLES20.GL_TRIANGLES, numIndices,
    GLES20.GL_UNSIGNED_SHORT, indexBuffer);
}
```

Now that we have a solid color lighting material and shaders, we can add them to the `Sphere` class to be used in our project.

Adding a Material to a Sphere

To use this `Material` with the `Sphere`, we'll define a new constructor (`Sphere`) that calls a helper method (`createSolidColorLightingMaterial`) to create the material and set the buffers. Here's the code:

```
public Sphere(float[] color) {
    super();
    allocateBuffers();
    createSolidColorLightingMaterial(color);
}

public Sphere createSolidColorLightingMaterial(float[] color){
    SolidColorLightingMaterial mat = new
    SolidColorLightingMaterial(color);
    mat.setBuffers(vertexBuffer, normalBuffer, indexBuffer,
    numIndices);
    material = mat;
    return this;
}
```

Okay, we can now add the sphere to our scene.

Viewing the Sphere

Let's see how this looks! We'll create a scene with a sphere, a light, and a camera. Remember that, fortunately, the `RenderBox` class creates the default `Camera` and `Light` instances for us. We just need to add the `Sphere` component.

Edit your `MainActivity.java` file to add the sphere in `setup`. We'll color it yellowish and position it at *x, y, z* location (2, -2, 5):

```
private Transform sphere;

@Override
public void setup() {
    sphere = new Transform();
    float[] color = new float[]{1, 1, 0.5f, 1};
    sphere.addComponent(new Sphere(color));
    sphere.setLocalPosition(2.0f, -2.f, -5.0f);
}
```

Here's what it should look like, a stereoscopic pair of golden globes:

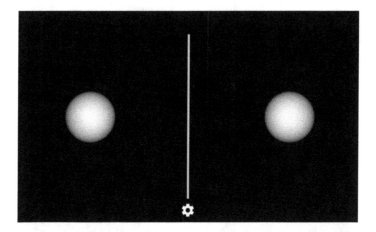

If you see what I see, you deserve an award for that!

Adding the Earth texture material

Next, we'll terraform our sphere into a globe of the Earth by rendering a texture onto the surface of the sphere.

Shaders can get quite complex, implementing all kinds of specular highlights, reflections, shadows, and so on. A simpler algorithm that still makes use of a color texture and lighting is a diffuse material. This is what we'll use here. The word diffuse refers to the fact that light diffuses across the surface, as opposed to being reflective or shiny (specular lighting).

A texture is just an image file (for example, `.jpg`) that can be mapped (projected) onto a geometric surface. Since a sphere isn't easily flattened or unpeeled into a two-dimensional map (as centuries of cartographers can attest), the texture image will look distorted. The following is the texture we'll use for the Earth. (A copy of this file is provided with the download files for this book and similar ones can be found on the Internet at `http://www.solarsystemscope.com/nexus/textures/`):

- In our application, we plan to make use of the standard practice of packaging image assets into the `res/drawable` folder. If necessary, create this folder now.

- Add the `earth_tex.png` file to it.

The `earth_tex` texture is shown in the following image:

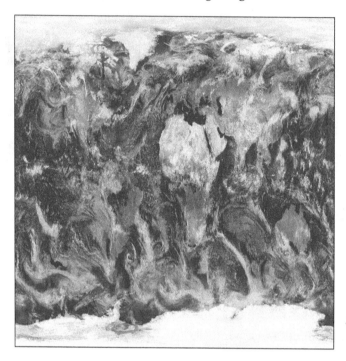

Loading a texture file

We now need a function to load the texture into our app. We can add it to `MainActivity`. Or, you can add it directly to the `RenderObject` class of your `RenderBox` lib. (It's fine in `MainActivity` for now, and we'll move it along with our other extensions to the library at the end of this chapter.) Add the code, as follows:

```
public static int loadTexture(final int resourceId){
    final int[] textureHandle = new int[1];

    GLES20.glGenTextures(1, textureHandle, 0);

    if (textureHandle[0] != 0)
    {
        final BitmapFactory.Options options = new
        BitmapFactory.Options();
        options.inScaled = false;    // No pre-scaling

        // Read in the resource
        final Bitmap bitmap = BitmapFactory.decodeResource
        (RenderBox.instance.mainActivity.getResources(),
        resourceId, options);
```

```
        // Bind to the texture in OpenGL
        GLES20.glBindTexture(GLES20.GL_TEXTURE_2D,
        textureHandle[0]);

        // Set filtering
        GLES20.glTexParameteri(GLES20.GL_TEXTURE_2D,
        GLES20.GL_TEXTURE_MIN_FILTER, GLES20.GL_NEAREST);
        GLES20.glTexParameteri(GLES20.GL_TEXTURE_2D,
        GLES20.GL_TEXTURE_MAG_FILTER, GLES20.GL_NEAREST);

        // Load the bitmap into the bound texture.
        GLUtils.texImage2D(GLES20.GL_TEXTURE_2D, 0,
        bitmap, 0);

        // Recycle the bitmap, since its data has been loaded
        // into OpenGL.
        bitmap.recycle();
    }

    if (textureHandle[0] == 0)
    {
        throw new RuntimeException("Error loading texture.");
    }

    return textureHandle[0];
}
```

The loadTexture method returns an integer handle that can be used to reference the loaded texture data.

Diffuse lighting shaders

As you may now be familiar, we are going to create a new Material, which uses new shaders. We'll write the shaders now. Create the two files in the res/raw folder named diffuse_lighting_vertex.shader and diffuse_lighting_fragment.shader, and define them as follows.

File: res/raw/diffuse_lighting_vertex.shader

```
uniform mat4 u_MVP;
uniform mat4 u_MV;

attribute vec4 a_Position;
attribute vec3 a_Normal;
attribute vec2 a_TexCoordinate;
```

```
varying vec3 v_Position;
varying vec3 v_Normal;
varying vec2 v_TexCoordinate;

void main() {
    // vertex in eye space
    v_Position = vec3(u_MV * a_Position);

    // pass through the texture coordinate.
    v_TexCoordinate = a_TexCoordinate;

    // normal's orientation in eye space
    v_Normal = vec3(u_MV * vec4(a_Normal, 0.0));

    // final point in normalized screen coordinates
    gl_Position = u_MVP * a_Position;
}
```

File: res/raw/diffuse_lighting_fragment.shader

```
precision highp float;
// default high precision for floating point ranges of the planets

uniform vec3 u_LightPos;        // light position in eye space
uniform vec4 u_LightCol;
uniform sampler2D u_Texture;    // the input texture

varying vec3 v_Position;
varying vec3 v_Normal;
varying vec2 v_TexCoordinate;

void main() {
    // distance for attenuation.
    float distance = length(u_LightPos - v_Position);

    // lighting direction vector from the light to the vertex
    vec3 lightVector = normalize(u_LightPos - v_Position);

    // dot product of the light vector and vertex normal.
    // If the normal and light vector are
    // pointing in the same direction then it will get max
    // illumination.
    float diffuse = max(dot(v_Normal, lightVector), 0.01);
```

```
    // Add a tiny bit of ambient lighting (this is outerspace)
    diffuse = diffuse + 0.025;

    // Multiply the color by the diffuse illumination level and
    // texture value to get final output color
    gl_FragColor = texture2D(u_Texture, v_TexCoordinate) *
    u_LightCol * diffuse;
}
```

These shaders add attributes to a light source and utilize geometry normal vectors on the vertices to calculate the shading. You might have noticed that the difference between this and the solid color shader is the use of texture2D, which is a **sampler function**. Also, note that we declared u_Texture as sampler2D. This variable type and function make use of the texture units, which are built into the GPU hardware, and can be used with UV coordinates to return the color values from a texture image. There are a fixed number of texture units, depending on graphics hardware. You can query the number of texture units using OpenGL. A good rule of thumb for mobile GPUs is to expect eight texture units. This means that any shader may use up to eight textures simultaneously.

Diffuse lighting material

Now we can write a Material to use a texture and shaders. In the materials/ folder, create a new Java class, DiffuseLightingMaterial, as follows:

```
public class DiffuseLightingMaterial extends Material {
    private static final String TAG = "diffuselightingmaterial";
```

Add the variables for the texture ID, program references, and buffers, as shown in the following code:

```
int textureId;
static int program = -1;
//Initialize to a totally invalid value for setup state
static int positionParam;
static int texCoordParam;
static int textureParam;
static int normalParam;
static int MVParam;
static int MVPParam;
static int lightPosParam;
static int lightColParam;
```

```
FloatBuffer vertexBuffer;
FloatBuffer texCoordBuffer;
FloatBuffer normalBuffer;
ShortBuffer indexBuffer;
int numIndices;
```

Now we can add a constructor, which sets up the shader program and loads the texture for the given resource ID, as follows:

```
public DiffuseLightingMaterial(int resourceId){
    super();
    setupProgram();
    this.textureId = MainActivity.loadTexture(resourceId);
}
```

As we've seen earlier, the setupProgram method creates the shader program and obtains references to its parameters:

```
public static void setupProgram(){
    //Already setup?
    if (program != -1) return;

    //Create shader program
    program = createProgram(R.raw.diffuse_lighting_vertex,
    R.raw.diffuse_lighting_fragment);
    RenderBox.checkGLError("Diffuse Texture Color Lighting
    shader compile");

    //Get vertex attribute parameters
    positionParam = GLES20.glGetAttribLocation(program,
    "a_Position");
    normalParam = GLES20.glGetAttribLocation(program,
    "a_Normal");
    texCoordParam = GLES20.glGetAttribLocation(program,
    "a_TexCoordinate");

    //Enable them (turns out this is kind of a big deal ;)
    GLES20.glEnableVertexAttribArray(positionParam);
    GLES20.glEnableVertexAttribArray(normalParam);
    GLES20.glEnableVertexAttribArray(texCoordParam);

    //Shader-specific parameters
    textureParam = GLES20.glGetUniformLocation(program,
    "u_Texture");
    MVParam = GLES20.glGetUniformLocation(program, "u_MV");
    MVPParam = GLES20.glGetUniformLocation(program, "u_MVP");
```

```
lightPosParam = GLES20.glGetUniformLocation(program,
"u_LightPos");
lightColParam = GLES20.glGetUniformLocation(program,
"u_LightCol");

RenderBox.checkGLError("Diffuse Texture Color Lighting
params");
    }
```

Likewise, we add a `setBuffers` method that is called by the `RenderObject`
component (`Sphere`):

```
public void setBuffers(FloatBuffer vertexBuffer, FloatBuffer
normalBuffer, FloatBuffer texCoordBuffer, ShortBuffer
indexBuffer, int numIndices){
    //Associate VBO data with this instance of the material
    this.vertexBuffer = vertexBuffer;
    this.normalBuffer = normalBuffer;
    this.texCoordBuffer = texCoordBuffer;
    this.indexBuffer = indexBuffer;
    this.numIndices = numIndices;
}
```

Lastly, add the `draw` code, which will be called from the `Camera` component, to
render the geometry prepared in the buffers (via `setBuffers`). The `draw` method
looks like this:

```
@Override
public void draw(float[] view, float[] perspective) {
    GLES20.glUseProgram(program);

    // Set the active texture unit to texture unit 0.
    GLES20.glActiveTexture(GLES20.GL_TEXTURE0);

    // Bind the texture to this unit.
    GLES20.glBindTexture(GLES20.GL_TEXTURE_2D, textureId);

    // Tell the texture uniform sampler to use this texture in
    // the shader by binding to texture unit 0.
    GLES20.glUniform1i(textureParam, 0);

    //Technically, we don't need to do this with every draw
    //call, but the light could move.
    //We could also add a step for shader-global parameters
    //which don't vary per-object
```

```
GLES20.glUniform3fv(lightPosParam, 1,
RenderBox.instance.mainLight.lightPosInEyeSpace, 0);
GLES20.glUniform4fv(lightColParam, 1,
RenderBox.instance.mainLight.color, 0);

Matrix.multiplyMM(modelView, 0, view, 0,
RenderObject.lightingModel, 0);
// Set the ModelView in the shader, used to calculate
// lighting
GLES20.glUniformMatrix4fv(MVParam, 1, false,
modelView, 0);
Matrix.multiplyMM(modelView, 0, view, 0,
RenderObject.model, 0);
Matrix.multiplyMM(modelViewProjection, 0, perspective, 0,
modelView, 0);
// Set the ModelViewProjection matrix for eye position.
GLES20.glUniformMatrix4fv(MVPParam, 1, false,
modelViewProjection, 0);

//Set vertex attributes
GLES20.glVertexAttribPointer(positionParam, 3,
GLES20.GL_FLOAT, false, 0, vertexBuffer);
GLES20.glVertexAttribPointer(normalParam, 3,
GLES20.GL_FLOAT, false, 0, normalBuffer);
GLES20.glVertexAttribPointer(texCoordParam, 2,
GLES20.GL_FLOAT, false, 0, texCoordBuffer);

GLES20.glDrawElements(GLES20.GL_TRIANGLES, numIndices,
GLES20.GL_UNSIGNED_SHORT, indexBuffer);

RenderBox.checkGLError("Diffuse Texture Color Lighting
draw");
    }
  }
```

Comparing this with the SolidColorLightingMaterial class that we defined earlier, you will notice that it's quite similar. We've replaced the single color with a texture ID, and we've added the requirements for a texture coordinate buffer (texCoordBuffer) given by a Sphere component. Also, note that we are setting the active texture unit to GL_TEXTURE0 and binding the texture.

Adding diffuse lighting texture to a Sphere component

To add the new material to the Sphere component, we'll make an alternative constructor that receives a texture handle. It then creates an instance of the DiffuseLightingMaterial class and sets the buffers from the sphere.

Let's add the material to the Sphere component by defining a new constructor (Sphere) that takes the texture ID and calls a new helper method named createDiffuseMaterial, as follows:

```
public Sphere(int textureId){
    super();
    allocateBuffers();
    createDiffuseMaterial(textureId);
}

public Sphere createDiffuseMaterial(int textureId){
    DiffuseLightingMaterial mat = new
    DiffuseLightingMaterial(textureId);
    mat.setBuffers(vertexBuffer, normalBuffer, texCoordBuffer,
    indexBuffer, numIndices);
    material = mat;
    return this;
}
```

Now, we can use the textured material.

Viewing the Earth

To add the Earth texture to our sphere, modify the setup method of MainActivity to specify the texture resource ID instead of a color, as follows:

```
@Override
public void setup() {
    sphere = new Transform();
    sphere.addComponent(new Sphere(R.drawable.earth_tex));
    sphere.setLocalPosition(2.0f, -2.f, -2.0f);
}
```

There you have it, *Home Sweet Home!*

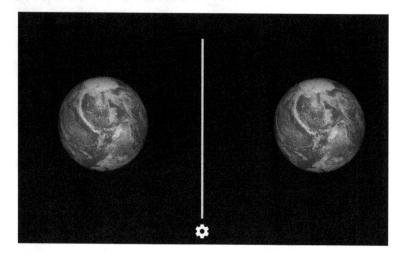

That looks really cool. Oops, it's upside down! Although there's not really a specific up versus down in outer space, our Earth looks upside down from what we're used to seeing. Let's flip it in the `setup` method so that it starts at the correct orientation, and while we're at it, let's take advantage of the fact that the `Transform` methods return themselves, so we can chain the calls, as follows:

```
public void setup() {
    sphere = new Transform()
        .setLocalPosition(2.0f, -2.f, -2.0f)
        .rotate(0, 0, 180f)
        .addComponent(new Sphere(R.drawable.earth_tex));
}
```

Naturally, the Earth is supposed to spin. Let's animate it to rotate it like we'd expect the Earth to do. Add this to the `preDraw` method, which gets called before each new frame. It uses the `Time` class's `getDeltaTime` method, which returns the current fraction of a second change since the previous frame. If we want it to rotate, say, -10 degrees per second, we use *-10 * deltaTime*:

```
public void preDraw() {
    float dt = Time.getDeltaTime();
    sphere.rotate( 0, -10f * dt, 0);
}
```

That looks good to me! How about you?

Changing the camera position

One more thing. We seem to be looking at the Earth in line with the light source. Let's move the camera view so that we can see the Earth from the side. That way, we can see the lighted shading better.

Suppose we leave the light source position at the origin, (0,0,0) as if it were the Sun at the center of the Solar System. The Earth is 147.1 million km from the Sun. Let's place the sphere that many units to the right of the origin, and place the camera at the same relative position. Now, the setup method looks like the following code:

```
public void setup() {
    sphere = new Transform()
        .setLocalPosition(147.1f, 0, 0)
        .rotate(0, 0, 180f)
        .addComponent(new Sphere(R.drawable.earth_tex));
    RenderBox.mainCamera.getTransform().setLocalPosition(
        147.1f, 2f, 2f);
}
```

Run it and this is what you will see:

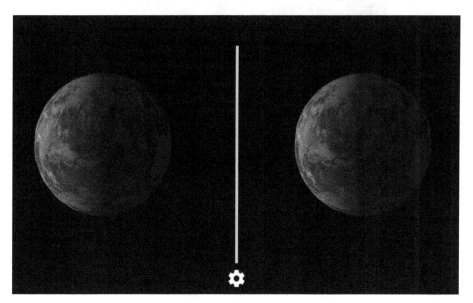

Does that look virtually realistic or what? NASA would be proud!

Day and night material

Honestly though, the back of the Earth looks uncannily dark. I mean, this isn't the 18th century. So much nowadays is 24 x 7, especially our cities. Let's represent this with a separate Earth night texture that has city lights.

We have a file for you to use named `earth_night_tex.jpg`. Drag a copy of the file into your `res/drawable/` folder.

It may be a little difficult to discern on this book's page, but this is what the texture image looks like:

Day/night shader

To support this, we will create a new `DayNightMaterial` class that takes both versions of the Earth texture. The material will also incorporate the corresponding fragment shader that takes into consideration the normal vector of the surface relative to the light source direction (using dot products, if you're familiar with vector math) to decide whether to render using the day or night texture image.

In your `res/raw/` folder, create files for `day_night_vertex.shader` and `day_night_fragment.shader`, and then define them, as follows.

File: day_night_vertex.shader

```
uniform mat4 u_MVP;
uniform mat4 u_MV;

attribute vec4 a_Position;
attribute vec3 a_Normal;
attribute vec2 a_TexCoordinate;

varying vec3 v_Position;
varying vec3 v_Normal;
varying vec2 v_TexCoordinate;

void main() {
    // vertex to eye space
    v_Position = vec3(u_MV * a_Position);

    // pass through the texture coordinate
    v_TexCoordinate = a_TexCoordinate;

    // normal's orientation in eye space
    v_Normal = vec3(u_MV * vec4(a_Normal, 0.0));

    // final point in normalized screen coordinates
    gl_Position = u_MVP * a_Position;
}
```

Except for the addition of v_Texcoordinate, this is exactly the same as our SolidColorLighting shader.

File: day_night_fragment.shader

```
precision highp float;
// default high precision for floating point ranges of the
// planets
uniform vec3 u_LightPos;      // light position in eye space
uniform vec4 u_LightCol;
uniform sampler2D u_Texture;  // the day texture.
uniform sampler2D u_NightTexture;  // the night texture.

varying vec3 v_Position;
varying vec3 v_Normal;
varying vec2 v_TexCoordinate;

void main() {
```

```
// lighting direction vector from the light to the vertex
vec3 lightVector = normalize(u_LightPos - v_Position);

// dot product of the light vector and vertex normal. If the
// normal and light vector are
// pointing in the same direction then it will get max
// illumination.
float ambient = 0.3;
float dotProd = dot(v_Normal, lightVector);
float blend = min(1.0, dotProd * 2.0);
if(dotProd < 0.0){
    //flat ambient level of 0.3
    gl_FragColor = texture2D(u_NightTexture, v_TexCoordinate)
    * ambient;
} else {
    gl_FragColor = (
        texture2D(u_Texture, v_TexCoordinate) * blend
        + texture2D(u_NightTexture, v_TexCoordinate) * (1.0 -
        blend)
    ) * u_LightCol * min(max(dotProd * 2.0, ambient), 1.0);
}
}
```

As always, for lighting, we calculate the dot product (dotProd) of the vertex normal vector and the light direction vector. When that value is negative, the vertex is facing away from the light source (the Sun), so we'll render using the night texture. Otherwise, we'll render using the regular daytime earth texture.

The lighting calculations also include a blend value. This is basically a way of squeezing the transitional zone closer around the terminator when calculating the gl_FragColor variable. We are multiplying the dot product by 2.0 so that it follows a steeper slope, but still clamping the blend value between 0 and 1. It's a little complicated, but once you think about the math, it should make some sense.

We are using two textures to draw the same surface. While this might seem unique to this day/night situation, it is actually a very common method known as multitexturing. You may not believe it, but 3D graphics actually got quite far before introducing the ability to use more than one texture at a time. These days, you see multitexturing almost everywhere, enabling techniques such as normal mapping, decal textures, and displacement/parallax shaders, which create greater detail with simpler meshes.

The DayNightMaterial class

Now we can write the `DayNightMaterial` class. It's basically like the
`DiffuseLightingMaterial` class that we created earlier but supports both the
textures. Therefore, the constructor takes two texture IDs. The `setBuffers` method
is identical to the earlier one, and the `draw` method is nearly identical but with the
added binding of the night texture.

Here's the complete code, highlighting the lines that differ from
`DiffuseLightingMaterial`:

```
public class DayNightMaterial extends Material {
    private static final String TAG = "daynightmaterial";
```

As with our other materials, declare the variables we'll need, including the texture ID
for both the day and night:

```
    int textureId;
    int nightTextureId;

    static int program = -1;
    //Initialize to a totally invalid value for setup state
    static int positionParam;
    static int texCoordParam;
    static int textureParam;
    static int nightTextureParam;
    static int normalParam;
    static int MVParam;
    static int MVPParam;
    static int lightPosParam;
    static int lightColParam;

    FloatBuffer vertexBuffer;
    FloatBuffer texCoordBuffer;
    FloatBuffer normalBuffer;
    ShortBuffer indexBuffer;
    int numIndices;
```

Define the constructor that takes both the resource IDs and the `setupProgram`
helper method:

```
    public DayNightMaterial(int resourceId, int nightResourceId){
        super();
        setupProgram();
        this.textureId = MainActivity.loadTexture(resourceId);

        this.nightTextureId = MainActivity.
```

```
            loadTexture(nightResourceId);
    }

    public static void setupProgram(){
        if(program != -1) return;
        //Create shader program
        program = createProgram(R.raw.day_night_vertex,
        R.raw.day_night_fragment);

        //Get vertex attribute parameters
        positionParam = GLES20.glGetAttribLocation(program,
        "a_Position");
        normalParam = GLES20.glGetAttribLocation(program,
        "a_Normal");
        texCoordParam = GLES20.glGetAttribLocation(program,
        "a_TexCoordinate");

        //Enable them (turns out this is kind of a big deal ;)
        GLES20.glEnableVertexAttribArray(positionParam);
        GLES20.glEnableVertexAttribArray(normalParam);
        GLES20.glEnableVertexAttribArray(texCoordParam);

        //Shader-specific parameters
        textureParam = GLES20.glGetUniformLocation(program,
        "u_Texture");
        nightTextureParam = GLES20.glGetUniformLocation(program,
        "u_NightTexture");
        MVParam = GLES20.glGetUniformLocation(program, "u_MV");
        MVPParam = GLES20.glGetUniformLocation(program, "u_MVP");
        lightPosParam = GLES20.glGetUniformLocation(program,
        "u_LightPos");
        lightColParam = GLES20.glGetUniformLocation(program,
        "u_LightCol");

        RenderBox.checkGLError("Day/Night params");
    }

    public void setBuffers(FloatBuffer vertexBuffer, FloatBuffer
    normalBuffer, FloatBuffer texCoordBuffer, ShortBuffer
    indexBuffer, int numIndices){
        //Associate VBO data with this instance of the material
        this.vertexBuffer = vertexBuffer;
        this.normalBuffer = normalBuffer;
        this.texCoordBuffer = texCoordBuffer;
        this.indexBuffer = indexBuffer;
        this.numIndices = numIndices;
    }
```

Lastly, the `draw` method that cranks it all out to the screen:

```
@Override
public void draw(float[] view, float[] perspective) {
    GLES20.glUseProgram(program);

    // Set the active texture unit to texture unit 0.
    GLES20.glActiveTexture(GLES20.GL_TEXTURE0);

    // Bind the texture to this unit.
    GLES20.glBindTexture(GLES20.GL_TEXTURE_2D, textureId);

    GLES20.glActiveTexture(GLES20.GL_TEXTURE1);
    GLES20.glBindTexture(GLES20.GL_TEXTURE_2D,
    nightTextureId);

    // Tell the texture uniform sampler to use this texture in
    // the shader by binding to texture unit 0.
    GLES20.glUniform1i(textureParam, 0);
    GLES20.glUniform1i(nightTextureParam, 1);

    //Technically, we don't need to do this with every draw
    //call, but the light could move.
    //We could also add a step for shader-global parameters
    //which don't vary per-object
    GLES20.glUniform3fv(lightPosParam, 1,
    RenderBox.instance.mainLight.lightPosInEyeSpace, 0);
    GLES20.glUniform4fv(lightColParam, 1,
    RenderBox.instance.mainLight.color, 0);

    Matrix.multiplyMM(modelView, 0, view, 0,
    RenderObject.lightingModel, 0);
    // Set the ModelView in the shader, used to calculate
    // lighting
    GLES20.glUniformMatrix4fv(MVParam, 1, false,
    modelView, 0);
    Matrix.multiplyMM(modelView, 0, view, 0,
    RenderObject.model, 0);
    Matrix.multiplyMM(modelViewProjection, 0, perspective, 0,
    modelView, 0);
    // Set the ModelViewProjection matrix for eye position.
    GLES20.glUniformMatrix4fv(MVPParam, 1, false,
    modelViewProjection, 0);

    //Set vertex attributes
    GLES20.glVertexAttribPointer(positionParam, 3,
    GLES20.GL_FLOAT, false, 0, vertexBuffer);
    GLES20.glVertexAttribPointer(normalParam, 3,
    GLES20.GL_FLOAT, false, 0, normalBuffer);
```

```
GLES20.glVertexAttribPointer(texCoordParam, 2,
GLES20.GL_FLOAT, false, 0, texCoordBuffer);

GLES20.glDrawElements(GLES20.GL_TRIANGLES, numIndices,
GLES20.GL_UNSIGNED_SHORT, indexBuffer);

RenderBox.checkGLError("DayNight Texture Color Lighting
draw");
    }
}
```

Rendering with day/night

Now we're ready to integrate the new material into our `Sphere` component and see how it looks.

In `Sphere.java`, add a new constructor and the `createDayNightMaterial` helper method, as follows:

```
public Sphere(int textureId, int nightTextureId){
    super();
    allocateBuffers();
    createDayNightMaterial(textureId, nightTextureId);
}

public Sphere createDayNightMaterial(int textureId,
int nightTextureId){
    DayNightMaterial mat = new DayNightMaterial(textureId,
    nightTextureId);
    mat.setBuffers(vertexBuffer, normalBuffer, texCoordBuffer,
    indexBuffer, numIndices);
    material = mat;
    return this;
}
```

Let's call it from the `setup` method of `MainActivity`, and replace the call with the new `Sphere` instance passing both the textures' resource IDs:

```
.addComponent(new Sphere(R.drawable.earth_tex,
R.drawable.earth_night_tex));
```

Run it now. That looks really cool! Classy! Unfortunately, it doesn't make a lot of sense to paste a screenshot here because the city night lights won't show very well. You'll just have to see it for yourself in your own Cardboard viewer. Believe me when I tell you, it's worth it!

Next, *here comes the Sun, and I say, it's alright...*

Creating the Sun

The Sun will be rendered as a textured sphere. However, it's not shaded with front and back sides like our Earth. We need to render it unlit or rather unshaded. This means we need to create the UnlitTextureMaterial.

We have a texture file for the Sun, too (and all the planets as well).We won't show all of them in the chapter although they're included with the downloadable files for the book.

Drag a copy of the sun_tex.png file onto your res/drawable/ folder.

Unlit texture shaders

As we've seen earlier in this book, unlit shaders are much simpler than ones with lighting. In your res/raw/ folder, create files for unlit_tex_vertex.shader and unlit_tex_fragment.shader, and then define them, as follows.

File: unlit_tex_vertex.shader

```
uniform mat4 u_MVP;

attribute vec4 a_Position;
attribute vec2 a_TexCoordinate;

varying vec3 v_Position;
varying vec2 v_TexCoordinate;

void main() {
   // pass through the texture coordinate
   v_TexCoordinate = a_TexCoordinate;

   // final point in normalized screen coordinates
   gl_Position = u_MVP * a_Position;
}
```

File: unlit_tex_fragment.shader

```
precision mediump float;       // default medium precision
uniform sampler2D u_Texture;   // the input texture

varying vec3 v_Position;
varying vec2 v_TexCoordinate;

void main() {
```

```
    // Send the color from the texture straight out
    gl_FragColor = texture2D(u_Texture, v_TexCoordinate);
}
```

Yup, that's simpler than our earlier shaders.

Unlit texture material

Now, we can write the `UnlitTexMaterial` class. Here's the initial code:

```
public class UnlitTexMaterial extends Material {
    private static final String TAG = "unlittex";

    int textureId;

    static int program = -1;
    //Initialize to a totally invalid value for setup state
    static int positionParam;
    static int texCoordParam;
    static int textureParam;
    static int MVPParam;

    FloatBuffer vertexBuffer;
    FloatBuffer texCoordBuffer;
    ShortBuffer indexBuffer;
    int numIndices;
```

Here are the constructor, `setupProgram`, and `setBuffers` methods:

```
    public UnlitTexMaterial(int resourceId){
        super();
        setupProgram();
        this.textureId = MainActivity.loadTexture(resourceId);
    }

    public static void setupProgram(){
        if(program != -1) return;
        //Create shader program
        program = createProgram(R.raw.unlit_tex_vertex,
        R.raw.unlit_tex_fragment);

        //Get vertex attribute parameters
        positionParam = GLES20.glGetAttribLocation(program,
        "a_Position");
```

```
    texCoordParam = GLES20.glGetAttribLocation(program,
    "a_TexCoordinate");

    //Enable them (turns out this is kind of a big deal ;)
    GLES20.glEnableVertexAttribArray(positionParam);
    GLES20.glEnableVertexAttribArray(texCoordParam);

    //Shader-specific parameters
    textureParam = GLES20.glGetUniformLocation(program,
    "u_Texture");
    MVPParam = GLES20.glGetUniformLocation(program, "u_MVP");

    RenderBox.checkGLError("Unlit Texture params");
}

public void setBuffers(FloatBuffer vertexBuffer, FloatBuffer
texCoordBuffer, ShortBuffer indexBuffer, int numIndices){
    //Associate VBO data with this instance of the material
    this.vertexBuffer = vertexBuffer;
    this.texCoordBuffer = texCoordBuffer;
    this.indexBuffer = indexBuffer;
    this.numIndices = numIndices;
}
```

It will be handy to have getter and setter methods for the texture ID (in later projects, not used here):

```
public void setTexture(int textureHandle){
    textureId = textureHandle;
}

  public int getTexture(){
      return textureId;
  }
```

Lastly, here's the `draw` method:

```
@Override
public void draw(float[] view, float[] perspective) {
    GLES20.glUseProgram(program);

    // Set the active texture unit to texture unit 0.
    GLES20.glActiveTexture(GLES20.GL_TEXTURE0);

    // Bind the texture to this unit.
```

```
GLES20.glBindTexture(GLES20.GL_TEXTURE_2D, textureId);

// Tell the texture uniform sampler to use this texture in
// the shader by binding to texture unit 0.
GLES20.glUniform1i(textureParam, 0);

Matrix.multiplyMM(modelView, 0, view, 0,
RenderObject.model, 0);
Matrix.multiplyMM(modelViewProjection, 0, perspective, 0,
modelView, 0);
// Set the ModelViewProjection matrix in the shader.
GLES20.glUniformMatrix4fv(MVPParam, 1, false,
modelViewProjection, 0);

// Set the vertex attributes
GLES20.glVertexAttribPointer(positionParam, 3,
GLES20.GL_FLOAT, false, 0, vertexBuffer);
GLES20.glVertexAttribPointer(texCoordParam, 2,
GLES20.GL_FLOAT, false, 0, texCoordBuffer);

GLES20.glDrawElements(GLES20.GL_TRIANGLES, numIndices,
GLES20.GL_UNSIGNED_SHORT, indexBuffer);

RenderBox.checkGLError("Unlit Texture draw");
    }
}
```

Rendering with an unlit texture

We're ready to integrate the new material into our `Sphere` class and see how it looks.

In `Sphere.java`, add a new constructor that takes a `boolean` parameter, indicating that the texture should be lighted, and the `createUnlitTexMaterial` helper method:

```
public Sphere(int textureId, boolean lighting){
    super();
    allocateBuffers();
    if (lighting) {
        createDiffuseMaterial(textureId);
    } else {
        createUnlitTexMaterial(textureId);
    }
}

public Sphere createUnlitTexMaterial(int textureId){
```

```
UnlitTexMaterial mat = new UnlitTexMaterial(textureId);
mat.setBuffers(vertexBuffer, texCoordBuffer, indexBuffer,
numIndices);
material = mat;
return this;
}
```

Notice that the way in which we've defined constructors, you can call either new
`Sphere(texId)` or `Sphere(texId, true)` to get lighted renders. But for unlit, you
must use the second one as `Sphere(texId, false)`. Also note that setting up the
whole component in the constructor is not the only way to go. We only do it this way
because it keeps our `MainActivity` code concise. In fact, as we start expanding our
use of `RenderBox` and its shader library, it will become necessary to put most of this
code into our `MainActivity` class. It would be impossible to create a constructor for
every type of material. Ultimately, a materials system is necessary to allow you to
create and set materials without having to create a new class for each one.

Adding the Sun

Now, all we need to do is add the Sun sphere to the `setup` method of `MainActivity`.
Let's make it big, say, at a scale of 6.963 (remember that's in millions of kms). This
value may seem arbitrary now, but you'll see where it comes from when we run the
calculations on the Solar System geometry and scale the planets as well.

Add the following code to the `setup` method of `MainActivity`:

```
public void setup() {
    Transform origin = new Transform();

    //Sun
    Transform sun = new Transform()
        .setParent(origin, false)
        .setLocalScale(6.963f, 6.963f, 6.963f)
        .addComponent(new Sphere(R.drawable.sun_tex, false));

    //"Sun" light
    RenderBox.instance.mainLight.transform.
    setPosition( origin.getPosition());
    RenderBox.instance.mainLight.color = new float[]{1, 1,
    0.8f, 1};

    //Earth…
```

We start by defining an origin transform that will be the center of the Solar System. Then, we create the Sun, parented to the origin, with the given scale. Then, add a new sphere component with the Sun texture. We've also given our light a slightly yellowish color, which will blend with the Earth's texture colors.

Here's what the rendered Sun looks like, which seems to illuminate the Earth:

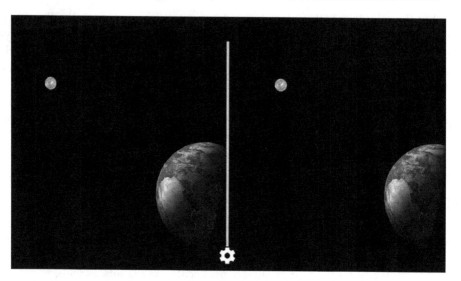

Now, let's move on to the rest of the Solar System.

Creating a Planet class

As we build our Solar System, it will be useful to abstract out a `Planet` class to be used for each planet.

Planets have a number of different attributes that define their unique characteristics in addition to their texture resource IDs. Planets have a distance from the Sun, size (radius), and an orbital speed. Planets all orbit around the Sun as their origin.

- The distance will be its distance from the Sun measured in millions of kilometers.

- The radius will be the planet's size in kilometers (actually in millions of kilometers, to be consistent).

- Rotation is the rate at which the planet rotates about its own axis (one of its days).

- Orbit is the rate at which the planet rotates about the Sun (one of its years). We will assume a perfectly circular orbit.

- TexId is the resource ID of the texture image for the planet.

- origin is the center of its orbit. For planets, this will be the Sun's transform. For a moon, this will be the moon's planet.

The Solar System is a really big thing. The distances and radii are measured in millions of kilometers. The planets are really far apart and relatively small compared to the size of their orbits. The rotation and orbit values are relative rates. You'll note that we'll normalize them to 10 seconds per Earth day.

From these attributes, a planet maintains two transforms: one transform for the planet itself and another transform that describes its location in orbit. In this way, we can rotate each planet's separate parent transform which, when the planet is at a local position whose magnitude is equal to the orbital radius, causes the planet to move in a circular pattern. Then we can rotate the planet itself using its transform.

For the Moon, we'll also use the Planet class (yeah, I know, maybe we should have named it HeavenlyBody?) but set its origin as the Earth. The moon does not rotate.

In your app (for example, app/java/com/cardbookvr/solarsystem/), create a Java class and name it Planet. Add variables for its attributes (distance, radius, rotation, orbit, orbitTransform, and transform), as follows:

```
public class Planet {
    protected float rotation, orbit;
    protected Transform orbitTransform, transform;

    public float distance, radius;
```

Define a constructor that takes the planet's attribute values, initializes the variables, and calculates the initial transforms:

```
    public Planet(float distance, float radius, float rotation,
    float orbit, int texId, Transform origin){
        setupPlanet(distance, radius, rotation, orbit, origin);
        transform.addComponent(new Sphere(texId));
    }

    public void setupPlanet(float distance, float radius, float
    rotation, float orbit, Transform origin){
        this.distance = distance;
        this.radius = radius;
        this.rotation = rotation;
        this.orbit = orbit;
        this.orbitTransform = new Transform();
        this.orbitTransform.setParent(origin, false);

        transform = new Transform()
```

```
            .setParent(orbitTransform, false)
            .setLocalPosition(distance, 0, 0)
            .setLocalRotation(180, 0, 0)
            .setLocalScale(radius, radius, radius);
}
```

The constructor generates an initial transform for the planet and adds a `Sphere` component with the given texture.

On each new frame, we will update the `orbitTransform` rotation around the Sun (year) and the planet's rotation about its own axis (day):

```
public void preDraw(float dt){
    orbitTransform.rotate(0, dt * orbit, 0);
    transform.rotate(0, dt * -rotation, 0);
}
```

We can also provide a couple of accessor methods for the `Planet` class's transforms:

```
public Transform getTransform() { return transform; }
public Transform getOrbitransform() { return orbitTransform; }
```

Now, let's take a look at the geometry of our Solar System.

Formation of the Solar System

This is our chance to throw some real science into our project. The following table shows the actual distance, size, rotation, and orbit values for each of the planets. (Most of this data came from `http://www.enchantedlearning.com/subjects/astronomy/planets/`.)

Planet	Distance from Sun (millions km)	Radius size (km)	Day length (Earth hours)	Year length (Earth years)
Mercury	57.9	2440	1408.8	0.24
Venus	108.2	6052	5832	0.615
Earth	147.1	6371	24	1.0
Earth's Moon	0.363 (from Earth)	1737	0	
Mars	227.9	3390	24.6	2.379
Jupiter	778.3	69911	9.84	11.862
Saturn	1427.0	58232	10.2	29.456
Uranus	2871.0	25362	17.9	84.07
Neptune	4497	24622	19.1	164.81
Pluto (still counts)	5913	1186	6.39	247.7

We also have texture images for each of the planets. These files are included with the downloads for this book. They should be added to the `res/drawable` folder, named `mercury_tex.png`, `venus_tex.png`, and so on. The following table identifies the sources we have used and where you can find them as well:

Planet	Texture
Mercury	`http://laps.noaa.gov/albers/sos/mercury/mercury/mercury_rgb_cyl_www.jpg`
Venus	`http://csdrive.srru.ac.th/55122420119/texture/venus.jpg`
Earth	`http://www.solarsystemscope.com/nexus/content/tc-earth_texture/tc-earth_daymap.jpg` Night: `http://www.solarsystemscope.com/nexus/content/tc-earth_texture/tc-earth_nightmap.jpg`
Earth's Moon	`https://farm1.staticflickr.com/120/263411684_ea405ffa8f_o_d.jpg`
Mars	`http://lh5.ggpht.com/-2aLH6cYiaKs/TdOsBtnpRqI/AAAAAAAAAP4/bnMOdD9OMjk/s9000/mars%2Btexture.jpg`
Jupiter	`http://laps.noaa.gov/albers/sos/jupiter/jupiter/jupiter_rgb_cyl_www.jpg`
Saturn	`http://www.solarsystemscope.com/nexus/content/planet_textures/texture_saturn.jpg`
Uranus	`http://www.astrosurf.com/nunes/render/maps/full/uranus.jpg`
Neptune	`http://www.solarsystemscope.com/nexus/content/planet_textures/texture_neptune.jpg`
Pluto	`http://www.shatters.net/celestia/files/pluto.jpg`
Sun	`http://www.solarsystemscope.com/nexus/textures/texture_pack/assets/preview_sun.jpg`
Milky Way	`http://www.geckzilla.com/apod/tycho_cyl_glow.png` (by Judy Schmidt, `http://geckzilla.com/`)

Setting up planets in MainActivity

We're going to set up all the planets in `MainActivity` using a `setupPlanets` method that will be called from `setup`. Let's go for it.

At the top of the class, declare a `planets` array:

```
Planet[] planets;
```

Then, we declare a number of constants which we'll explain in a moment:

```
// tighten up the distances (millions km)
float DISTANCE_FACTOR = 0.5f;
// this is 100x relative to interplanetary distances
float SCALE_FACTOR = 0.0001f;
// animation rate for one earth rotation (seconds per
rotation)
float EDAY_RATE = 10f;
// rotation scale factor e.g. to animate earth: dt * 24 *
// DEG_PER_EHOUR
float DEG_PER_EHOUR = (360f / 24f / EDAY_RATE);
// animation rate for one earth rotation (seconds per orbit)
// (real is EDAY_RATE * 365.26)
float EYEAR_RATE = 1500f;
// orbit scale factor
float DEG_PER_EYEAR = (360f / EYEAR_RATE);
```

The `setupPlanets` method uses our celestial data and builds new planets accordingly. First, let's define the physical data, as follows:

```
public void setupPlanets(Transform origin) {

    float[] distances = new float[] { 57.9f, 108.2f, 149.6f,
    227.9f, 778.3f, 1427f, 2871f, 4497f, 5913f };
    float[] fudged_distances = new float[] { 57.9f, 108.2f,
    149.6f, 227.9f, 400f, 500f, 600f, 700f, 800f };

    float[] radii = new float[] { 2440f, 6052f, 6371f, 3390f,
    69911f, 58232f, 25362f, 24622f, 1186f };

    float[] rotations = new float[] { 1408.8f * 0.05f, 5832f *
    0.01f, 24f, 24.6f, 9.84f, 10.2f, 17.9f, 19.1f, 6.39f };

    float[] orbits = new float[] { 0.24f, 0.615f, 1.0f,
    2.379f, 11.862f, 29.456f, 84.07f, 164.81f, 247.7f };
```

The `distances` array has the distance of each planet from the Sun in millions of km. This is really huge, especially for the outer planets that are really far away and are not very visible relative to other planets. To make things more interesting, we'll fudge the distance of those planets (Jupiter through Pluto), so the values that we'll use are in the `fudged_distances` array.

The `radii` array has the actual size of each planet in kms.

The `rotations` array has the day length, in Earth hours. Since Mercury and Venus spin really fast compared to the Earth, we'll artificially slow them down by arbitrary scale factors.

The `orbits` array has the length of each planet's year in Earth years and the time it takes for one complete rotation around the Sun.

Now, let's set up the texture IDs for each planet's materials:

```
int[] texIds = new int[]{
        R.drawable.mercury_tex,
        R.drawable.venus_tex,
        R.drawable.earth_tex,
        R.drawable.mars_tex,
        R.drawable.jupiter_tex,
        R.drawable.saturn_tex,
        R.drawable.uranus_tex,
        R.drawable.neptune_tex,
        R.drawable.pluto_tex
};
```

Now initialize the `planets` array, creating a new `Planet` object for each:

```
planets = new Planet[distances.length + 1];
for(int i = 0; i < distances.length; i++){
    planets[i] = new Planet(
            fudged_distances[i] * DISTANCE_FACTOR,
            radii[i] * SCALE_FACTOR,
            rotations[i] * DEG_PER_EHOUR,
            orbits[i] * DEG_PER_EYEAR *
            fudged_distances[i]/distances[i],
            texIds[i],
            origin);
}
```

While we fudged some of the planets' actual distances so that they'd be closer to the inner Solar System, we also multiply all the distances by a DISTANCE_FACTOR scalar, mostly to not blow up our float precision calculations. We scale all the planet sizes by a different SCALE_FACTOR variable to make them relatively larger than life (a factor of 0.0001 is actually a factor of 100 because radii are calculated in km while the distance is calculated in millions of km).

The rotation animation rate is the actual length of the day of the planet scaled by how fast we want to animate a day in VR. We default to 10 seconds per Earth day.

Lastly, the planetary orbit animation has its own scale factor. We've sped it up about 2 X. You can also adjust the orbit rate of the distance fudge factors (for example, Pluto orbits the Sun once every 247 Earth years, but we've moved it a lot closer so it needs to slow down).

Then, we add the Earth's moon. We've used some artistic license here as well, adjusting the distance and radius and speeding up its orbit rate to make it compelling to watch in VR:

```
// Create the moon
planets[distances.length] = new Planet(7.5f, 0.5f, 0, -
0.516f, R.drawable.moon_tex, planets[2].getTransform());}
```

Let's take a look at one more method: `goToPlanet`. It'll be convenient to position the `Camera` near a specific planet. Since the planets are located at data-driven positions and will be moving in orbit, it's best to make the camera a child of the planet's transform. This is one of the reasons why we separated out the orbiting transform from the planet's transform. We don't want the camera to spin around with the planet—you might get sick! Here's the implementation:

```
void goToPlanet(int index){
    RenderBox.mainCamera.getTransform().
    setParent( planets[index].getOrbitransform(), false);
    RenderBox.mainCamera.getTransform().
    setLocalPosition( planets[index].distance,
    planets[index].radius * 1.5f, planets[index].radius * 2f);
}
```

 Note that the scale and distance values we finally use in the code are derived from but not the actual celestial measurements. For a lovely VR experience of the Solar System with real educational value, check out Titans of Space (http://www.titansofspacevr.com/).

Camera's planet view

The `gotoPlanet` function is called with a planet index (for example, Earth is 2), so we can position the camera near the specified planet. The `Camera` component gets parented to the planet's `orbitTransform` variable as a way to obtain the planet's current orbit rotation. Then, it's positioned as the planet's distance from the Sun, and then offset a bit, relative to the planet's size.

In `MainActivity` class's setup method, we have already set up the Sun and the Earth. We'll replace the Earth sphere with a call to a `setupPlanets` helper method:

```
public void setup() {
    //Sun ...

    // Planets
```

```
        setupPlanets(origin);

        // Start looking at Earth
        goToPlanet(2);
    }
```

If you build and run the project now, you will see the Earth, the Sun, and maybe some of the planets. But not until they're moving in their orbits will they come to life.

Animating the heavenly bodies

Now that we have all the planets instantiated, we can animate their orbit and axis rotations. All it takes is updating their transforms in the MainAcitvity class's preDraw method:

```
@Override
public void preDraw() {
    float dt = Time.getDeltaTime();
    for(int i = 0; i < planets.length; i++){
        planets[i].preDraw(dt);
    }
}
```

Run! Oh, wow! I feel like a god. Well, not exactly, because it's dark outside. We need stars!

A starry sky dome

What if the Universe was just a giant ball and we're inside it? That's what we're going to imagine to implement a starry sky spherical background.

In computer graphics, you can create backgrounds to make the scene look bigger than it really is. You can use a spherical texture, or skydome, as we will use here. (A common alternative in many game engines is a cuboid skybox, constructed from six internal faces of a cube.)

Among the set of textures that we provided with this book is milky_way_tex.png. Drag a copy of this file into your res/drawable/ directory, if it's not there already.

Now, we can add the starry sky dome to our scene. Add the following code to MainActivity.setup():

```
        //Stars in the sky
        Transform stars = new Transform()
                .setParent(RenderBox.mainCamera.transform, false)
```

```
.setLocalScale(Camera.Z_FAR * 0.99f, Camera.Z_FAR
* 0.99f, Camera.Z_FAR * 0.99f)
.addComponent(new Sphere(R.drawable.milky_way_tex,
false));
```

This looks so much more celestial.

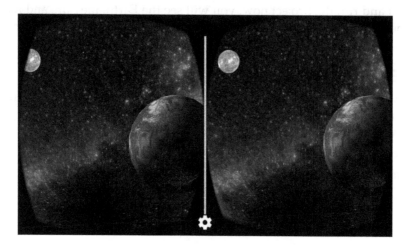

You might be wondering what that 0.99 factor is all about. Different GPUs deal with floating point numbers differently. While some might render a vertex at the draw distance one way, others might exhibit render glitches when the geometry is "on the edge" due to a floating point precision. In this case, we just pull the skybox toward the camera by an arbitrarily small factor. It is especially important in VR that the skybox be as far away as possible, so that it is not drawn with parallax. The fact that the skybox is in the same exact place for the left and right eye is what tricks your brain into thinking that it's infinitely far away. You may find that you need to tweak this factor to avoid holes in the skybox.

Fine tuning the Earth

If you're a space geek, you might be thinking that there are a few things we could do to our Earth model. For one, we should add the night view texture. (Mars and the other planets don't need one because their cities shut off all their lights at night.) Also, the Earth is slightly tilted on its axis. We can fix that.

The night texture

First, let's add the night texture. To do this, let's make an `Earth` Java class a subclass of a `Planet`. Right-click on your Java `solarsystem` folder, select **New** | **Java Class**, and name it `Earth`. Then, start defining it like this:

```
public class Earth extends Planet {

    public Earth(float distance, float radius, float rotation,
    float orbit, int texId, int nightTexId, Transform origin) {
        super(distance, radius, rotation, orbit, origin);
        transform.addComponent(new Sphere(texId, nightTexId));
    }

}
```

This requires that we add a new constructor to the `Planet` class, which omits `texId`, since the Earth constructor creates the new `Sphere` component, this time with two textures, `textId` and `nightTexId`.

In `Planet.java`, add the following code:

```
public Planet(float distance, float radius, float rotation,
float orbit, Transform origin){
    setupPlanet(distance, radius, rotation, orbit, origin);
}
```

Now, in `MainActivity`, let's create an Earth separately from the other planets. In `setupPlanets`, modify the loop to handle this case:

```
for(int i = 0; i < distances.length; i++){
    if (i == 2) {
        planets[i] = new Earth(
                fudged_distances[i] * DISTANCE_FACTOR,
                radii[i] * SCALE_FACTOR,
                rotations[i] * DEG_PER_EHOUR,
                orbits[i] * DEG_PER_EYEAR *
                fudged_distances[i] / distances[i],
                texIds[i],
                R.drawable.earth_night_tex,
                origin);
    } else {
        planets[i] = new Planet(
```

Axis tilt and wobble

Among all its greatness, like all nature and mankind, the Earth is not perfect. In this case, we're talking about tilt and wobble. The Earth's axis of rotation is not exactly perpendicular to the orbital plane. It also suffers from a slight wobble as it rotates. We can show this in our virtual model.

Modify the `Earth` class constructor to read as follows:

```
Transform wobble;

public Earth(float distance, float radius, float rotation,
float orbit, int texId, int nightTexId, Transform origin) {
    super(distance, radius, rotation, orbit, origin);

    wobble = new Transform()
            .setLocalPosition(distance, 0, 0)
            .setParent(orbitTransform, false);

    Transform tilt = new Transform()
            .setLocalRotation(-23.4f,0,0)
            .setParent(wobble, false);

    transform
            .setParent(tilt, false)
            .setLocalPosition(0,0,0)
            .addComponent(new Sphere(texId, nightTexId));
}
```

Now, the Earth's rotation on each frame is against this wobble transform, so give Earth its own `preDraw` method, as follows:

```
public void preDraw(float dt){
    orbitTransform.rotate(0, dt * orbit, 0);
    wobble.rotate(0, dt * 5, 0);
    transform.rotate(0, dt * -rotation, 0);
}
```

Changing the camera location

The final feature of our Solar System is to make it more interactive. I mean all these planets look so cool, but you can't really see them from so far away. How about clicking on the Cardboard trigger to jump from planet to planet, nice and up close?

Fortunately, we already have a `goToPlanet` method that we used to set our initial view from the Earth. Because `MainActivity` extends `CardboardActivity`, we can use the Cardboard SDK's `onCardboardTrigger` method (refer to `https://developers.google.com/cardboard/android/latest/reference/com/google/vrtoolkit/cardboard/CardboardActivity.html#onCardboardTrigger()`).

Add the following code to `MainActivity`:

```
int currPlanet = 2;

public void onCardboardTrigger(){
    if (++currPlanet >= planets.length)
        currPlanet = 0;
    goToPlanet(currPlanet);
}
```

The app will start with the camera near the Earth (index 2). When the user presses the cardboard trigger (or touches the screen), it'll go to Mars (3). Then, Jupiter, and so on, and then cycle back to Mercury (0).

Possible enhancements

Can you think of other enhancements to this project? Here are a few you could consider and try to implement:

* Add rings to Saturn. (A cheap way to implement might be a plane with transparency.)
* Improve `goToPlanet` so that your camera position animates between positions.
* Add controls to allow you to change the perspective or fly freely through space.
* Add a top-down view option, for a "traditional" picture of the Solar System. (Be aware of float precision issues at scale.)
* Add moons to each of the other planets. (This can be implemented just like we did for the Earth's moon, with its mother planet as its origin.)
* Represent the asteroid belt between Mars and Jupiter.
* Add tilt and wobble to the other planets. Did you know that Uranus spins on its side?
* Add text labels to each planet that use the planet's transform but always face the camera. In lieu of 3D text objects, the labels could be prepared images.
* Add background music.
* Improve the positional accuracy in such a way that it accurately represents the relative positions of each planet on a given date.

Updating the RenderBox library

With the Solar System project implemented and our code stabilized, you might realize that we've built some code that is not necessarily specific to this application, which can be reused in other projects, and ought to make its way back to the RenderBox library. That's what we'll do now.

We recommend you do this directly within Android Studio, selecting and copying from this project's hierarchy view to the other's. Perform the following steps:

1. Move all the .shader files from the Solar System's res/raw/ directory into the res/raw/ directory of the RenderBox lib's RenderBox module. If you've been following along, there will be eight files for the vertex and fragment .shader files for day_night, diffuse_lighting, solid_color_lighting, and unilt_tex.

2. Move all the Component and Material .java files from the Solar System's RenderBoxExt module folder to the corresponding folders in RenderBox lib's RenderBox module. Remove all invalid references to MainActivity in the source code.

3. In the Solar System project, we implemented a method named loadTexture in MainActivity. It rightfully belongs to the RenderBox library. Find the declaration for loadTexture in the Solar System's MainActivity.java file, and cut the code. Then, open the RenderObject.java file in RenderBox lib and paste the definition into the RenderObject class.

4. In the RenderBox lib, replace (refactor) all the instances of MainActivity. loadTexture with RenderObject.loadTexture. These will be found in several Material Java files, where we load material textures.

5. In RenderBox.java, the reset() method destroys the handles of any materials. Add the calls for the new materials that we just introduced:
   ◦ DayNightMaterial.destroy()
   ◦ DiffuseLightingMaterial.destroy()
   ◦ SolidColorLightingMaterial.destroy()
   ◦ UnlitTexMaterial.destroy()

6. Resolve any package name mismatches, and fix any other compile-time errors, including removing any references to solarsystem throughout.

Now, you should be able to successfully rebuild the library (**Build | Make Module 'renderbox'**) to generate an updated renderbox[-debug].aar library file.

Lastly, the Solar System project can now use the new `.aar` library. Copy the `renderbox[-debug].aar` file from the `RenderBoxLib` project's `renderbox/build/output` folder into the SolarSystem `renderbox/` folder, replacing the older version of the same file with the newly built one. Build and run the Solar System project with this version of the library.

Summary

Congratulations! You received an "A" on your Solar System science project!

In this chapter, we built a Solar System simulation that can be viewed in virtual reality using a Cardboard VR viewer and an Android phone. This project uses and expands the `RenderBox` library, as discussed in *Chapter 5, RenderBox Engine*.

To begin, we added a `Sphere` component to our repertoire. Initially, it was rendered using a solid color lighting material. Then, we defined a diffuse lighting material and rendered the sphere with an Earth image texture, resulting in a rendered globe. Next, we enhanced the material to accept two textures, adding an additional one to the back/"night" side of the sphere. And lastly, we created an unlit texture material, which is used for the Sun. Armed with actual sizes of the planets and distances from the Sun, we configured a Solar System scene with nine planets, the Earth's moon, and the Sun. We added a star field as a sky dome, and we animated the heavenly bodies for their appropriate rotation (day) and orbit (year). We also implemented some interaction, responding to Cardboard trigger events by moving the camera view from planet to planet.

In the next chapter, we'll get to use our sphere again, this time, to view your library of 360-degree photos.

7
360-Degree Gallery

360-degree photos and videos are a different approach to virtual reality. Rather than rendering 3D geometry in real time with OpenGL, you're letting users look around a prerendered or photographed scene. 360-degree viewers are a great way to introduce consumers to VR because they give a very natural experience and are easy to produce. It is much easier to take a photo than to render a photorealistic scene of objects in real time. Images are easy to record with a new generation of 360-degree cameras, or the photosphere feature in the Google Camera app. Viewing prerecorded images requires much less computer power than rendering full 3D scenes, and this works well on mobile Cardboard viewers. Battery power should also be less of an issue.

Non-VR 360-degree media has become fairly common. For example, for many years real-estate listing sites have provided panoramic walkthroughs with a web-based player that lets you interactively view the space. Similarly, YouTube supports the uploading and playback of 360-degree videos and provides a player with interactive controls to look around during playback. Google Maps lets you upload 360-degree still photosphere images, much like their Street View tool, that you can create with an Android or iOS app (for more information, visit `https://www.google.com/maps/about/contribute/photosphere/`) or a consumer 360 camera. The Internet is teeming with 360-degree media!

Viewing 360-degree media in VR is surprisingly immersive, even for still photos (and even without a pair of stereoscopic images). You're standing at the center of a sphere with an image projected onto the inside surface, but you feel like you're really there in the captured scene. Simply turn your head to look around.

In this project, we'll build a photo gallery that lets you browse photos on your phone. Regular flat pictures and panoramas will appear projected on a large screen to your left. But 360-degree photospheres will fully immerse you inside the spherical projection. We will accomplish this project by performing the following steps:

- Setting up the new project
- Viewing a 360-degree photosphere
- Viewing a regular photo on a large virtual projection screen
- Adding a frame border to the photos
- Loading and displaying a photo image from your device's camera folder
- Adjusting a photo's orientation and aspect ratio
- Creating a user interface with a grid of thumbnail images for selecting the photo to be viewed with scrolling
- Ensuring a good, responsive VR experience with thread-safe operations
- Launching an Android image view intent app

The source code for this project can be found on the Packt Publishing website, and on GitHub at `https://github.com/cardbookvr/gallery360` (with each topic a separate commit).

Setting up the new project

To build this project, we're going to use our `RenderBox` library created in *Chapter 5, RenderBox Engine*. You can use yours, or grab a copy from the download files provided with this book or our GitHub repo (use the commit tagged `after-ch6` — `https://github.com/cardbookvr/renderboxlib/releases/tag/after-ch6`). For a more detailed description of how to import the `RenderBox` library, refer to the final section, *Using RenderBox in future projects*, in *Chapter 5, RenderBox Engine*. To do this, perform the following steps:

1. With Android Studio opened, create a new project. Let's name it `Gallery360` and target **Android 4.4 KitKat (API 19)** with an **Empty Activity**.
2. Create new modules for the `renderbox`, `common`, and `core` packages, using **File | New Module | Import .JAR/.AAR Package**.
3. Set the modules as dependencies for the app, using **File | Project Structure**.
4. Edit the `build.gradle` file as explained in *Chapter 2, The Skeleton Cardboard Project*, to compile against SDK 22.
5. Update `/res/layout/activity_main.xml` and `AndroidManifest.xml`, as explained in the previous chapters.

6. Edit `MainActivity` as class `MainActivity` extends `CardboardActivity` implements `IRenderBox`, and implement the interface method stubs (*Ctrl + I*).

We can go ahead and define the `onCreate` method in `MainActivity`. The class now has the following code:

```
public class MainActivity extends CardboardActivity implements
IRenderBox {
    private static final String TAG = "Gallery360";
    CardboardView cardboardView;
    @Override
    protected void onCreate(Bundle savedInstanceState) {
        super.onCreate(savedInstanceState);
        setContentView(R.layout.activity_main);

        cardboardView = (CardboardView)
        findViewById(R.id.cardboard_view);
        cardboardView.setRenderer(new RenderBox(this, this));
        setCardboardView(cardboardView);
    }
    @Override
    public void setup() {

    }
    @Override
    public void preDraw() {
        // code run beginning each frame
    }
    @Override
    public void postDraw() {
        // code run end of each frame
    }
}
```

While we implement this project, we will be creating new classes that could be good extensions to `RenderBoxLib`. We'll make them regular classes in this project at first. Then, at the end of the chapter, we'll help you move them into the `RenderBoxLib` project and rebuild the library. Perform the following steps:

1. Right-click on the `gallery360` folder (`com.cardbookvr.gallery360`) and go to **New** | **Package**, and name the package `RenderBoxExt`.

2. Within `RenderBoxExt`, create package subfolders named `components` and `materials`.

There's no real technical need to make it a separate package but this helps organize our files, because the ones in RenderBoxExt will be moved into our reusable library at the end of this chapter.

You can add a cube to the scene, temporarily, to help ensure that everything is set up properly. Add it to the setup method as follows:

```
public void setup() {
    new Transform()
        .setLocalPosition(0,0,-7)
        .setLocalRotation(45,60,0)
        .addComponent(new Cube(true));
}
```

If you remember, a cube is a component that's added to a transform. The cube defines its geometry (for example, vertices). The transform defines its position, rotation, and scale in 3D space.

You should be able to click on **Run 'app'** with no compile errors, and see the cube and Cardboard split screen view on your Android device.

Viewing a 360-degree photo

Ever since it was discovered that the Earth is round, cartographers and mariners have struggled with how to project the spherical globe onto a two-dimensional chart. The result is an inevitable distortion of some areas of the globe.

To learn more about map projections and spherical distortions, visit http://en.wikipedia.org/wiki/Map_projection.

For 360-degree media, we typically use an equirectangular (or a meridian) projection where the sphere is unraveled into a cylindrical projection, stretching the texture as you progress toward the North and South poles while keeping the meridians as equidistant vertical straight lines. To illustrate this, consider Tissot's Indicatrix (visit http://en.wikipedia.org/wiki/Tissot%27s_indicatrix for more information) that shows a globe with strategically arranged identical circles (an illustration by Stefan Kühn):

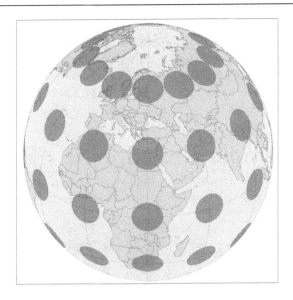

The following image shows the globe unwrapped with an equirectangular projection (https://en.wikipedia.org/wiki/Equirectangular_projection):

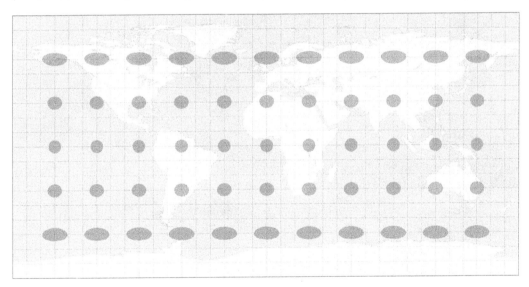

We will use an equirectangular mesh for our photospheres and an appropriately projected (warped) image for its texture map. To view, we place the camera viewpoint at the center of the sphere and render the image onto the inside surface.

You may have noticed that our Earth and other planet textures had the same sort of distortion on them. It's a pretty common way to map spherical images to flat ones, and in fact, we've been "doing the math" on this problem ever since we created the UVs for our sphere in *Chapter 6, Solar System*! You'll have to get clever with UV offsets to keep them from appearing stretched, but you should also be able to display panoramic photos on a sphere in the same way.

Viewing a sample photosphere

You may choose any 360-degree equirectangular image for this topic. We've included the following beach photo with this book, named `sample360.jpg`:

Add it to your project.

Copy the image you want to view into the project's `res/drawable/` folder. Now add the following code to the `MainActivity.java` file:

```
final int DEFAULT_BACKGROUND = R.drawable.sample360;

Sphere photosphere;

@Override
public void setup() {
    setupBackground();
}

void setupBackground() {
    photosphere = new Sphere(DEFAULT_BACKGROUND, false);
    new Transform()
```

```
        .setLocalScale(Camera.Z_FAR * 0.99f, -Camera.Z_FAR *
        0.99f, Camera.Z_FAR * 0.99f)
        .addComponent(photosphere);
    }
```

Note that multiplying the scale by 0.99 avoids unwanted clipping of the background image due to floating point precision errors on some phones. Using a negative scale *y* axis compensates for inverted rendering by the texture shader (alternatively you could modify the shader code).

You can replace the drawable filename, R.drawable.sample360, with yours, as defined in the DEFAULT_BACKGROUND variable. This variable must be final, as required by the Android resource system.

In the setup method, we create a Sphere component as we have been doing all along. Start with a new transform, scale it, then add a new Sphere component with our resource ID to the transform. We're naming the object background because later on, this object will be the default background for the app.

Run the app, and insert your phone into a Cardboard viewer. Voila! You're in Margaritaville!! If that seemed really easy, you're right; it was! Really, the hard work was done for us by the photosphere app or whatever transformed the image into an equirectangular projection. The rest of it is the standard UV projection math we've been doing all along!

Using the background image

We're going to make a gallery that lets the user pick from a number of images. It would be nice if the user saw something more neutral when they first started the app. A more appropriate background image is included with the downloadable files for this book. It is named `bg.png` and contains a regular grid. Copy it to your `res/drawable/` folder. Then, change `DEFAULT_BACKGROUND` to `R.drawable.bg`.

Rerun the app, and it should look like this:

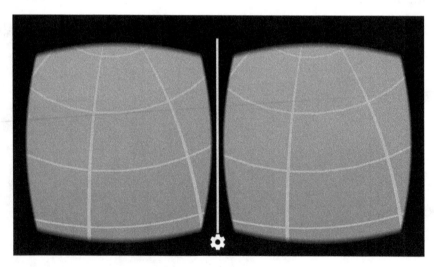

Viewing a regular photo

Now that we got that done, let's prepare our app to also be able to view regular flat photos. We'll do this by rendering them onto a plane. So first we need to define a `Plane` component.

Defining the Plane component and allocating buffers

The `Plane` component rightfully belongs to the `RenderBox` library, but for the time being, we'll add it directly to the app.

Create a new Java class file in the `RenderBoxExt/components/` folder, and name it `Plane`. Define it as `extends RenderObject`, as follows:

```
public class Plane extends RenderObject {
}
```

As with other geometry in the `RenderBox` library, we'll define the plane with triangles. Simply two adjacent triangles are required, a total of six indices. The following data arrays define our default plane's 3D coordinates, UV texture coordinates, vertex colors (middle gray), normal vectors, and corresponding indices. Add the following code at the top of the class:

```
public static final float[] COORDS = new float[] {
        -1.0f, 1.0f, 0.0f,
        1.0f, 1.0f, 0.0f,
        -1.0f, -1.0f, 0.0f,
        1.0f, -1.0f, 0.0f
};
public static final float[] TEX_COORDS = new float[] {
        0.0f, 1.0f,
        1.0f, 1.0f,
        0f, 0f,
        1.0f, 0f,
};
public static final float[] COLORS = new float[] {
        0.5f, 0.5f, 0.5f, 1.0f,
        0.5f, 0.5f, 0.5f, 1.0f,
        0.5f, 0.5f, 0.5f, 1.0f,
        0.5f, 0.5f, 0.5f, 1.0f
};
```

```
public static final float[] NORMALS = new float[] {
        0.0f, 0.0f, -1.0f,
        0.0f, 0.0f, -1.0f,
        0.0f, 0.0f, -1.0f,
        0.0f, 0.0f, -1.0f
};
public static final short[] INDICES = new short[] {
        0, 1, 2,
        1, 3, 2
};
```

Now, we can define the `Plane` constructor that calls an `allocateBuffers` helper method that allocates buffers for vertices, normals, textures, and indexes. Let's declare variables for these at the top of the class, and write the methods:

```
public static FloatBuffer vertexBuffer;
public static FloatBuffer colorBuffer;
public static FloatBuffer normalBuffer;
public static FloatBuffer texCoordBuffer;
public static ShortBuffer indexBuffer;
public static final int numIndices = 6;

public Plane(){
    super();
    allocateBuffers();
}

public static void allocateBuffers(){
    //Already allocated?
    if (vertexBuffer != null) return;
    vertexBuffer   = allocateFloatBuffer(COORDS);
    texCoordBuffer = allocateFloatBuffer(TEX_COORDS);
    colorBuffer    = allocateFloatBuffer(COLORS);
    normalBuffer   = allocateFloatBuffer(NORMALS);
    indexBuffer    = allocateShortBuffer(INDICES);
}
```

Again, we ensure that `allocateBuffers` is run only once by checking whether `vertexBuffer` is null. (Note that we've decided to declare the buffers `public` to afford future flexibility to create arbitrary texture materials for objects.)

Adding materials to the Plane component

Next, we can add an appropriate material to the `Plane`, one that uses a texture image. Using a constructor API pattern that is consistent with the built-in `Sphere` component in *Chapter 6, Solar System*, we'll add the ability to call a new `Plane` with an image texture ID and an optional lighting Boolean flag. Then, we'll add helper methods to allocate the corresponding `Material` objects and set their buffers:

```
public Plane(int textureId, boolean lighting) {
    super();
    allocateBuffers();
    if (lighting) {
        createDiffuseMaterial(textureId);
    } else {
        createUnlitTexMaterial(textureId);
    }
}

public Plane createDiffuseMaterial(int textureId) {
    DiffuseLightingMaterial mat = new
    DiffuseLightingMaterial(textureId);
    mat.setBuffers(vertexBuffer, normalBuffer, texCoordBuffer,
    indexBuffer, numIndices);
    material = mat;
    return this;
}

public Plane createUnlitTexMaterial(int textureId) {
    UnlitTexMaterial mat = new UnlitTexMaterial(textureId);
    mat.setBuffers(vertexBuffer, texCoordBuffer, indexBuffer,
    numIndices);
    material = mat;
    return this;
}
```

Adding an image screen to the scene

We can now add an image to the scene in `MainActivity`. Soon we will take a look at the phone's photos folder for pictures, but at this point, you can just use the same (photosphere) one that we used earlier (or drop another in your `res/drawable` folder). Note that you might have issues displaying an image that is too large for a phone's GPU. We will take a look at this issue later, so try to keep it less than 4,096 pixels in either dimension.

Name the object `screen` because later on, we'll use it to project whichever photo the user selects from a gallery.

In `MainActivity.java`, update the `setup` function to add the image to the scene, as follows:

```
Plane screen;

public void setup() {
    setupBackground();
    setupScreen();
}

void setupScreen() {
    screen = new Plane(R.drawable.sample360, false);
    new Transform()
            .setLocalScale(4, 4, 1)
            .setLocalPosition(0, 0, -5)
            .setLocalRotation(0, 0, 180)
            .addComponent(screen);
}
```

The screen is scaled to 4 units (in X and Y) and placed 5 units in front of the camera. That's like sitting 5 meters (15 feet) from an 8 meter wide movie screen!

Also, note that we rotate the plane 180 degrees on the *z* axis; otherwise, the image will appear upside down. Our world coordinate system has the up-direction along the positive *y* axis. However, UV space (for rendering textures) typically has the origin in the upper-left corner and positive is downward. (If you remember, in the previous chapter, this is why we also had to flip the Earth). Later in this chapter, when we implement an `Image` class, we'll read the actual orientation from the image file and set the rotation accordingly. Here's our screen plane with the image (viewed from an angle):

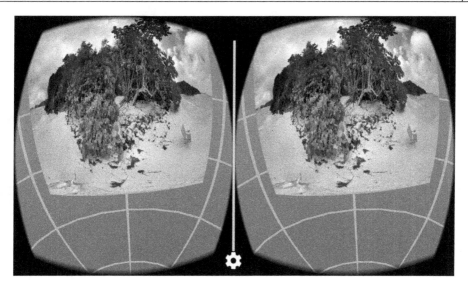

It will be convenient to separate the screen plane (with its image texture) from the placement and size of the screen. We will see why this is important later, but it has to do with scaling and rotating based on image parameters. Let's refactor the code so that the screen is parented by a screenRoot transform as follows:

```
void setupScreen() {
    Transform screenRoot = new Transform()
            .setLocalScale(4, 4, 1)
            .setLocalRotation(0, 0, 180)
            .setLocalPosition(0, 0, -5);

    screen = new Plane(R.drawable.sample360, false);

    new Transform()
            .setParent(screenRoot, false)
            .addComponent(screen);
}
```

Putting a border frame on the image

Pictures look best in a frame. Let's add one now. There are a number of ways to accomplish this, but we are going to use shaders. The frame will also be used for the thumbnail images and will enable us to change colors to highlight when the user selects an image. Furthermore, it helps define a region of contrast, which ensures that you can see the edge of any image on any background.

Border shaders

We can start by writing the shader programs which, among other things, define the variables they will need from the Material object that uses it.

If necessary, create a resource directory for the shaders, res/raw/. Then, create the border_vertex.shader and border_fragment.shader files. Define them as follows.

The border_vertex shader is identical to the unlit_tex_vertex shader that we were using.

File: res/raw/border_vertex.shader

```
uniform mat4 u_MVP;

attribute vec4 a_Position;
attribute vec2 a_TexCoordinate;

varying vec3 v_Position;
varying vec2 v_TexCoordinate;

void main() {
    // pass through the texture coordinate
    v_TexCoordinate = a_TexCoordinate;

    // final point in normalized screen coordinates
    gl_Position = u_MVP * a_Position;
}
```

For the border_fragement shader, we add variables for a border color (u_Color) and width (u_Width). Then, add a bit of logic to decide whether the current coordinate being rendered is on the border or in the texture image:

File: `res/raw/border_fragment.shader`

```
precision mediump float;
uniform sampler2D u_Texture;

varying vec3 v_Position;
varying vec2 v_TexCoordinate;
uniform vec4 u_Color;
uniform float u_Width;

void main() {
    // send the color from the texture straight out unless in
    // border area
    if(
        v_TexCoordinate.x > u_Width
        && v_TexCoordinate.x < 1.0 - u_Width
        && v_TexCoordinate.y > u_Width
        && v_TexCoordinate.y < 1.0 - u_Width
    ){
        gl_FragColor = texture2D(u_Texture, v_TexCoordinate);
    } else {
        gl_FragColor = u_Color;
    }
}
```

Note that this technique cuts off the edges of the image. We found this to be acceptable, but if you really want to see the entire image, you can offset the UV coordinates within the `texture2D` sampler call. It would look something like this:

```
float scale = 1.0 / (1 - u_Width * 2);
Vec2 offset = vec(
    v_TexCoordinate.x * scale - u_Width,
    v_TexCoordinate.x * scale - u_Width);
gl_FragColor = texture2D(u_Texture, offset);
```

Finally, observant readers might notice that when the plane is scaled non-uniformly (to make it a rectangle), the border will be scaled so that the vertical borders might be thicker or thinner than the horizontal borders. There are a number of ways to fix this, but this is left as an exercise for the (over-achieving) reader.

The border material

Next, we define the material for the border shader. Create a new Java class in RenderBoxExt/materials/ named BorderMaterial and define it as follows:

```java
public class BorderMaterial extends Material {
    private static final String TAG = "bordermaterial";

}
```

Add material variables for the texture ID, border width, and color. Then, add variables for the shader program references and buffers, as shown in the following code:

```java
int textureId;
public float borderWidth = 0.1f;
public float[] borderColor = new float[]{0, 0, 0, 1};
// black
static int program = -1;
//Initialize to a totally invalid value for setup state
static int positionParam;
static int texCoordParam;
static int textureParam;
static int MVPParam;
static int colorParam;
static int widthParam;

FloatBuffer vertexBuffer;
FloatBuffer texCoordBuffer;
ShortBuffer indexBuffer;
int numIndices;
```

Now we can add a constructor. As we've seen earlier, it calls a setupProgram helper method that creates the shader program and obtains references to its parameters:

```java
public BorderMaterial() {
    super();
    setupProgram();
}

public static void setupProgram() {
    //Already setup?
    if (program > -1) return;
    //Create shader program
    program = createProgram(R.raw.border_vertex,
    R.raw.border_fragment);

    //Get vertex attribute parameters
    positionParam = GLES20.glGetAttribLocation(program,
    "a_Position");
```

```
texCoordParam = GLES20.glGetAttribLocation(program,
"a_TexCoordinate");

//Enable them (turns out this is kind of a big deal ;)
GLES20.glEnableVertexAttribArray(positionParam);
GLES20.glEnableVertexAttribArray(texCoordParam);

//Shader-specific parameters
textureParam = GLES20.glGetUniformLocation(program,
"u_Texture");
MVPParam = GLES20.glGetUniformLocation(program, "u_MVP");
colorParam = GLES20.glGetUniformLocation(program,
"u_Color");
widthParam = GLES20.glGetUniformLocation(program,
"u_Width");
RenderBox.checkGLError("Border params");
}
```

Likewise, we add a `setBuffers` method to be called by the `RenderObject` component (`Plane`):

```
public void setBuffers(FloatBuffer vertexBuffer, FloatBuffer
texCoordBuffer, ShortBuffer indexBuffer, int numIndices){
    //Associate VBO data with this instance of the material
    this.vertexBuffer = vertexBuffer;
    this.texCoordBuffer = texCoordBuffer;
    this.indexBuffer = indexBuffer;
    this.numIndices = numIndices;
}
```

Provide a setter method for the texture ID:

```
public void setTexture(int textureHandle) {
    textureId = textureHandle;
}
```

Add the draw code, which will be called from the `Camera` component, to render the geometry prepared in the buffers (via `setBuffer`). The draw method looks like this:

```
@Override
public void draw(float[] view, float[] perspective) {
    GLES20.glUseProgram(program);

    // Set the active texture unit to texture unit 0.
    GLES20.glActiveTexture(GLES20.GL_TEXTURE0);
```

```
    // Bind the texture to this unit.
    GLES20.glBindTexture(GLES20.GL_TEXTURE_2D, textureId);

    // Tell the texture uniform sampler to use this texture in
    // the shader by binding to texture unit 0.
    GLES20.glUniform1i(textureParam, 0);

    Matrix.multiplyMM(modelView, 0, view, 0,
    RenderObject.model, 0);
    Matrix.multiplyMM(modelViewProjection, 0, perspective, 0,
    modelView, 0);
    // Set the ModelViewProjection matrix for eye position.
    GLES20.glUniformMatrix4fv(MVPParam, 1, false,
    modelViewProjection, 0);

    GLES20.glUniform4fv(colorParam, 1, borderColor, 0);
    GLES20.glUniform1f(widthParam, borderWidth);

    //Set vertex attributes
    GLES20.glVertexAttribPointer(positionParam, 3,
    GLES20.GL_FLOAT, false, 0, vertexBuffer);
    GLES20.glVertexAttribPointer(texCoordParam, 2,
    GLES20.GL_FLOAT, false, 0, texCoordBuffer);

    GLES20.glDrawElements(GLES20.GL_TRIANGLES, numIndices,
    GLES20.GL_UNSIGNED_SHORT, indexBuffer);

    RenderBox.checkGLError("Border material draw");
}
```

One more thing; let's provide a method to destroy an existing material:

```
public static void destroy(){
    program = -1;
}
```

Using the border material

To use the BorderMaterial class instead of the default UnlitTexMaterial class, we wrote in the Plane class previously, we can add it to the Plane Java class, as follows. We plan to create the material outside the Plane class (in MainActivity), so we just need to set it up. In Plane.java, add the following code:

```
public void setupBorderMaterial(BorderMaterial material){
    this.material = material;
    material.setBuffers(vertexBuffer, texCoordBuffer,
    indexBuffer, numIndices);
}
```

In `MainActivity`, modify the `setupScreen` method to use this material instead of the default one, as follows. We first create the material and set the texture to our sample image. We don't need to set the color, which will default to black. Then we create the screen plane and set its material. And then create the transform and add the screen component:

```
void setupScreen() {
    //...
    Screen = new Plane();
    BorderMaterial screenMaterial = new BorderMaterial();
    screenMaterial.setTexture(RenderBox.loadTexture(
    R.drawable.sample360));
    screen.setupBorderMaterial(screenMaterial);
    //...

}
```

When you run it now, it should look something like this:

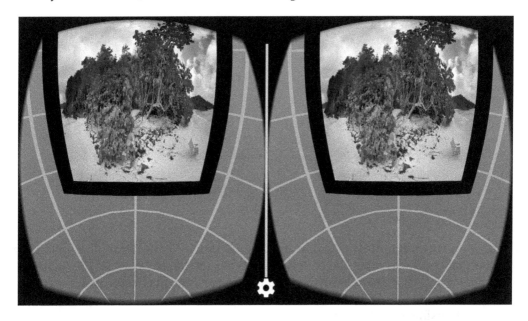

Loading and displaying a photo image

So far, we've used images in the project's `drawable` resource folder. The next step is to read photo images from the phone and display one on our virtual screen.

Defining the image class

Let's make a placeholder `Image` class. Later on, we'll build the attributes and methods. Define it as follows:

```java
public class Image {
    final static String TAG = "image";
    String path;
    public Image(String path) {
        this.path = path;
    }
    public static boolean isValidImage(String path){
        String extension = getExtension(path);
        if(extension == null)
            return false;
        switch (extension){
            case "jpg":
                return true;
            case "jpeg":
                return true;
            case "png":
                return true;
        }
        return false;
    }
    static String getExtension(String path){
        String[] split = path.split("\\.");
        if(split== null || split.length < 2)
            return null;
        return split[split.length - 1].toLowerCase();
    }
}
```

We define a constructor that takes the image's full path. We also provide a validation method that checks whether the path is actually for an image, based on the filename extension. We don't want to load and bind the image data on construction because we don't want to load all the images at once; as you'll see, we will manage these intelligently using a worker thread.

Reading images into the app

Now in `MainActivity`, access the photos folder on the phone and build a list of images in our app. The following `getImageList` helper method looks in the given folder path and instantiates a new `Image` object for each file found:

```
final List<Image> images = new ArrayList<>();

int loadImageList(String path) {
    File f = new File(path);
    File[] file = f.listFiles();
    if (file==null)
        return 0;
    for (int i = 0; i < file.length; i++) {
        if (Image.isValidImage(file[i].getName())) {
            Image img = new Image(path + "/" +
            file[i].getName());
            images.add(img);
        }
    }
    return file.length;
}
```

Use this method in the `setup` method, passing in the name of the camera images folder path, as follows (your path may vary):

```
final String imagesPath = "/storage/emulated/0/DCIM/Camera";

public void setup() {
    ...

    loadImageList(imagesPath);
}
```

Also, ensure that the following line is included in your `AndroidManifest.xml` file, giving the app the permission to read the device's external storage. Technically, you should already have this permission when using the Cardboard SDK:

```
<uses-permission
android:name="android.permission.READ_EXTERNAL_STORAGE" />
```

You can add a log message to the `getImageList` loop and run it to verify that it is finding files. If not, you may need to discover the actual path to your photos folder.

This is the first project where we need to be really careful about permissions. Up until this point, the Cardboard SDK itself was the only thing which needed access to the filesystem, but now we need it for the app itself to function. If you are using a device with Andriod 6.0, and you don't make sure to compile the app against SDK 22, you will not be able to load the image files, and the app will either do nothing, or crash.

If you are compiling against SDK 22 and you have the permission set up correctly in the manifest but you still get an empty file list, try looking for the correct path on your device with a file browser. It could very well be that the path we provided doesn't exist or is empty. And, of course, make sure that you have actually taken a picture with that device!

Image load texture

If you remember, in *Chapter 6, Solar System,* we wrote a `loadTexture` method that reads a static image from the project's `res/drawable` folder into a memory bitmap and binds it to the texture in OpenGL. Here, we're going to do something similar but source the images from the phone's camera path and provide methods for additional processing, such as resizing and rotating its orientation.

At the top of the `Image` class, add a variable to hold the current texture handle:

```
int textureHandle;
```

The image's `loadTexture` method, given a path to an image file, will load an image file into a bitmap and then convert it to a texture. (This method will be called from `MainActivity` with the app's `CardboardView` class.) Write it as follows:

```
public void loadTexture(CardboardView cardboardView) {
    if (textureHandle != 0)
        return;
    final Bitmap bitmap = BitmapFactory.decodeFile(path);
    if (bitmap == null){
        throw new RuntimeException("Error loading bitmap.");
    }
    textureHandle = bitmapToTexture(bitmap);
}
```

We added a small (but important) optimization, checking whether the texture has already been loaded; don't do it again if not needed.

Our implementation of `bitmapToTexture` is shown in the following code. Given a bitmap, it binds the bitmap to an OpenGL ES texture (with some error checking). Add the following code to `Image`:

```
public static int bitmapToTexture(Bitmap bitmap){
    final int[] textureHandle = new int[1];

    GLES20.glGenTextures(1, textureHandle, 0);
    RenderBox.checkGLError("Bitmap GenTexture");

    if (textureHandle[0] != 0) {
        // Bind to the texture in OpenGL
        GLES20.glBindTexture(GLES20.GL_TEXTURE_2D,
        textureHandle[0]);

        // Set filtering
        GLES20.glTexParameteri(GLES20.GL_TEXTURE_2D,
        GLES20.GL_TEXTURE_MIN_FILTER, GLES20.GL_NEAREST);
        GLES20.glTexParameteri(GLES20.GL_TEXTURE_2D,
        GLES20.GL_TEXTURE_MAG_FILTER, GLES20.GL_NEAREST);

        // Load the bitmap into the bound texture.
        GLUtils.texImage2D(GLES20.GL_TEXTURE_2D, 0,
        bitmap, 0);
    }
    if (textureHandle[0] == 0){
        throw new RuntimeException("Error loading texture.");
    }

    return textureHandle[0];
}
```

Showing an image on the screen

Let's show one of our camera images in the app, say, the first one.

To show an image on the virtual screen, we can write a show method that takes the current CardboardView object and the Plane screen. It'll load and bind the image texture and pass its handle to the material. In the Image class, implement the show method as follows:

```
public void show(CardboardView cardboardView, Plane screen) {
    loadTexture(cardboardView);
    BorderMaterial material = (BorderMaterial)
    screen.getMaterial();
    material.setTexture(textureHandle);
}
```

Now let's use this stuff! Go to MainActivity and write a separate showImage method to load the image texture. And, temporarily, call it from setup with the first image that we find (you will need at least one image in your camera folder):

```
public void setup() {
    setupBackground();
    setupScreen();
    loadImageList(imagesPath);
    showImage(images.get(0));
}

void showImage(Image image) {
    image.show(cardboardView, screen);
}
```

It now also makes sense to modify setupScreen, so it creates the screen but doesn't load an image texture onto it. Remove the call to screenMaterial.setTexture in there.

Now run the app, and you will see your own image on the screen. Here's mine:

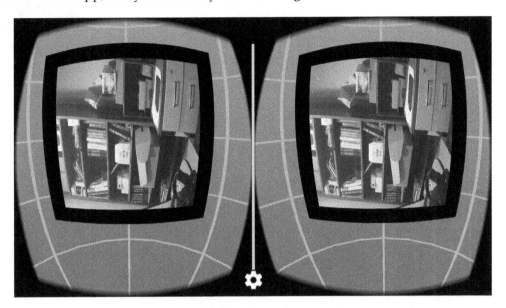

Rotating to the correct orientation

Some image file types keep track of their image orientation, particularly JPG files (`.jpg` or `.jpeg`). We can get the orientation value from the EXIF metadata included with the file written by the camera app. (For example, refer to `http://sylvana. net/jpegcrop/exif_orientation.html`. Note that some devices may not be compliant or contain different results.)

If the image is not JPG, we'll skip this step.

At the top of the `Image` class, declare a variable to hold the current image rotation:

```
Quaternion rotation;
```

The `rotation` value is stored as a `Quaternion` instance, as defined in our RenderBox math library. If you remember *Chapter 5, RenderBox Engine*, a quaternion represents a rotational orientation in three-dimensional space in a way that is more precise and less ambiguous than Euler angles. But Euler angles are more human-friendly, specifying an angle for each *x*, *y*, and *z* axes. So, we'll set the quaternion using Euler angles based on the image orientation. Ultimately, we use a `Quaternion` here because it is the underlying type of `Transform.rotation`:

```
void calcRotation(Plane screen){
    rotation = new Quaternion();
```

```
// use Exif tags to determine orientation, only available
// in jpg (and jpeg)
String ext = getExtension(path);
if (ext.equals("jpg") || ext.equals("jpeg")) {

    try {
        ExifInterface exif = new ExifInterface(path);
        switch (exif.getAttribute
        (ExifInterface.TAG_ORIENTATION)) {
            // Correct orientation, but flipped on the
            // horizontal axis
            case "2":
                rotation = new
                Quaternion().setEulerAngles(180, 0, 0);
                break;
            // Upside-down
            case "3":
                rotation = new
                Quaternion().setEulerAngles(0, 0, 180);
                break;
            // Upside-Down & Flipped along horizontal axis
            case "4":
                rotation = new
                Quaternion().setEulerAngles(180, 0, 180);
                break;
            // Turned 90 deg to the left and flipped
            case "5":
                rotation = new
                Quaternion().setEulerAngles(0, 180, 90);
                break;
            // Turned 90 deg to the left
            case "6":
                rotation = new
                Quaternion().setEulerAngles(0, 0, -90);
                break;
            // Turned 90 deg to the right and flipped
            case "7":
                rotation = new
                Quaternion().setEulerAngles(0, 180, 90);
                break;
            // Turned 90 deg to the right
            case "8":
                rotation = new
                Quaternion().setEulerAngles(0, 0, 90);
                break;
```

```
                    //Correct orientation--do nothing
                    default:
                        break;
                }
            } catch (IOException e) {
                e.printStackTrace();
            }
        }
        screen.transform.setLocalRotation(rotation);
    }
```

Now we set the screen's rotation in the `show` method of the `Image` class, as follows:

```
public void show(CardboardView cardboardView, Plane screen) {
    loadTexture(cardboardView);
    BorderMaterial material = (BorderMaterial)
    screen.getMaterial();
    material.setTexture(textureHandle);
    calcRotation(screen);
}
```

Run your project again. The image should be correctly oriented. Note that it is possible that your original image was fine all along. It will become easier to check whether your rotation code works once we get the thumbnail grid going.

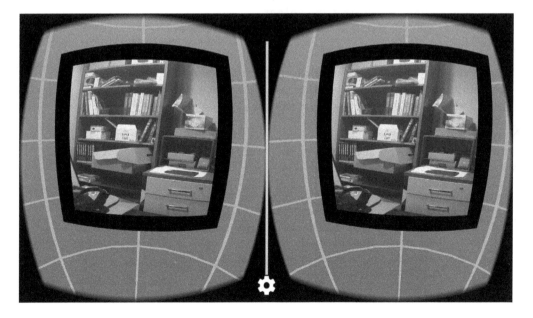

Dimensions to correct the width and height

Square images are easy. But usually, photos are rectangular. We can get the actual width and height of the image and scale the screen accordingly, so the display won't show up distorted.

At the top of the `Image` class, declare variables to hold the current image width and height:

```
int height, width;
```

Then, set them in `loadTexture` using bitmap options in the `decodeFile` method, as follows:

```
public void loadTexture(CardboardView cardboardView) {
    if (textureHandle != 0)
        return;
    BitmapFactory.Options options = new
    BitmapFactory.Options();
    final Bitmap bitmap = BitmapFactory.decodeFile(path,
    options);
    if (bitmap == null){
        throw new RuntimeException("Error loading bitmap.");
    }
    width = options.outWidth;
    height = options.outHeight;
    textureHandle = bitmapToTexture(bitmap);
}
```

The `decodeFile` call returns the image's width and height (among other information) in the options (refer to `http://developer.android.com/reference/android/graphics/BitmapFactory.Options.html`).

Now we can set the screen size in the `show` method of the `Image` class. We'll normalize the scale so that the longer side is of size 1.0 and the shorter one is calculated as the image aspect ratio:

```
public void show(CardboardView cardboardView, Plane screen) {
    loadTexture(cardboardView);
    BorderMaterial material = (BorderMaterial)
    screen.getMaterial();
    material.setTexture(textureHandle);
    calcRotation(screen);
    calcScale(screen);
}
```

```
void calcScale(Plane screen) {
    if (width > 0 && width > height) {
        screen.transform.setLocalScale(1, (float) height /
        width, 1);
    } else if(height > 0) {
        screen.transform.setLocalScale((float) width / height,
        1, 1);
    }
}
```

If you run it now, the screen will have the correct aspect ratio for the image:

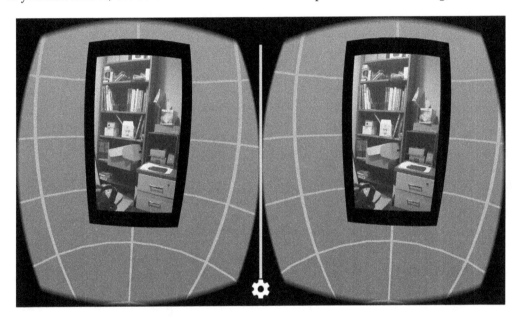

Sample image down to size

The camera in your phone is probably awesome! It's probably really mega awesome!
Many-megapixel images are important when printing or doing lots of cropping. But
for viewing in our app, we don't need the full resolution image. In fact, you might
already be having trouble running this project if the image size generates a texture
that's too big for your device's hardware.

We can accommodate this issue by constraining the maximum size and scaling our bitmaps to fit within these constraints when loading the texture. We will ask OpenGL ES to give us its current maximum texture size. We'll do this in `MainActivity`, so it's generally available (and/or move this into the `RenderBox` class in your `RenderBox` library project). Add the following to `MainActivity`:

```
static int MAX_TEXTURE_SIZE = 2048;

void setupMaxTextureSize() {
    //get max texture size
    int[] maxTextureSize = new int[1];
    GLES20.glGetIntegerv(GLES20.GL_MAX_TEXTURE_SIZE,
    maxTextureSize, 0);
    MAX_TEXTURE_SIZE = maxTextureSize[0];
    Log.i(TAG, "Max texture size = " + MAX_TEXTURE_SIZE);
}
```

We call it as the first line of the `setup` method of the `MainActivity` class.

As for scaling the image, unfortunately, Android's `BitmapFactory` does not let you directly request a new size of a sampled image. Instead, given an arbitrary image, you can specify the sampling rate, such as every other pixel (2), every fourth pixel (4), and so on. It must be a power of two.

Back to the `Image` class. First, we will add a `sampleSize` argument to `loadTexture`, which can be used as an argument to `decodeFile`, as follows:

```
public void loadTexture(CardboardView cardboardView, int
sampleSize) {
    if (textureHandle != 0)
        return;
    BitmapFactory.Options options = new
    BitmapFactory.Options();
    options.inSampleSize = sampleSize;
    final Bitmap bitmap = BitmapFactory.decodeFile(path,
    options);
    if(bitmap == null){
        throw new RuntimeException("Error loading bitmap.");
    }
    width = options.outWidth;
    height = options.outHeight;
    textureHandle = bitmapToTexture(bitmap);
}
```

To determine an appropriate sample size for images, we need to first find out its full dimensions and then figure out what sample size will get it closest but less than the maximum texture size we're going to use. The math isn't too difficult, but instead of going through that, we'll use a procedural method to search for the best size value.

Fortunately, one of the input options of `decodeFile` is to only retrieve the image bounds, and not actually load the image. Write a new load texture method named `loadFullTexture`, as follows:

```
public void loadFullTexture(CardboardView cardboardView) {
    // search for best size
    int sampleSize = 1;
    BitmapFactory.Options options = new
    BitmapFactory.Options();
    options.inJustDecodeBounds = true;
    do {
        options.inSampleSize = sampleSize;
        BitmapFactory.decodeFile(path, options);
        sampleSize *= 2;
    } while (options.outWidth > MainActivity.MAX_TEXTURE_SIZE
    || options.outHeight > MainActivity.MAX_TEXTURE_SIZE);
    sampleSize /= 2;
    loadTexture(cardboardView, sampleSize);
}
```

We keep bumping up the sample size until we find one that produces a bitmap within the MAX_TEXTURE_SIZE bounds, and then call `loadTexture`.

Use `loadFullTexture` in the `show` method instead of the other `loadTexture` one:

```
public void show(CardboardView cardboardView, Plane screen) {
    loadFullTexture(cardboardView);
    BorderMaterial material = (BorderMaterial)
    screen.getMaterial();
    . . .
```

Run the project. It should look the same as the earlier one. But if your camera is too good, maybe it's not crashing like it was before.

This sampling will also be useful to display thumbnail versions of the images in the user interface. There's no point in loading the full-sized bitmap for a thumbnail view.

Loading and displaying a photosphere image

So far, we've been handling all the images in the same manner. But some of them may be 360-degree images. These should be displayed on the photosphere and not on the virtual screen.

If you do not have any 360-degree photos in your device's camera folder yet, you can create them using the Google Camera app.

 If the default camera app on your phone does not include a **Photosphere** mode, you may need to download the Google Camera app from the Play Store. Third-party cameras might use a different name. For example, Samsung calls their photosphere feature **Surround Shot**.

Some images include the XMP metadata that will include information of whether the image is distorted for an equirectangular projection. This can be useful to distinguish spherical images from flat ones. However, the Android API doesn't include an XMP interface, so integrating XMP header parsing is beyond the scope of this book.

For now, we'll just check whether the filename is prefixed with PANO_. Add the following variable to the Image class and set it in the constructor method:

```
public boolean isPhotosphere;

public Image(String path) {
    this.path = path;
    isPhotosphere = path.toLowerCase().contains("pano");
}
```

We can now build the MainActivity show method to handle regular photos (displayed on the virtual screen) versus photospheres (displayed on the background sphere). Furthermore, it should handle switching between a flat image displayed on the virtual screen and rendering the photosphere and vice versa.

We want to remember the texture handle ID of the background photosphere texture. Add a bgTextureHandle handle at the top of the MainActivity class:

```
int bgTextureHandle;
```

Then, set it in `setupBackground` by calling `getTexture`:

```
void setupBackground() {
    photosphere = new Sphere(DEFAULT_BACKGROUND, false);
    new Transform()
            .setLocalScale(Camera.Z_FAR * 0.99f,
            -Camera.Z_FAR * 0.99f, Camera.Z_FAR * 0.99f)
            .addComponent(photosphere);
    UnlitTexMaterial mat = (UnlitTexMaterial)
    photosphere.getMaterial();
    bgTextureHandle = mat.getTexture();
}
```

Now we can update the `showImage` method, as follows:

```
void showImage(Image image) {
    UnlitTexMaterial bgMaterial = (UnlitTexMaterial)
    photosphere.getMaterial();
    image.loadFullTexture(cardboardView);
    if (image.isPhotosphere) {
        bgMaterial.setTexture(image.textureHandle);
        screen.enabled = false;
    } else {
        bgMaterial.setTexture(bgTextureHandle);
        screen.enabled = true;
        image.show(cardboardView, screen);
    }
}
```

When the image is a photosphere, we set the background photosphere texture to the image and hide the screen plane. When the image is a regular photo, we set the background texture back to the default one and show the image on the virtual screen.

Until we implement the user interface (next) to test this, you will need to know which image in the images list is a photosphere. If you make a new photosphere now, it'll be the last one in the list, and you can change the `setup` method to call `showImage` on it. For example, run the following code:

```
showImage(images.get(images.size()-1));
```

Run the project again and be happy!

The image gallery user interface

Before we go ahead and implement a user interface for this project, let's talk about how we want it to work.

The purpose of this project is to allow the user to select a photo from their phone's storage and view it in VR. The phone's photo collection will be presented in a scrollable grid of thumbnail images. If a photo is a normal 2D one, it'll be displayed on the virtual screen plane we just made. If it's a photosphere, we'll view it as a fully immersive 360-degree spherical projection.

A sketch of our proposed scene layout is shown in the following diagram. The user camera is centered at the origin, and the photosphere is represented by the gray circle, which surrounds the user. In front of the user (determined by the calibration at launch), there will be a 5 x 3 grid of thumbnail images from the phone's photo gallery. This will be a scrollable list. To the left of the user, there is the image projection screen.

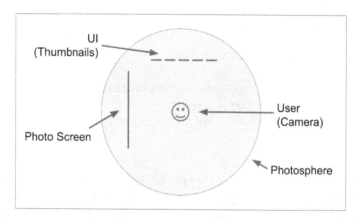

Specifically, the UI will implement the following features:

- Displays up to 15 thumbnail images in a 5 x 3 grid.

- Allows the user to select one of the thumbnail images by looking at it and then clicking on the Cardboard trigger. Thumbnails will be highlighted when in the sightline.

- Selecting a regular photo will display it on the virtual projection screen in the scene (and clear the photosphere to the background image).

- Selecting a photosphere will hide the virtual projection screen and load the image into the photosphere projection.
- Allows the user to scroll through thumbnail images by selecting the up/down arrows.

Some of our UI considerations are unique to virtual reality. Most importantly, all of the user interface elements and controls are in world coordinate space, That is, they're integrated into the scene as geometric objects with a position, rotation, and scale like any other component. This is in contrast with most mobile games where the UI is implemented as a screen space overlay.

Why? Because in VR, in order to create the stereoscopic effect, each eye has a separate viewpoint, offset by the interpupillary distance. This can be simulated in screen space by horizontally offsetting the position of screen space objects, so they appear to have a parallax (a technique we used in *Chapter 4, Launcher Lobby*). But when mixed with 3D geometry, camera, lighting, and rendering, that technique proves inadequate. A world space UI is required for an effective user experience and immersion.

Another feature that's unique to VR is gaze-based selection. In this case, where you look will highlight an image thumbnail, and then you click on the Cardboard trigger to open the image.

Lastly, as mentioned earlier, since we're working in world space and making selections based on where we're looking, the layout of our 3D space is an important consideration. Remember that we're in VR and not constrained by rectangular edges of a phone screen. Objects in the scene can be placed all around you. On the other hand, you don't want users twisting and turning all the time (unless that's an intended part of the experience). We'll pay attention to comfort zones to place our UI controls and image screen.

Furthermore, Google and researchers elsewhere have begun to develop best practices for the user interface design, including the optimal distance for menus and UI controls from the camera, approximately 5 to 15 feet (1.5 to 5 meters). This distance is close enough to enjoy a 3D parallax effect but not so close to make you look cross-eyed to focus on the objects.

Okay, let's begin with the UI implementation.

Positioning the photo screen on the left

Firstly, let's move the screen from in front to the side, that is, rotate it 90 degrees to the left. Our transform math does the position after the rotation, so we now offset it along the *x* axis. Modify the setupScreen method of the MainActivity class, as follows:

```
void setupScreen() {
    Transform screenRoot = new Transform()
            .setLocalScale(4, 4, 1)
            .setLocalRotation(0, -90, 0)
            .setLocalPosition(-5, 0, 0);
    ...
```

Displaying thumbnails in a grid

A thumbnail is a mini version of the full image. Therefore, we don't need to load a full-sized texture bitmap. For the sake of simplicity, let's just always sample it down by 4 (to 1/16th the original size).

The thumbnail image

In the Image class, the show method loads the full texture. Let's write a similar showThumbnail method that uses a smaller sampling. In the Image class, add the following code:

```
public void showThumbnail(CardboardView cardboardView, Plane
thumb) {
    loadTexture(cardboardView, 4);
    BorderMaterial material = (BorderMaterial)
    thumb.getMaterial();
    material.setTexture(textureHandle);
    calcRotation(thumb);
    calcScale(thumb);
}
```

The Thumbnail class

Create a new `Thumbnail` class for the project that will contain a small `Plane` object and an `Image` object to show on it. It also gets the current `cardboardView` instance, which `Image` will require:

```
public class Thumbnail {
    final static String TAG = "Thumbnail";

    public Plane plane;
    public Image image;
    CardboardView cardboardView;

    public Thumbnail(CardboardView cardboardView) {
        this.cardboardView = cardboardView;
    }
}
```

Define a `setImage` method that loads the image texture and shows it as a thumbnail:

```
public void setImage(Image image) {
    this.image = image;
    // Turn the image into a GPU texture
    image.loadTexture(cardboardView, 4);
    // TODO: wait until texture binding is done
    // show it
    image.showThumbnail(cardboardView, plane);
}
```

Lastly, make a quick toggle for the thumbnail visibility:

```
public void setVisible(boolean visible) {
    plane.enabled = visible;
}
```

The thumbnail grid

The plan is to display the phone photos in a 5 x 3 grid of thumbnail images. At the top of the `MainActivity` class, declare a `thumbnails` variable to hold the list of thumbnails:

```
final int GRID_X = 5;
final int GRID_Y = 3;


final List<Thumbnail> thumbnails = new ArrayList<>();
```

Build the list in a new method named `setupThumbnailGrid`. The first thumbnail is positioned in the upper-left corner of the page (-4, 3, -5) and each thumb spaced 2.1 units in *x* and 3 units in *y*, as follows:

```
void setupThumbnailGrid() {
    int count = 0;
    for (int i = 0; i < GRID_Y; i++) {
        for (int j = 0; j < GRID_X; j++) {
            if (count < images.size()) {
                Thumbnail thumb = new
                    Thumbnail(cardboardView);
                thumbnails.add(thumb);

                Transform image = new Transform();
                image.setLocalPosition(-4 + j * 2.1f,
                3 - i * 3, -5);
                Plane imgPlane = new Plane();
                thumb.plane = imgPlane;
                imgPlane.enabled = false;
                BorderMaterial material = new
                BorderMaterial();
                imgPlane.setupBorderMaterial(material);
                image.addComponent(imgPlane);
            }
            count++;
        }
    }
}
```

Now we need to add image textures to the planes. We'll write another method, `updateThumbnails`, as follows. It will show the first 15 images in the grid (or less if you don't have that many):

```
void updateThumbnails() {
    int count = 0;
    for (Thumbnail thumb : thumbnails) {
```

```
        if (count < images.size()) {
            thumb.setImage(images.get(count));
            thumb.setVisible(true);
        } else {
            thumb.setVisible(false);
        }
        count++;
    }
}
```

Add these new methods to `setup`:

```
public void setup() {
    setupMaxTextureSize();
    setupBackground();
    setupScreen();
    loadImageList(imagesPath);
    setupThumbnailGrid();
    updateThumbnails();
}
```

When you run the project, it should look something like this:

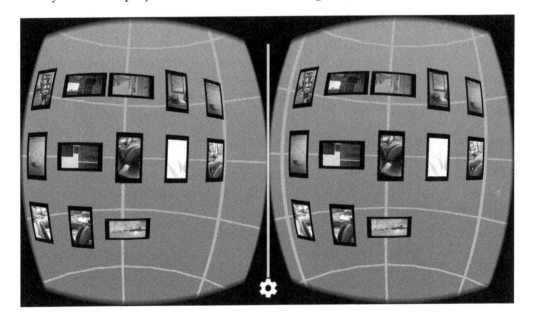

Note that the thumbnails' sizes are adjusted to match the image aspect ratio, and are properly oriented, because we implemented those features in the `Image` class earlier.

If you don't have more than 15 photos already in your phone, add a loop to `loadImageList` to load duplicates. For example, run the following code:

```
for(int j = 0; j < 3; j++) { //Repeat image list
    for (int i = 0; i < file.length; i++) {
        if (Image.isValidImage(file[i].getName())) {
            ...
```

Gaze to load

We want to detect when the user looks at a thumbnail and highlight the image by changing its border color. If users move their gaze away from the thumbnail, it will unhighlight. When the user clicks on the Cardboard trigger, that image is loaded.

Gaze-based highlights

Fortunately, we implemented the `isLooking` detection in the `RenderBox` library at the end of *Chapter 5, RenderBox Engine*. If you remember, the technique determines whether the user is looking at the plane by checking whether the vector between the camera and the plane position is the same as the camera's view direction, within a threshold of tolerance.

We can use this in `MainActivity`. We'll write a `selectObject` helper method that checks whether any of the objects in the scene are selected and highlights them. First, let's declare some variables at the top of the `MainActivity` class. The `selectedThumbnail` object holds the currently selected thumbnail index. We define border colors for normal and selected states:

```
final float[] selectedColor = new float[]{0, 0.5f, 0.5f, 1};
final float[] invalidColor = new float[]{0.5f, 0, 0, 1};
final float[] normalColor = new float[]{0, 0, 0, 1};
Thumbnail selectedThumbnail = null;
```

Now the `selectObject` method goes through each thumbnail, checks whether it's `isLooking`, and highlights (or unhighlights) it accordingly:

```
void selectObject() {
    selectedThumbnail = null;
    for (Thumbnail thumb : thumbnails) {
        if (thumb.image == null)
            return;
        Plane plane = thumb.plane;
        BorderMaterial material = (BorderMaterial)
        plane.getMaterial();
        if (plane.isLooking) {
            selectedThumbnail = thumb;
            material.borderColor = selectedColor;
        } else {
            material.borderColor = normalColor;
        }
    }
}
```

`RenderBox` provides hooks, including `postDraw` where we'll check for selected objects. We want to use `postDraw` because we need to wait until `draw` is called on all of `RenderObjects` before we know which one the user is looking at. In `MainActivity`, add a call to the `selectObject` method as follows:

```
@Override
public void postDraw() {
    selectObject();
}
```

Run the project. As you gaze at a thumbnail image, it should get highlighted!

Selecting and showing photos

Well, now that we can pick an image from the thumbnail grid, we need a way to click on it and show that image. That'll happen in `MainActivity` using the Cardboard SDK hook, `onCardboardTrigger`.

With all the work we've done so far, it's not going to take much more to implement this:

```java
@Override
public void onCardboardTrigger() {
    if (selectedThumbnail != null) {
        showImage(selectedThumbnail.image);
    }
}
```

Try and run it. Now highlight an image and pull the trigger. If you're lucky, it'll work...mine crashes.

Queue events

What's going on? We're running into thread-safe issues. So far, we've been executing all of our code from the render thread, which is started by the `GLSurfaceView`/`CardboardView` class via the Cardboard SDK. This thread owns the access to the GPU and to the particular surface we're rendering on. The call to `onCardboardTrigger` originates from a thread that is not the render thread. This means that we can't make any OpenGL calls from here. Luckily, `GLSurfaceView` provides a nifty way to execute arbitrary code on the render thread through a method called `queueEvent`. The `queueEvent` method takes a single `Runnable` argument, which is a Java class meant to create one-off procedures such as these (refer to `http://developer.android.com/reference/android/opengl/GLSurfaceView.html#queueEvent(java.lang.Runnable)`).

Modify `showImage` to wrap it inside a `Runnable` argument, as follows:

```java
void showImage(final Image image) {
    cardboardView.queueEvent(new Runnable() {
        @Override
        public void run() {

            UnlitTexMaterial bgMaterial = (UnlitTexMaterial)
            photosphere.getMaterial();
            image.loadFullTexture(cardboardView);
            if (image.isPhotosphere) {
                Log.d(TAG, "!!! is photosphere");
                bgMaterial.setTexture(image.textureHandle);
                screen.enabled = false;
            } else {
                bgMaterial.setTexture(bgTextureHandle);
```

```
                        screen.enabled = true;
                        image.show(cardboardView, screen);
                }

            }
        });
    }
```

Note that any data passed to the anonymous class, such as our image, must be declared `final` to be accessible from the new procedure.

Try to run the project again. It should work. You can gaze at a thumbnail, click on the trigger, and that image will be shown, either on the virtual screen or in the background photosphere.

Using a vibrator

No worries, we're keeping it clean. We want to provide some haptic feedback to the user when an image has been selected, using the phone's vibrator. And fortunately, in Android, that's straightforward.

First, make sure that your `AndroidManifest.xml` file includes the following line of code:

```
<uses-permission android:name="android.permission.VIBRATE" />
```

At the top of the `MainActivity` class, declare a `vibrator` variable:

```
private Vibrator vibrator;
```

Then, in `onCreate`, add the following code to initialize it:

```
vibrator = (Vibrator)
getSystemService(Context.VIBRATOR_SERVICE);
```

Then, use it in `onCardboardTrigger`, as follows:

```
vibrator.vibrate(25);
```

Run it again. Click on it and you'll feel it. *Ahhh!* But don't get carried away, it's not that kind of vibrator.

Enable scrolling

Our thumbnail grid has 15 images. If your phone has more than 15 photos, you'll need to scroll through the list. For this project, we'll implement a simple mechanic to scroll the list up and down, using triangular scroll buttons.

Creating the Triangle component

Like other `RenderObjects` in our `RenderBox`, the `Triangle` component defines coordinates, normals, indices, and other data that describes a triangle. We create a constructor method that allocates buffers. Like the `Plane` component, we want to use the `BorderMaterial` class so that it can be highlighted when selected. And like the `Plane` component, it will determine when the user is looking at it. Without further ado, here's the code.

Create a new Java class file, `Triangle.java`, in the `RenderBoxExt/components` folder. We begin by declaring it `extends RenderObject` and by declaring the following variables:

```
public class Triangle extends RenderObject {

    /*
    Special triangle for border shader

    *    0/3 (0,1,0)/(0,1,0) (0,1)/(1,1)
              /|\
             / | \
           *--*--*
           1  2  4
    */

    private static final float YAW_LIMIT = 0.15f;
    private static final float PITCH_LIMIT = 0.15f;
    public static final float[] COORDS = new float[] {
            0f, 1.0f, 0.0f,
            -1.0f, -1.0f, 0.0f,
            0.0f, -1.0f, 0.0f,
            0f, 1.0f, 0.0f,
            1.0f, -1.0f, 0.0f,
    };
    public static final float[] TEX_COORDS = new float[] {
            0f, 1f,
            0f, 0f,
            0.5f, 0f,
            1f, 1f,
```

```
            1f, 0f
    };
    public static final float[] COLORS = new float[] {
            0.5f, 0.5f, 0.5f, 1.0f,
            0.5f, 0.5f, 0.5f, 1.0f,
            0.5f, 0.5f, 0.5f, 1.0f,
            0.5f, 0.5f, 0.5f, 1.0f,
            0.5f, 0.5f, 0.5f, 1.0f
    };
    public static final float[] NORMALS = new float[] {
            0.0f, 0.0f, -1.0f,
            0.0f, 0.0f, -1.0f,
            0.0f, 0.0f, -1.0f,
            0.0f, 0.0f, -1.0f,
            0.0f, 0.0f, -1.0f
    };
    public static final short[] INDICES = new short[] {
            1, 0, 2,
            2, 3, 4
    };

    private static FloatBuffer vertexBuffer;
    private static FloatBuffer colorBuffer;
    private static FloatBuffer normalBuffer;
    private static FloatBuffer texCoordBuffer;
    private static ShortBuffer indexBuffer;
    static final int numIndices = 6;

    static boolean setup;
}
```

In case it's not clear as to why we need this 2-triangle triangle, it has to do with how the UVs work. You can't get a full border with just one triangle, at least not the way we've written the border shader.

Add a constructor, along with an `allocateBuffers` helper:

```
    public Triangle(){
        super();
        allocateBuffers();
    }

    public static void allocateBuffers(){
        //Already allocated?
        if (vertexBuffer != null) return;
```

```
    vertexBuffer = allocateFloatBuffer(COORDS);
    texCoordBuffer = allocateFloatBuffer(TEX_COORDS);
    colorBuffer = allocateFloatBuffer(COLORS);
    normalBuffer = allocateFloatBuffer(NORMALS);
    indexBuffer = allocateShortBuffer(INDICES);
}
```

We can create various materials, but we really only plan to use `BorderMaterial`, so let's support this like we did with `Plane`:

```
public void setupBorderMaterial(BorderMaterial material){
    this.material = material;
    material.setBuffers(vertexBuffer, texCoordBuffer,
    indexBuffer, numIndices);
}
```

Adding triangles to the UI

In `MainActivity`, we can add the `up` and `down` triangle buttons to scroll the thumbnails. At the top of the `MainActivity` class, declare variables for the triangles and their materials:

```
Triangle up, down;
BorderMaterial upMaterial, downMaterial;
boolean upSelected, downSelected;
```

Define a `setupScrollButtons` helper as follows:

```
void setupScrollButtons() {
    up = new Triangle();
    upMaterial = new BorderMaterial();
    up.setupBorderMaterial(upMaterial);
    new Transform()
        .setLocalPosition(0,6,-5)
        .addComponent(up);

    down = new Triangle();
    downMaterial = new BorderMaterial();
    down.setupBorderMaterial(downMaterial);
    new Transform()
        .setLocalPosition(0,-6,-5)
        .setLocalRotation(0,0,180)
        .addComponent(down);
}
```

Then, call it from the `setup` method:

```
public void setup() {
    setupMaxTextureSize();
    setupBackground();
    setupScreen();
    loadImageList(imagesPath);
    setupThumbnailGrid();
    setupScrollButtons();
    updateThumbnails();
}
```

When you run the project, you will see the arrows:

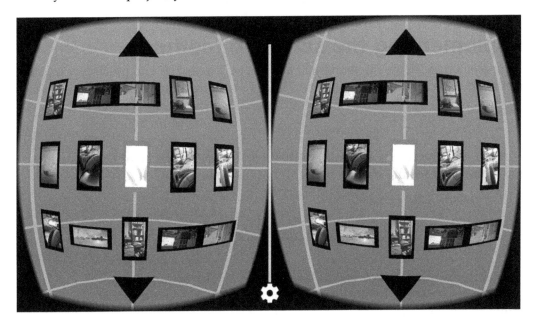

Interacting with the scroll buttons

Now we will detect when the user is looking at a triangle, by using `isLooking` in `selectObject` (which is called from the `postDraw` hook):

```
void selectObject() {
    ...

    if (up.isLooking) {
        upSelected = true;
        upMaterial.borderColor = selectedColor;
```

```
        } else {
            upSelected = false;
            upMaterial.borderColor = normalColor;
        }

        if (down.isLooking) {
            downSelected = true;
            downMaterial.borderColor = selectedColor;
        } else {
            downSelected = false;
            downMaterial.borderColor = normalColor;
        }
    }
```

Implementing the scrolling method

To implement scrolling the thumbnail images, we'll keep the grid planes in place and just scroll the textures. Use an offset variable to hold the index of the first image in the grid:

```
static int thumbOffset = 0;
```

Now, modify the updateThumbnails method to populate the plane textures using the thumb offset as the starting index of the image textures:

```
void updateThumbnails() {
    int count = thumbOffset;
    for (Thumbnail thumb : thumbnails) {
        . . .
```

We can perform scrolling when the up or down arrows are pressed in onCardboardTrigger by shifting the thumbOffset variable one row at a time (GRID_X):

```
public void onCardboardTrigger() {
    if (selectedThumbnail != null) {
        vibrator.vibrate(25);
        showImage(selectedThumbnail.image);
    }
    if (upSelected) {
        // scroll up
        thumbOffset -= GRID_X;
        if (thumbOffset < 0) {
            thumbOffset = images.size() - GRID_X;
        }
```

```
        vibrator.vibrate(25);
        updateThumbnails();
    }
    if (downSelected) {
        // scroll down
        if (thumbOffset < images.size()) {
            thumbOffset += GRID_X;
        } else {
            thumbOffset = 0;
        }
        vibrator.vibrate(25);
        updateThumbnails();
    }
}
```

As with `showImage`, the `updateThumbnails` method needs to run on the render thread:

```
void updateThumbnails() {
    cardboardView.queueEvent(new Runnable() {
        @Override
        public void run() {
            . . .
```

Run the project. You can now click on the up and down arrows to scroll through your photos.

Stay responsive and use threads

There are a few problems with our loading and scrolling code, all related to the fact that loading images and converting bitmaps is compute-intensive. Attempting to do this for 15 images all at once causes the app to appear frozen. You may have also noticed that the app takes significantly longer to start up since we added the thumbnail grid.

In conventional apps, it might be annoying but somewhat acceptable for the app to lock up while waiting for data to load. But in VR, the app needs to stay alive. The app needs to continue responding to the head movement and update the display for each frame with a view corresponding to the current view direction. If the app is locked while loading files, it will feel stuck, that is, stuck to your face! In a fully immersive experience, and on a desktop HMD that is strapped on, visual lockup is the most severe cause of nausea, or *sim sickness*.

The solution is a worker thread. The key to successful multithreaded support is providing the ability for the procedures to signal each other with semaphores (Boolean flags). We'll use the following:

- `Image.loadLock`: This is true when waiting for the GPU to generate a texture
- `MainActivity.cancelUpdate`: This is true when the thread should stop due to a user event
- `MainActivity gridUpdateLock`: This is true when the grid is updating; ignore other user events

Let's declare these. At the top of the `Image` class, add the following code:

```
public static boolean loadLock = false;
```

At the top of the `MainActivity` class, add the following:

```
public static boolean cancelUpdate = false;
static boolean gridUpdateLock = false;
```

First, let's identify the compute-intensive part of our code. Feel free to do your own investigation, but let's assume that `BitmapFactory.decodeFile` is the culprit. Ideally, any code that wasn't directly related to rendering should be done on a worker thread, but beware of pre-optimization. We're doing this work because we've noticed an issue, so we should be able to identify the new code which is causing it. An educated guess points to this business of loading arbitrary images into textures.

Where do we do this operation? Well, the actual call to `BitmapFactory.decodeFile` comes from `Image.loadTexture`, but more generally, all of this is kicked off in `MainActivity.updateGridTextures` and `MainActivity.showImage`. Let's update these last two functions now.

Lucky for us, `showImage` has already been wrapped in `Runnable` for the purpose of redirecting its execution to the render thread. Now we want to actually ensure that it always happens off the render thread. We'll be using `queueEvent` in a different place to avoid the error that we encountered earlier. We replace the previous `Runnable` code with `Thread`. For example, `showImage` now looks like this:

```
void showImage(final Image image) {
    new Thread() {
        @Override
        public void run() {
            UnlitTexMaterial bgMaterial = (UnlitTexMaterial)
            photosphere.getMaterial();
                ...
        }
    }.start();
}
```

Do the same to `updateThumbnails`. While we're here, add the `gridUpdateLock` flag that remains set while it's running, and handle the `cancelUpdate` flag, so the loops can be interrupted:

```
void updateThumbnails() {
    gridUpdateLock = true;
    new Thread() {
        @Override
        public void run() {
            int count = thumbOffset;
            for (Thumbnail thumb : thumbnails) {
                if (cancelUpdate)
                    return;
                if (count < images.size()) {
                    thumb.setImage(images.get(count));
                    thumb.setVisible(true);
                } else {
                    thumb.setVisible(false);
                }
                count++;
            }
            cancelUpdate = false;
            gridUpdateLock = false;
        }
    }.start();
}
```

Focusing on the `Image` class's `loadTexture` method, we need to redirect the GPU calls back to the render thread with `queueEvent`. If you try to run the app now, it will crash right out of the gate. This is because `showImage` is now always run in its own thread, and when we eventually make the OpenGL calls to generate the texture, we'll get the invalid operation error that we got earlier when we added the trigger input. To fix this, modify `loadTexture` as follows:

```
public void loadTexture(CardboardView cardboardView,
int sampleSize) {
    if (textureHandle != 0)
        return;
    BitmapFactory.Options options = new
    BitmapFactory.Options();
    options.inSampleSize = sampleSize;
    final Bitmap bitmap = BitmapFactory.decodeFile(path,
    options);
    if(bitmap == null){
```

```
            throw new RuntimeException("Error loading bitmap.");
    }
    width = options.outWidth;
    height = options.outHeight;

    loadLock = true;
    cardboardView.queueEvent(new Runnable() {
                @Override
                public void run() {
                    if (MainActivity.cancelUpdate)
                        return;
                    textureHandle =
                    bitmapToTexture(bitmap);
                    bitmap.recycle();
                    loadLock = false;
                }
            }
    });
    while (loadLock){
        try {
            Thread.sleep(100);
        } catch (InterruptedException e) {
            e.printStackTrace();
        }
    }
}
```

We changed it so that `bitmapToTexture` is now called on the GPU thread. We use the `loadLock` flag to indicate that the loading is busy. When it's done, the flag is reset. Meanwhile, `loadTexture` waits for it to finish before returning because we need this `textureHandle` value for later. But since we're always calling this from a worker thread, the app isn't hung waiting. This change will also improve the start-up time.

Similarly, we do the same thing in the `Thumbnail` class; its `setImage` method also loads the image texture. Modify it so that it looks like this:

```
public void setImage(Image image) {
    this.image = image;
    // Turn the image into a GPU texture
    image.loadTexture(cardboardView, 4);
    // wait until texture binding is done
    try {
        while (Image.loadLock) {
```

```
                if (MainActivity.cancelUpdate)
                    return;
                Thread.sleep(10);
            }
        } catch (InterruptedException e) {
            e.printStackTrace();
        }
        // show it
        . . .

    }
```

You might have noticed a subtler issue in all of this. If we try to close the app in the middle of one of these worker thread operations, it will crash. The underlying issue is that the thread persists, but the graphics context has been destroyed, even if you are just switching apps. Trying to generate textures with an invalid graphics context results in a crash, and the user gets little notification. Bad news. What we want to do is stop the worker thread when the app closes. This is where cancelUpdate comes into play. In MainActivity, we'll set its value in the onCreate method, and add the methods to the onStart, onResume, and onPause hook methods, as follows:

```
@Override
protected void onCreate(Bundle savedInstanceState) {
    cancelUpdate = false;
    //...
}

@Override
protected void onStart(){
    super.onStart();
    cancelUpdate = true;
}
@Override
protected void onResume(){
    super.onResume();
    cancelUpdate = false;
}
@Override
protected void onPause(){
    super.onPause();
    cancelUpdate = true;
}
```

If you try to click on something while the grid is updating, it shouldn't let you to do so. Add the following code to the top of `onCardboardTrigger`:

```
if (gridUpdateLock) {
    vibrator.vibrate(new long[]{0,50,30,50}, -1);
    return;
}
```

This new `long[]{0,50,30,50}` business is a way of programming a sequence into the vibrator. In this case, two short (50 milliseconds) pulses in a row are used to indicate the nuh-uh reaction.

We can even go one beautiful step further and highlight selectable objects in `selectObject` with a disabled color during `gridUpdateLock` like this:

```
if (plane.isLooking) {
    selectedThumbnail = thumb;
    if(gridUpdateLock)
        material.borderColor = invalidColor;
    else
        material.borderColor = selectedColor;

    . . .
```

Your project should run as before. But now it's more responsive, better behaved, and doesn't get stuck waiting for images to load.

An explanation of threading and virtual reality

OpenGL is not thread-safe. This sounds like a design flaw. In reality, it's more like a design requirement. You want your graphics API to draw frames as quickly and frequently as possible. As you may know, or will soon learn, waiting is something that threads end up doing a lot of the time. If you introduce multithreaded access to your graphics hardware, you introduce periods where the hardware might be waiting on the CPU simply to figure out its thread scheduling and who needs access at the time. It's much simpler and faster to say "only one thread may access the GPU." Technically speaking, as graphics APIs become more advanced (DirectX 12 and Vulkan), this is not strictly true, but we will not be getting into multithreaded rendering in this book.

Let's first take a step back and ask the question, "Why do we need to use threads?" To some of you who are more experienced application developers, the answer should be obvious. But not all programmers need to use threads, and, even worse, many programmers use threads inappropriately, or when they aren't needed in the first place. For those of you still in the dark, a thread is a fancy term for "a way to run two procedures at the same time." On a practical level, the operating system takes control of scheduling threads to run one after another, or on different CPU cores, but as programmers, we assume that all threads are running "simultaneously."

Incidentally, while we are only allowed one CPU thread to control the GPU, the whole point of a GPU is that it is massively multithreaded. Mobile GPUs are still getting there, but high-end Tegra chips have hundreds of cores (currently, the X1 is at 256 cores), lagging behind their desktop equivalents with thousands of cores (Titan Black @ 2880 cores). A GPU is set up to process each pixel (or other similar small datum) on a separate thread, and there is some hardware magic going on that schedules all of them automatically with zero overhead. Think of your render thread as a slow taskmaster instructing a tiny army of CPUs to do your bidding and report back with the results, or in most cases, just draw them right to the screen. This means that the CPU is already doing a fair amount of waiting on behalf of the GPU, freeing your other worker threads to do their tasks and then wait when there is more CPU render work to be done.

Threads are generally useful when you want to run a process which will take a while, and you want to avoid blocking the program's execution, or main, thread. The most common place where this comes up is starting a background process and allowing the UI to continue to update. If you're creating a media encoder program, you don't want it to be unresponsive for 30 minutes while it decodes a video. Instead, you'd like the program to run as normal, allowing the user to click on buttons and see progress updates from the background work. In this scenario, you have to let the UI and background threads take a break now and then to send and check messages passed between the two. Adjusting the length of the break, or sleep time, and thread priority values allows you to avoid one thread hogging too much CPU time.

Back to OpenGL and graphics programming. It is common in a game engine to split the work into a few, distinct threads (render, physics, audio, input, and so on). However, the render thread is always a kind of *orchestrator* because rendering still tends to be the most time-sensitive job and must happen at least 30 times per second. In VR, this constraint is even more important. We're not worried about physics and audio, perhaps, but we still need to make sure that our renderer can draw things as quickly as possible, or the feeling of presence is lost. Furthermore, we can never stop rendering, as long as the person is looking at the screen. We need threads to avoid "hiccups" or unacceptably long periods between render frames.

Head tracking is essential to a VR experience. A person who is moving their head, looking only at a fixed image, will start to experience nausea, or *simsickness*. Even some text on a black background, if it is not compensated by some sort of fixed horizon, will eventually cause discomfort. Sometimes, we do have to block the render thread for significant periods of time, and the best option is to first fade the image to a solid color, or void. This can be comfortable for a short period of time. The worst thing that can happen in VR is periodic hiccups or frame rate drops due to extensive work being done on the render thread. If you don't maintain a constant, smooth, frame rate, your VR experience is worthless.

In our case, we need to decode a series of rather large bitmaps and load them into GPU textures. Unfortunately, the decode step takes a few hundred milliseconds and causes those hiccups we were just talking about. However, since this isn't GPU work, it doesn't have to happen on the render thread! If we want to avoid any heavy lifting in our `setup()`, `preDraw()`, and `postDraw()` functions, we should create a thread any time that we want to decode a bitmap. In the case of updating our grid of previews, we should probably just create a single thread, which can run the whole update process, waiting in between each bitmap. In the CPU land, the OS needs to use some resources to schedule threads and allocate their resources. It's much more efficient to just create a single thread to run through the entire job, rather than spinning up and taking down a thread for each bitmap.

Of course, we're going to need to make use of our old friend `queueEvent` in order to do any graphics work, in this case generating and loading the texture. As it turns out, updating the display of the image is not graphics work, since it just involves changing a value on our material. We do, however, need to wait on the graphics work in order to get this new value. As a result of these optimizations and constraints, we need a locking system in order to allow one thread to wait on the others to finish its work, and to prevent the user from interrupting or restarting this procedure before it has completed. This is what we just implemented in the previous topic.

Launch with an intent

Wouldn't it be cool if you could launch this app any time you go to view an image on your phone, especially 360-degree photospheres?

One of the more powerful features of the Android operating system is the ability to communicate between apps with intents. An **intent** is a message that any app can send to the Android system, which declares its intent to use another app for a certain purpose. The intent object contains a number of members to describe what type of action needs to be done, and, if any, the data on which it needs to be done. As a user, you may be familiar with the default action picker, which displays a number of app icons, and the choices, **Just Once**, or **Always**. What you're seeing is the result of the app you were just using broadcasting a new intent to the system. When you choose an app, and Android launches a new activity from that app, which has been registered to respond to intents of that type.

In your `AndroidManifest.xml` file, add an intent filter to the activity block. Let Android know that the app can be used as an image viewer. Add the following XML code:

```
<intent-filter>
    <action android:name="android.intent.action.VIEW" />
    <category android:name="android.intent.category.DEFAULT" />
    <data android:mimeType="image/*" />
</intent-filter>
```

We just need to handle the situation so an intent image is the default image loaded when the app starts. In `MainActivity`, we'll write a new function that shows an image given its URI, as follows. The method gets the URI path and translates it into a file pathname, calls the new `Image` object on that path, and then the `showImage` method. (For reference, visit `http://developer.android.com/guide/topics/providers/content-provider-basics.html`):

```
void showUriImage(final Uri uri) {
    Log.d(TAG, "intent data " + uri.getPath());
    File file = new File(uri.getPath());
    if(file.exists()){
        Image img = new Image(uri.getPath());
        showImage(img);
    } else {
        String[] filePathColumn =
        {MediaStore.Images.Media.DATA};
        Cursor cursor = getContentResolver().query(uri,
        filePathColumn, null, null, null);
        if (cursor == null)
            return;
```

```
        if (cursor.moveToFirst()) {
            int columnIndex =
            cursor.getColumnIndex(filePathColumn[0]);
            String yourRealPath =
            cursor.getString(columnIndex);
            Image img = new Image(yourRealPath);
            showImage(img);
        }
        // else report image not found error?
        cursor.close();

    }
```

Then, add a call to showUriImage from setup, as follows:

```
public void setup() {
    BorderMaterial.destroy();
    setupMaxTextureSize();
    setupBackground();
    setupScreen();
    loadImageList(imagesPath);
    setupThumbnailGrid();
    setupScrollButtons();
    Uri intentUri = getIntent().getData();
    if (intentUri != null) {
        showUriImage(intentUri);
    }
    updateThumbnails();
}
```

We've also added a call to BorderMaterial.destroy() since the intent launches a second instance of the activity. If we don't destroy the materials, the new activity instance, which has its own graphics context, will throw errors when it tries to use shaders compiled on the first activity's graphics context.

Now with the project built and installed on the phone, when you choose an image file, for example, from a file folder browser app such as **My Files** (Samsung), you're given a choice of apps with an intent to view images. Your Gallery360 app (or whatever you have actually named it) will be one of the choices, as shown in the following screenshot. Pick it and it will launch with that image file view as the default.

Showing/hiding the grid with tilt-up gestures

Back in the early days of Cardboard, you had one button. That was all. The one button and head tracking were the only ways for the user to interact with the app. And because the button was a nifty magnet thing, you couldn't even press and hold the one button. With Cardboard 2.0, the screen turned into the button, and we also realized that we could briefly take the box off of our face, tilt the phone up, put it back on, and interpret that as a gesture. Thus, a second input was born! At the time of writing, the sample Cardboard apps use this as a back gesture.

We will be using tilt-up to show and hide the grid and arrows so that you can fully immerse yourself in the selected photosphere. Since it's less work, we'll also let the user do this anytime, and not just while looking at photospheres. As with the vibration feedback, this is actually a pretty painless feature to add. Most of the hard work is done by an `OrientationEventListener` class.

At the top of the `MainActivity` class, add a variable for the state of the grid, the orientation event listener, and ones for a tilt detection timer, as follows:

```
static boolean setupComplete = false;

boolean interfaceVisible = true;
OrientationEventListener orientationEventListener;
int orientThreshold = 10;
boolean orientFlip = false;
long tiltTime;
int tiltDamper = 250;
```

First, we can write a method that toggles the thumbnail grid menu on/off. Check whether there are less images than planes since empty ones are already disabled in `updateThumbnails`:

```
void toggleGridMenu() {
    interfaceVisible = !interfaceVisible;
    if (up != null)
        up.enabled = !up.enabled;
    if (down != null)
        down.enabled = !down.enabled;
    int texCount = thumbOffset;
    for (Thumbnail thumb : thumbnails) {
        if (texCount < images.size() && thumb != null) {
            thumb.setVisible(interfaceVisible);
        }
        texCount++;
    }
}
```

Next, write a `setupOrientationListener` helper method, which provides a callback function when the device orientation changes. If the orientation gets close to vertical after being in landscape mode, we can call our toggle function, and once the device returns to landscape and goes vertical again, we toggle again:

```
void setupOrientationListener() {
    orientationEventListener = new
    OrientationEventListener(this,
    SensorManager.SENSOR_DELAY_NORMAL) {
        @Override
        public void onOrientationChanged(int orientation) {
            if(gridUpdateLock || !setupComplete)
                return;
            if(System.currentTimeMillis() - tiltTime > tiltDamper)
            {
```

```
                    if(Math.abs(orientation) < orientThreshold ||
                    Math.abs(orientation - 180) <
                    orientThreshold){
                    //"close enough" to portrait mode
                        if(!orientFlip) {
                            Log.d(TAG, "tilt up! " + orientation);
                            vibrator.vibrate(25);
                            toggleGridMenu();
                        }
                        orientFlip = true;
                    }
                    if(Math.abs(orientation - 90) <
                    orientThreshold || Math.abs(orientation - 270)
                    < orientThreshold) {
                     //"close enough" to landscape mode
                        orientFlip = false;
                    }
                        tiltTime = System.currentTimeMillis();
                }
            }
        };
        if(orientationEventListener.canDetectOrientation())
            orientationEventListener.enable();
    }
```

Then, add it to `onCreate`:

```
    protected void onCreate(Bundle savedInstanceState) {
        ...
        setupOrientationListener();
    }
```

The `setupComplete` flag prevents the grid from being toggled while it is still being created. Let's reset the complete flag after `updateThumbnails`:

```
    void updateThumbnails() {
        . . .
                cancelUpdate = false;
                gridUpdateLock = false;
                setupComplete = true;
```

It's prudent to destroy it in `onDestroy`:

```
    @Override
    protected void onDestroy(){
        super.onDestroy();
        orientationEventListener.disable();
    }
```

The onOrientationChanged callback will fire whenever the phone changes orientation. We'll only be interested in the times when it changes from landscape to portrait, and we also want to make sure that it doesn't happen too often, hence the **tilt damper** feature. You might want to tweak the value (currently 250 milliseconds) to your liking. Too short, and you might falsely register two changes in a row. Too long, and the user might try to tiltup twice within the cutoff time.

Spherical thumbnails

Spherical 360-degree images deserve better than a plain ol' paint-chip thumbnail images, don't you think? I suggest that we display them as small balls. Maybe we should call them thumb-tips or thumb-marbles. Anyway, let's do a little hacking to make this happen.

Add a sphere to the Thumbnail class

In the Thumbnail class, add a sphere variable:

```
public Sphere sphere;
```

Modify setImage to recognize a photosphere image:

```
public void setImage(Image image) {
    // ...
    // show it
    if (image.isPhotosphere) {
        UnlitTexMaterial material = (UnlitTexMaterial)
        sphere.getMaterial();
        material.setTexture(image.textureHandle);
    } else {
        image.showThumbnail(cardboardView, plane);
    }
}
```

We must also change setVisible to handle both the plane and sphere variables, as follows:

```
public void setVisible(boolean visible) {
    if(visible) {
        if(image.isPhotosphere){
            plane.enabled = false;
            sphere.enabled = true;
        } else{
            plane.enabled = true;
            sphere.enabled = false;
```

```
            }
        } else {
            plane.enabled = false;
            sphere.enabled = false;
        }
    }
}
```

Next, in the `MainActivity` class's `setupThumbnailGrid`, initialize a `Sphere` object in addition to a `Plane` object (inside the `GRID_Y` and `GRID_X` loops):

```
        . . .
        image.addComponent(imgPlane);

        Transform sphere = new Transform();
        sphere.setLocalPosition(-4 + j * 2.1f,
        3 - i * 3, -5);
        sphere.setLocalRotation(180, 0, 0);
        sphere.setLocalScale(normalScale, normalScale,
        normalScale);
        Sphere imgSphere = new Sphere(R.drawable.bg,
        false);
        thumb.sphere = imgSphere;
        imgSphere.enabled = false;
        sphere.addComponent(imgSphere);
```

Now the thumbnails have both a plane and a sphere that we can populate depending on the image type.

Lastly, we just need to modify the `selectObject` method to see how we highlight a sphere thumbnail. We highlight the rectangular ones by changing the border color. Our spheres don't have a border; in lieu of that we'll change their size.

At the top of `MainActivity`, add variables to the normal and selected scales:

```
        final float selectedScale = 1.25f;
        final float normalScale = 0.85f;
```

Now, change `selectObject` to behave differently when the image is a photosphere:

```
        void selectObject() {
            float deltaTime = Time.getDeltaTime();
            selectedThumbnail = null;
            for (Thumbnail thumb : thumbnails) {
                if (thumb.image == null)
                    return;
                if (thumb.image.isPhotosphere) {
                    Sphere sphere = thumb.sphere;
                    if (sphere.isLooking) {
                        selectedThumbnail = thumb;
```

```
                if (!gridUpdateLock)
                    sphere.transform.setLocalScale
                    (selectedScale, selectedScale,
                    selectedScale);
            } else {
                sphere.transform.setLocalScale(normalScale,
                normalScale, normalScale);
            }
            sphere.transform.rotate(0, 10 * deltaTime, 0);
        } else {
            Plane plane = thumb.plane;
            //...
        }
    }
}
//. . .
```

Whoo hoo! We even have the sphere spinning, so you can see its 360-ness in all its glory! This is so much fun, it should be illegal.

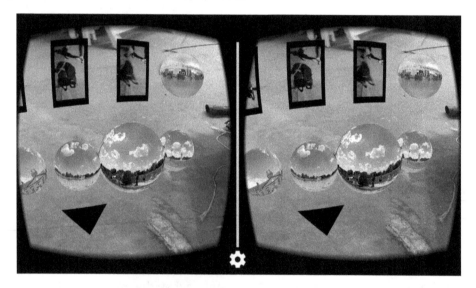

There you have it! A beautiful photo viewer app that supports both regular camera images as well as 360-degree photospheres.

Updating the RenderBox library

With the Gallery360 project implemented and our code stabilized, you might realize that we've built some code that is not necessarily specific to this application that can be reused in other projects, and ought to make its way back to the RenderBox library.

We did this at the end of the previous project in *Chapter 6, Solar System*. You can refer to that topic for details. Follow these steps to update the `RenderBoxLib` project:

1. Move the `Plane` and `Triangle` components from `RenderBoxExt/ components`.

2. Move the `BorderMaterial` component from `RenderBoxExt/materials`.

3. Move the border shader files from `res/raw`.

4. Refactor any invalid references to correct the package names.

5. Rebuild the library by clicking **Build** | **Make Project**.

Further possible enhancements

Whew, that was a lot of work! This thing is certainly done, isn't it? *Never!* Here are a few improvements just begging to be implemented:

- Better detection of phone images:

  ° Not everyone keeps all of their images in a specific path. In fact, some camera software uses completely different paths! Introduce a proper file browser.

- Better detection of photosphere images:

  ° There is a `Projection Type` attribute in the XMP header, another piece of metadata in some JPG files. Unfortunately, the Android API doesn't have a specific class to read this data, and integrating a third-party library is beyond the scope of this project. Feel free to try the following links:

    `https://github.com/dragon66/pixymeta-android`

    `https://github.com/drewnoakes/metadata-extractor`

    Don't use the pano technique because it picks up regular panoramas. Allow users to flag or fix photosphere or rotation metadata on images that are displayed incorrectly.

- Animate UI actions—scale/translate on select, smooth grid scrolling.

- A nifty technique to keep grid tiles from showing up behind the up/down arrows is known as **depth masking**. You can also just introduce a maximum and minimum Y value in the world space beyond which tiles would not be able to draw. But depth masks are cooler.

- Respond to the `GALLERY` intent to override the grid with a selection of images from another app.

- Accept image URLs from the web in VIEW intents.
- You need to first download the image, and then load it from the download path.

Summary

I hope you're as excited as I am with what we accomplished here! We built a truly practical Cardboard VR app to view a gallery of regular photos and 360-degree photospheres. The project uses the RenderBox library, as discussed in *Chapter 5, RenderBox Engine*.

To begin with, we illustrated how photospheres work and viewed one on Cardboard using the RenderBox library without any custom changes. Then, to view a regular photo, we created a Plane component to be used as a virtual projection screen. We wrote new materials and shaders to render images with a frame border.

Next, we defined a new Image class and loaded images from the phone's camera folder into a list, and wrote a method to show the image on the screen Plane, correcting its orientation and aspect ratio. Then, we built a user interface that shows a grid of thumbnail images and lets you select one by gazing at it and clicking on the Cardboard trigger to display the image. The grid is scrollable, which required us to add threading, so the app would not appear to lock up when files are loading. Lastly, we added a couple of bells and whistles to launch the app with the image view intent, toggle the menu grid by tilting the phone vertically, and spherical thumbanils for photospheres.

In the next chapter, we'll build another kind of viewer; this time to view full 3D models in OBJ files.

8
3D Model Viewer

Three-dimensional models are everywhere, from mechanical engineering of machine parts to medical imaging; from video game design to 3D printing. 3D models are as prolific as photos, videos, music, and other media. Yet, while browsers and apps have native support for other media types, 3D models do not have so much. One day 3D viewing standards will be integrated into the browser (such as WebGL and WebVR). Until then, we'll have to rely on plugins and sister apps to view our models. Free 3D file models in the OBJ format, for example, can be found online, including TF3DM (`http://tf3dm.com/`), TurboSquid (`http://www.turbosquid.com/`), and many others (`http://www.hongkiat.com/blog/60-excellent-free-3d-model-websites/`).

In this project, we will build an Android 3D model viewer app that lets you open and view models in 3D using a Cardboard VR headset. The file format that we'll use is OBJ, an open format first developed by Wavefront Technologies for cinematic 3D animation. OBJs can be created and exported by many 3D design applications, including open source ones, such as Blender and MeshLab, as well as commercial ones, such as 3D Studio Max and Maya. An OBJ is a noncompressed plain text file that stores a description of the surface mesh of a 3D object composed of triangles (or higher degree polygons).

To implement the viewer, we will read and parse OBJ file models and display them in 3D for viewing with Cardboard. We will accomplish this by performing the following steps:

- Setting up the new project
- Writing an OBJ file parser to import the geometry
- Displaying the 3D model
- Rotating the view of the object using the user's head motion

The source code for this project can be found on the Packt Publishing website, and on GitHub at `https://github.com/cardbookvr/modelviewer` (with each topic as a separate commit).

Setting up a new project

To build this project, we're going to use our `RenderBox` library created in *Chapter 5, RenderBox Engine*. You can use yours, or grab a copy from the downloadable files provided with this book or from our GitHub repository (use the commit tagged `after-ch7` — `https://github.com/cardbookvr/renderboxlib/releases/tag/after-ch7`). For a more detailed description of how to import the `RenderBox` library, refer to the final section, *Using RenderBox in future projects*, of *Chapter 5, RenderBox Engine*. To create a new project, perform the following steps:

1. With Android Studio opened, create a new project. Let's name it `Gallery360` and target **Android 4.4 KitKat (API 19)** with an **Empty Activity**.
2. Create new modules for the `renderbox`, `common` and `core` packages, using **File | New Module | Import .JAR/.AAR Package**.
3. Set the modules as dependencies for the app, using **File | Project Structure.**
4. Edit the `build.gradle` file as explained in *Chapter 2, The Skeleton Cardboard Project*, to compile against SDK 22.
5. Update `/res/layout/activity_main.xml` and `AndroidManifest.xml`, as explained in the previous chapters.
6. Edit `MainActivity` as `class MainActivity extends CardboardActivity implements IRenderBox`, and implement the interface method stubs (*Ctrl + I*).

We can go ahead and define the `onCreate` method in `MainActivity`. The class now has the following code:

```
public class MainActivity extends CardboardActivity implements
IRenderBox {
    private static final String TAG = "ModelViewer";
    CardboardView cardboardView;
    @Override
    protected void onCreate(Bundle savedInstanceState) {
        super.onCreate(savedInstanceState);
        setContentView(R.layout.activity_main);

        cardboardView = (CardboardView)
        findViewById(R.id.cardboard_view);
        cardboardView.setRenderer(new RenderBox(this, this));
```

```
        setCardboardView(cardboardView);
    }
    @Override
    public void setup() {
    }
    @Override
    public void preDraw() {
        // code run beginning each frame
    }
    @Override
    public void postDraw() {
        // code run end of each frame
    }
}
```

You can add a cube to the scene, temporarily, to help ensure that everything is set up properly. Add it to the `setup` method, as follows:

```
public void setup() {
    new Transform()
        .setLocalPosition(0,0,-7)
        .setLocalRotation(45,60,0)
        .addComponent(new Cube(true));
}
```

If you remember, a `Cube` is a `Component` that's added to a `Transform`. The `Cube` defines its geometry (for example, vertices). The `Transform` defines its position, rotation, and scale in 3D space.

You should be able to click on **Run 'app'** with no compile errors and see the cube and Cardboard split screen view on your Android device.

Understanding the OBJ file format

The goal of this project is to view 3D models in the Wavefront OBJ format. Before we begin coding, let's take a look at the file format. A reference can be found at `http://www.fileformat.info/format/wavefrontobj/egff.htm`.

As we know, 3D models can be represented as a mesh of X, Y, and Z vertices. Sets of vertices are connected to define a face of the mesh surface. A full mesh surface is a collection of these faces.

Each vertex can also be assigned a normal vector and/or a texture coordinate. The normal vector defines the outward facing direction at that vertex, used in lighting calculations. The UV texture coordinate can be used to map texture images onto the mesh surface. There are other features of the format, including free-form curves and materials, which we will not support in this project.

As a plain text file, an OBJ is organized as separate lines of text. Each nonblank line begins with a keyword and data for that keyword separated by spaces. Comments begin with # and are ignored by the parser.

The OBJ data keywords include:

- `v`: Geometric vertices (for example, `v   0.0   1.0   0.0`)
- `vt`: Texture vertices (for example, `vt   0.0   1.0   0.0`) [not supported in our project]
- `vn`: Vertex normals (for example, `vn   0.0   1.0   0.0`)
- `f`: Polygonal face indexes (for example, `f   1   2   3`)

The face values are indices pointing into the vertices list into the vertices (starting at 1 for the first one).

As for the `f` command specifying face indices, they're integer values that index into the vertex list. When there are three indices, it describes a triangle; four describes a quad, and so on.

When texture vertices exist, they are referenced as the second number after a slash, for example, `f   1/1   2/2   3/3`. We're not supporting them now, but we might need to parse them in an `f` command. When vertex normals exist, they are referenced as the third number after a slash, for example, `f   1//1   2//2   3//3` or `f   1/1/1   2/2/2   3/3/3`.

Indices can be negative, in which case they reference the last (most recently encountered) item as -1, the previous one as -2, and so on.

Other lines, including data that we are not supporting here, will be ignored.

For example, the following data represents a simple triangle:

```
# Simple Wavefront file
v 0.0 0.0 0.0
v 0.0 1.0 0.0
v 1.0 0.0 0.0
f 1 2 3
```

Our OBJ implementation is limited. It safely handles the example models included with this book, and perhaps others that you'll find on the Internet or make yourself. However, this is an example code and a demonstration project. Writing a robust data importer and supporting the many features of OBJ in our `RenderBox` engine is beyond the scope of this book.

Creating the ModelObject class

To begin with, we will define a `ModelObject` class that extends `RenderObject`. It will load model data from OBJ files and set up buffers needed by its material (and OpenGL ES shaders to be rendered in the VR scene).

Right-click on the `app/java/com.cardboardvr.modelviewer/` folder, go to **New | Java Class**, and name it `ModelObject`. Define it so that it extends `RenderObject`, as follows:

```
public class ModelObject extends RenderObject {
}
```

Just like we've done in the previous chapters, when introducing new kinds of `RenderObjects`, we'll have one or more constructors that can instantiate a `Material` and set up buffers. For `ModelObject`, we'll pass in a file resource handle, parse the file (refer to the next topic), and create a solid color material (initially, without lighting), as follows:

```
public ModelObject(int objFile) {
    super();
    InputStream inputStream = RenderBox.instance.mainActivity.
    getResources().openRawResource(objFile);
    if (inputStream == null)
        return; // error
    parseObj(inputStream);
    createMaterial();
}
```

Now add the material as follows. First, declare variables for the buffers (as we have done for other `RenderObjects` in the previous projects). These can be private, but our convention is to keep them public if we want to define new materials outside:

```
public static FloatBuffer vertexBuffer;
public static FloatBuffer colorBuffer;
public static FloatBuffer normalBuffer;
public static ShortBuffer indexBuffer;
public int numIndices;
```

Here's the `createMaterial` method (which is called from the constructor):

```
public ModelObject createMaterial(){
    SolidColorLightingMaterial scm = new
    SolidColorLightingMaterial(new float[]{0.5f, 0.5f,
    0.5f, 1});
    scm.setBuffers(vertexBuffer, normalBuffer, indexBuffer,
    numIndices);
    material = scm;
    return this;
}
```

Next, we implement the `parseObj` method.

Parse OBJ models

The `parseObj` method will open the resource file as an `InputStream`. It reads one line at a time, parsing the command and data, building the model's list of vertices, normals, and indexes. Then, we build the buffers from the data.

First, at the top of the `ModelObject` class, declare variables for the data lists:

```
Vector<Short> faces=new Vector<Short>();
Vector<Short> vtPointer=new Vector<Short>();
Vector<Short> vnPointer=new Vector<Short>();
Vector<Float> v=new Vector<Float>();
Vector<Float> vn=new Vector<Float>();
Vector<Material> materials=null;
```

Let's write `parseObj` with placeholders for helper methods. We open the file, process each line, build the buffers, and handle potential IO errors:

```
void parseObj(InputStream inputStream) {
    BufferedReader reader = null;
    String line = null;

    reader = new BufferedReader(new
    InputStreamReader(inputStream));
    if (reader == null)
        return; // error

    try { // try to read lines of the file
        while ((line = reader.readLine()) != null) {
            parseLine(line);
        }
        buildBuffers();
```

```
        } catch (IOException e) {
            e.printStackTrace();
        }
    }
```

The parseLine code is pretty straightforward. The first token of the line is the one-or-two character command (such as v, vn, or f), followed by data values (either float coordinates or integer indexes). Here's the code for parseLine and the parsers for the v and vn vertices:

```
    private void parseLine(String line) {
        Log.v("obj", line);
        if(line.startsWith("f")){//a polygonal face
            processFLine(line);
        }
        else
        if(line.startsWith("vn")){
            processVNLine(line);
        }
        else
        if(line.startsWith("v")){
        //line having geometric position of single vertex
            processVLine(line);
        }
    }

    private void processVLine(String line){
        String [] tokens=line.split("[ ]+");
        //split the line at the spaces
        int c=tokens.length;
        for(int i=1; i<c; i++){
        //add the vertex to the vertex array
            v.add(Float.valueOf(tokens[i]));
        }
    }

    private void processVNLine(String line){
        String [] tokens=line.split("[ ]+");
        //split the line at the spaces
        int c=tokens.length;
        for(int i=1; i<c; i++){
        //add the vertex to the vertex array
            vn.add(Float.valueOf(tokens[i]));
        }
    }
```

The f line needs to handle various value cases.

As for the f command that specifies face indices, they're integer values that index into the vertex list. When there are three indices, it describes a triangle, four describes a quad, and so on. Anything with more than three sides will need to be subdivided into triangles for our rendering with OpenGL ES.

Also, there can be any combination of index values, including formats such as v or v/vt or v/vt/vn, or even v//vn, /vt/vn, or //vn. (Remember that since we're not mapping textures, we will only use the first and third.)

Let's tackle the simplest case first, a triangle face:

```
private void processFLine(String line){
    String [] tokens=line.split("[ ]+");
    int c=tokens.length;

    if(tokens[1].matches("[0-9]+")){//f: v
        if(c==4){//3 faces
            for(int i=1; i<c; i++){
                Short s=Short.valueOf(tokens[i]);
                s--;
                faces.add(s);
            }
        }
    }
}
```

Now consider that there are more than three indices on the face. We need a method to triangulate the polygon. Let's write that now:

```
public static Vector<Short> triangulate(Vector<Short>
polygon){
    Vector<Short> triangles=new Vector<Short>();
    for(int i=1; i<polygon.size()-1; i++){
        triangles.add(polygon.get(0));
        triangles.add(polygon.get(i));
        triangles.add(polygon.get(i+1));
    }
    return triangles;
}
```

We can use it in `processFLine`:

```
private void processFLine(String line) {
    String[] tokens = line.split("[ ]+");
    int c = tokens.length;

    if (tokens[1].matches("[0-9]+") || //f: v
        tokens[1].matches("[0-9]+/[0-9]+")) {//f: v/vt

        if (c == 4) {//3 faces
            for (int i = 1; i < c; i++) {
                Short s = Short.valueOf(tokens[i]);
                s--;
                faces.add(s);
            }
        }
        else{//more faces
            Vector<Short> polygon=new Vector<Short>();
            for(int i=1; i<tokens.length; i++){
                Short s=Short.valueOf(tokens[i]);
                s--;
                polygon.add(s);
            }
            faces.addAll(triangulate(polygon));
            //triangulate the polygon and
            //add the resulting faces
        }
    }
    //if(tokens[1].matches("[0-9]+//[0-9]+")){//f: v//vn
    //if(tokens[1].matches("[0-9]+/[0-9]+/[0-9]+")){
    //f: v/vt/vn
}
```

This code is applied to the face value v and also v/vt since we are skipping textures. I've also commented out the other two permutations of the face index values. The rest of this is mostly just brute force string parsing. The v//vn case is as follows:

```
if(tokens[1].matches("[0-9]+//[0-9]+")){//f: v//vn
    if(c==4){//3 faces
        for(int i=1; i<c; i++){
            Short s=Short.valueOf(tokens[i].split("//")[0]);
            s--;
            faces.add(s);
```

```
                    s=Short.valueOf(tokens[i].split("//")[1]);
                    s--;
                    vnPointer.add(s);
                }
            }
        else{//triangulate
            Vector<Short> tmpFaces=new Vector<Short>();
            Vector<Short> tmpVn=new Vector<Short>();
            for(int i=1; i<tokens.length; i++){
                Short s=Short.valueOf(tokens[i].split("//")[0]);
                s--;
                tmpFaces.add(s);
                s=Short.valueOf(tokens[i].split("//")[1]);
                s--;
                tmpVn.add(s);
            }
            faces.addAll(triangulate(tmpFaces));
            vnPointer.addAll(triangulate(tmpVn));
        }
    }
```

Lastly, the `v/vt/vn` case is as follows:

```
    if(tokens[1].matches("[0-9]+/[0-9]+/[0-9]+")){//f: v/vt/vn
        if(c==4){//3 faces
            for(int i=1; i<c; i++){
                Short s=Short.valueOf(tokens[i].split("/")[0]);
                s--;
                faces.add(s);
                // (skip vt)
                s=Short.valueOf(tokens[i].split("/")[2]);
                s--;
                vnPointer.add(s);
            }
        }
        else{//triangulate
            Vector<Short> tmpFaces=new Vector<Short>();
            Vector<Short> tmpVn=new Vector<Short>();
            for(int i=1; i<tokens.length; i++){
                Short s=Short.valueOf(tokens[i].split("/")[0]);
                s--;
                tmpFaces.add(s);
                // (skip vt)
                s=Short.valueOf(tokens[i].split("/")[2]);
                s--;
```

```
            tmpVn.add(s);
        }
        faces.addAll(triangulate(tmpFaces));
        vnPointer.addAll(triangulate(tmpVn));
    }
}
```

As mentioned earlier, in the OBJ file format description, indices can be negative; in which case they need to be referenced from the end of the vertex list backward. This can be implemented by adding the index value to the size of the index list. To support this, in the preceding code, replace all s--; lines with the following:

```
if (s < 0)
    s = (short)(s + v.size());
else
    s--;
```

buildBuffers

The last step for the parseObj method is to build our shader buffers from the model data, that is, the vertexBuffer, normalBuffer, and indexBuffer variables. We can add that now to a buildBuffers method, as follows:

```
private void buildBuffers() {
    numIndices = faces.size();
    float[] tmp = new float[v.size()];
    int i = 0;
    for(Float f : v)
        tmp[i++] = (f != null ? f : Float.NaN);
    vertexBuffer = allocateFloatBuffer(tmp);

    i = 0;
    tmp = new float[vn.size()];
    for(Float f : vn)
        tmp[i++] = (f != null ? -f : Float.NaN);
        //invert normals
    normalBuffer = allocateFloatBuffer(tmp);

    i = 0;
    short[] indicies = new short[faces.size()];
    for(Short s : faces)
        indicies[i++] = (s != null ? s : 0);
    indexBuffer = allocateShortBuffer(indicies);
}
```

One caveat. We noticed that for the `RenderBox` coordinate system and shaders, it is necessary to invert the normals from the OBJ data (using `-f` rather than `f`). Actually, this depends on OBJ exporters (3Ds Max, Blender, and Maya). Some of them do and some don't flip normals. Unfortunately, there's no way to determine whether or not normals are flipped other than by viewing the model. For this reason, some OBJ importer/viewers provide (optional) functions to calculate normals from the face geometry rather than rely on the import data itself.

Model extents, scaling, and center

3D models come in all shapes and sizes. To view them in our app, we need to know the minimum and maximum boundaries of the model and its geometric center to scale and position it properly. Let's add this to `ModelObject` now.

At the top of the `ModelObject` class, add the following variables:

```
public Vector3 extentsMin, extentsMax;
```

Initialize the extents in the parser, before we parse the model data. The minimum extents are initialized to the maximum possible values; the maximum extents are initialized to the minimum possible values:

```
public ModelObject(int objFile) {
    super();
    extentsMin = new Vector3(Float.MAX_VALUE,
    Float.MAX_VALUE, Float.MAX_VALUE);
    extentsMax = new Vector3(Float.MIN_VALUE,
    Float.MIN_VALUE, Float.MIN_VALUE);
    . . .
```

Rather than calculating the extents after the model is loaded, we'll do it during the import process. As we add a new vertex to the vertex list, we'll calculate the current extents. Add a call to `setExtents` in the `processVLine` loop:

```
private void processVLine(String line) {
    String[] tokens = line.split("[ ]+");
    //split the line at the spaces
    int c = tokens.length;
    for (int i = 1; i < c; i++) {
    //add the vertex to the vertex array
        Float value = Float.valueOf(tokens[i]);
        v.add(value);
        setExtents(i, value);
    }
}
```

Then, the `setExtents` method can be implemented as follows:

```
private void setExtents(int coord, Float value) {
    switch (coord) {
        case 1:
            if (value < extentsMin.x)
                extentsMin.x = value;
            if (value > extentsMax.x)
                extentsMax.x = value;
            break;
        case 2:
            if (value < extentsMin.y)
                extentsMin.y = value;
            if (value > extentsMax.y)
                extentsMax.y = value;
            break;
        case 3:
            if (value < extentsMin.z)
                extentsMin.z = value;
            if (value > extentsMax.z)
                extentsMax.z = value;
            break;
    }
}
```

And let's add a scalar method that will be useful when we add the model to the scene (as you'll see in the next topic), to scale it to a normalized size with extents 1 to 1:

```
public float normalScalar() {
    float sizeX = (extentsMax.x - extentsMin.x);
    float sizeY = (extentsMax.y - extentsMin.y);
    float sizeZ = (extentsMax.z - extentsMin.z);
    return (2.0f / Math.max(sizeX, Math.max(sizeY, sizeZ)));
}
```

Now, let's try it out!

I'm a little teapot

For decades, 3D computer graphics researchers and developers have used this cute model of a teapot. It's a classic! The back story is that Martin Newell, the famous computer graphics pioneer and researcher, needed a model for his work, and his wife suggested that he model their teapot at home. The original is now on display at the Boston Computer Museum. We have included an OBJ version of this classic model with the downloadable files for this book.

Of course, you can choose your own OBJ file, but if you want to use the teapot, locate the `teapot.obj` file, and copy it to the `res/raw` folder (create the folder if necessary).

Now load the model and try it. In `MainActivity`, add a variable at the top of the `MainActivity` class to hold the current model:

```
Transform model;
```

Add the following code to the `setup` method. Notice that we're scaling it to a fraction of the original size and placing it 3 units in front of the camera:

```
public void setup() {
    ModelObject modelObj = new ModelObject(R.raw.teapot);
    float scalar = modelObj.normalScalar();
    model = new Transform()
            .setLocalPosition(0, 0, -3)
            .setLocalScale(scalar, scalar, scalar)
            .addComponent(modelObj);
}
```

Run the project, and it should look like this:

You can see that the model was successfully loaded and rendered. Unfortunately, the shading is difficult to discern. To get a better view of the shaded teapot, let's shift it down a bit. Modify the `setLocalPosition` method in setup, as follows:

```
.setLocalPosition(0, -2, -3)
```

The following screenshot is cropped and enlarged, so you can see the shaded teapot here similar to the way you'd see it in the Cardboard viewer:

I'm a little rotating teapot

Let's enhance the viewing experience by rotating the model as the user rotates his head. The effect will be different than a "normal" virtual reality experience. Ordinarily, moving one's head in VR rotates the subjective view of the camera in the scene to look around in unison with your head movement. In this project, the head movement will be like an input control rotating the model. The model is at a fixed position in front of you at all times.

To implement this feature is quite simple. The `RenderBox preDraw` interface method is called at the start of each frame. We'll get the current head angles and rotate the model accordingly, converting the head post-Euler angles into a Quaternion. (Combining multiple Euler angles can result in an unexpected final rotational orientation). We will also conjugate (that is, invert or reverse) the rotation, so that when you look up, you see the bottom of the object and so on. It feels more natural this way.

In `MainActivity`, add the following code to `preDraw`:

```
public void preDraw() {
    float[] hAngles = RenderBox.instance.headAngles;
    Quaternion rot = new Quaternion();
    rot.setEulerAnglesRad(hAngles[0], hAngles[1], hAngles[2]);
    model.setLocalRotation(rot.conjugate());
}
```

In `setup`, ensure that the `setLocalPosition` method positions the teapot straight in front of the camera:

```
.setLocalPosition(0, 0, -3)
```

Try and run it. We're almost there! The model rotates with the head, but we're still looking around the VR space as well.

To lock the head position, we just need to disable head tracking in `RenderBox`. If your version of `RenderBox` (as built in *Chapter 5, RenderBox Engine*) does not yet have this feature, add it to your separate `RenderBoxLib` lib project, as follows:

In the `Camera.java` file, first add a new public variable for `headTracking`:

```
public boolean headTracking = true;
```

Modify the `onDrawEye` method to conditionally update the view transform, as follows:

```
if (headTracking) {
    // Apply the eye transformation to the camera.
    Matrix.multiplyMM(view, 0, eye.getEyeView(), 0,
    camera, 0);
} else {
    // copy camera into view
    for (int i=0; i < camera.length; i++) { view[i] =
    camera[i]; }
}
```

Make sure that you copy the updated `.aar` file to the `ModelViewer` project's `RenderBox` module folder after you rebuild it.

Now, in the `MainActivity` class's `setup()`, add the following setting:

```
RenderBox.instance.mainCamera.headTracking = false;
```

Run it now, and as you move your head, the model remains relatively stationary but rotates as you turn your head. Neato! Much better.

Thread safe

In *Chapter 7, 360-Degree Gallery*, we explained the need for worker threads to offload processing from the render thread. In this project, we'll add threading to the `ModelObject` constructor where we read and parse the model files:

```java
public ModelObject(final int objFile) {
    super();
    extentsMin = new Vector3(Float.MAX_VALUE, Float.MAX_VALUE,
    Float.MAX_VALUE);
    extentsMax = new Vector3(Float.MIN_VALUE, Float.MIN_VALUE,
    Float.MIN_VALUE);

    SolidColorLightingMaterial.setupProgram();
    enabled = false;
    new Thread(new Runnable() {
        @Override
        public void run() {
            InputStream inputStream = RenderBox.instance.
            mainActivity.getResources().
            openRawResource(objFile);
            if (inputStream == null)
                return; // error
            createMaterial();
            enabled = true;
            float scalar = normalScalar();
            transform.setLocalScale(scalar, scalar, scalar);
        }
    }).start();
}
```

We have to declare the file handle, `objFile`, as `final` to be able to access it from within the inner class. You may have also noticed that we added a call to the material's `setup` program before starting the thread to ensure that it's properly set up in time and avoid crashing the app. This avoids the need to call `createMaterial` within a `queueEvent` procedure, since the shader compiler makes use of the graphics context. Similarly, we disable the object until it has completed loading its data. Finally, since the load is asynchronous, it's necessary to set the scale at the end of this procedure. Our previous method set the scale in `setup()`, which now completes before the model is done loading.

Launch with intent

In *Chapter 7, 360-Degree Gallery*, we introduced the use of Android intents to associate an app with a specific file type in order to launch our app as a viewer of those files. We'll do the same for OBJ files here.

An **intent** is a message that any app can send to the Android system that declares its intent to use another app for a certain purpose. The intent object contains a number of members to describe what type of action needs to be done, and, if any, the data on which it needs to be done. For the image gallery, we associated the intent filter with an image mime type. For this project, we'll associate an intent filter with a filename extension.

In your `AndroidManifest.xml` file, add an intent filter to the activity block. This lets Android know that the app can be used as an OBJ file viewer. We need to specify it as a file scheme and the filename pattern. The wildcard mime type and host are also required by Android. Add the following XML code:

```xml
<intent-filter>
    <action android:name="android.intent.action.VIEW"
    />
    <category android:name=
    "android.intent.category.DEFAULT" />
    <category android:name=
    "android.intent.category.BROWSABLE" />
    <data android:scheme="file" />
    <data android:mimeType="*/*" />
    <data android:pathPattern=".*\\.obj" />
    <data android:host="*" />
</intent-filter>
```

To handle the situation, we'll add a new constructor to `ModelObject` that takes a URI string instead of a resource ID, as we did earlier. Like the other constructor, we need to open an input stream and pass it to `parseObj`. Here's the constructor, including the worker thread:

```java
public ModelObject(final String uri) {
    super();
    extentsMin = new Vector3(Float.MAX_VALUE, Float.MAX_VALUE,
    Float.MAX_VALUE);
    extentsMax = new Vector3(Float.MIN_VALUE, Float.MIN_VALUE,
    Float.MIN_VALUE);
    SolidColorLightingMaterial.setupProgram();
    enabled = false;
```

```
            new Thread(new Runnable() {
                @Override
                public void run() {
                    File file = new File(uri.toString());
                    FileInputStream fileInputStream;
                    try {
                        fileInputStream = new FileInputStream(file);
                    } catch (IOException e) {
                        e.printStackTrace();
                        return; // error
                    }
                    parseObj(fileInputStream);
                    createMaterial();
                    enabled = true;
                    float scalar = normalScalar();
                    transform.setLocalScale(scalar, scalar, scalar);
                }
            }).start();
    }
```

Now in the `MainActivity` class's `setup`, we'll check whether the app is launched from an intent and use the intent URI. Otherwise, we'll view the default model, as we did earlier:

```
public void setup() {
    ModelObject modelObj;
    Uri intentUri = getIntent().getData();
    if (intentUri != null) {
        Log.d(TAG, "!!!! intent " + intentUri.getPath());
        modelObj = new ModelObject(intentUri.getPath());
    } else {
        // default object
        modelObj = new ModelObject(R.raw.teapot);
    }
    //...
```

Now with the project built and installed on the phone, let's try some web integration. Open the web browser and visit a 3D model download site.

Find the **Download** link for the interesting model to download it into the phone, and then when prompted, use the `ModelViewer` app to view it!

Practical and production ready

Note that, as mentioned earlier, we've created a limited implementation of the OBJ model format, so not every model that you find will view correctly (if at all) at this point. Then again, it might be sufficient, depending on the requirements of your own projects, for example, if you include specific models in the resource folder that can be viewed in the released version of your app. When you have complete control of the input data, you can cut corners.

While the basic structure of the OBJ file format is not very complicated, as we've demonstrated here, like many things in software (and in life) "the devil is in the details." Using this project as a starting point, and then building your own practical and production-ready OBJ file parser and renderer will require a considerable amount of additional work. You might also do some research on pre-existing packages, other model formats, or maybe even lifting some code from an open-source game engine like LibGDX. The features of OBJ that we omitted but are worth considering include the following:

- Texture vertices
- Material definitions
- Curve elements
- Grouping of geometry
- Color and other vertex attributes

Summary

In this project, we wrote a simple viewer for 3D models in the open OBJ file format. We implemented a `ModelObject` class that parses the model file and builds the vector and normal buffers needed by `RenderBox` to render the object in the scene. We then enabled shading. We then made the viewer interactive so that the model rotates as you move your head.

In the next chapter, we explore another type of media, your music. The music visualizer responds to the current music player to display dancing geometry in the VR world.

9
Music Visualizer

> *"See the music, hear the dance,"* said George Balanchine, famed Russian-born choreographer and father of the American ballet.

We won't attempt to raise the level of the art form, but still, maybe it'd be fun to visualize the playlists on our phones. In this project, we will create 3D animated abstract graphics that dance to the beat of your music. You might be familiar with music visualizations in 2D, but what would it look like in VR? To get inspired, try Googling for images using the phrase *geometry wars*, the classic game for XBox, for example!

A visualizer app takes input from the Android audio system and displays visualizations. In this project, we will take advantage of the Android `Visualizer` class, which lets an app capture part of the currently playing audio, not the full fidelity music details but a lower quality audio content sufficient for visualizations.

In this project, we will:

- Set up the new project
- Build a Java class architecture named VisualizerBox
- Capture waveform data from the phone's audio player
- Build a geometric visualization
- Build a texture-based visualization
- Capture the FFT data and build an FFT visualization
- Add a trippy trails mode
- Support multiple concurrent visualizations

The source code for this project can be found on the Packt Publishing website and on GitHub at `https://github.com/cardbookvr/visualizevr` (with each topic as a separate commit).

Setting up a new project

To build this project, we're going to use our RenderBox library created in *Chapter 5, RenderBox Engine*. You can use yours, or grab a copy from the downloadable files provided with this book or our GitHub repo (use the commit tagged `after-ch8` — `https://github.com/cardbookvr/renderboxlib/releases/tag/after-ch8`). For a more detailed description of how to import the `RenderBox` library, refer to the final section, *Using RenderBox in future projects*, of *Chapter 5, RenderBox Engine*. To create a new project, perform the following steps:

1. With Android Studio opened, create a new project. Let's name it `VisualizeVR` and target **Android 4.4 KitKat (API 19)** with an **Empty Activity**.

2. Create new modules for each of `renderbox`, `common`, and `core` packages, using **File | New Module | Import .JAR/.AAR Package**.

3. Set the modules as dependencies for the app, using **File | Project Structure**.

4. Edit the `build.gradle` file as explained in *Chapter 2, The Skeleton Cardboard Project*, to compile against SDK 22.

5. Update `/res/layout/activity_main.xml` and `AndroidManifest.xml`, as explained in the previous chapters.

6. Edit `MainActivity` as `class MainActivity extends CardboardActivity implements IRenderBox`, and implement the interface method stubs (*Ctrl + I*).

We can go ahead and define the `onCreate` method in `MainActivity`. The class now has the following code:

```
public class MainActivity extends CardboardActivity implements
IRenderBox {
    private static final String TAG = "MainActivity";
    CardboardView cardboardView;
    @Override
    protected void onCreate(Bundle savedInstanceState) {
        super.onCreate(savedInstanceState);
        setContentView(R.layout.activity_main);

        cardboardView = (CardboardView)
        findViewById(R.id.cardboard_view);
        cardboardView.setRenderer(new RenderBox(this, this));
        setCardboardView(cardboardView);
    }
    @Override
    public void setup() {
```

```
    }
    @Override
    public void preDraw() {
        // code run beginning each frame
    }
    @Override
    public void postDraw() {
        // code run end of each frame
    }
}
```

You can add a cube to the scene, temporarily, to ensure that everything is set up properly. Add it to the `setup` method as follows:

```
public void setup() {
    new Transform()
        .setLocalPosition(0,0,-7)
        .setLocalRotation(45,60,0)
        .addComponent(new Cube(true));
}
```

If you remember, a `Cube` is a `Component` that's added to a `Transform`. The `Cube` defines its geometry (for example, vertices). The `Transform` defines its position, rotation, and scale in 3D space.

You should be able to click on **Run 'app'** with no compile errors, and see the cube and Cardboard split screen view on your Android device.

Capturing audio data

Using the Android `Visualizer` class (http://developer.android.com/reference/android/media/audiofx/Visualizer.html), we can retrieve part of the audio data that is currently playing, at a specified sample rate. You can choose to capture data as waveform and/or frequency data:

- **Waveform**: This is an array of mono audio waveform bytes, or **pulse code modulation (PCM)** data, representing a sample series of audio amplitudes
- **Frequency**: This is an array of **Fast Fourier Transform (FFT)** bytes, representing a sampling of audio frequencies

The data is limited to 8 bits, so it's not useful for playback but is sufficient for visualizations. You can specify the sampling rate, although it must be a power of two.

Armed with this knowledge, we'll now go ahead and begin implementing an architecture that captures audio data and makes it available to visualization renderers that you can build.

A VisualizerBox architecture

Music visualizers often look really cool, especially at first. But after a time they may seem too repetitive, even boring. Therefore, in our design, we'll build the ability to queue up a number of different visualizations, and then, after a period of time, transition from one to the next.

To begin our implementation, we'll define an architecture structure that will be expandable and let us develop new visualizations as we go along.

However, even before that, we must ensure that the app has permission to use the Android audio features we need. Add the following directives to AndroidManifest.xml:

```
<!-- Visualizer permissions -->
<uses-permission
android:name="android.permission.RECORD_AUDIO" />
<uses-permission
android:name="android.permission.MODIFY_AUDIO_SETTINGS" />
```

Remember that the RenderBox library, first developed in *Chapter 5, RenderBox Engine,* allows MainActivity to delegate much of the graphics and Cardboard VR work to the RenderBox class and associated classes (Component, Material, and so on). We will follow a similar design pattern here, built on top of RenderBox. MainActivity can instantiate specific visualizations and then delegate the work to the VisualizerBox class.

The VisualizerBox class will provide the callback functions to the Android Visualizer class. Let's define a skeletal implementation of this first. Create a VisualizerBox Java class, as follows:

```
public class VisualizerBox {
    static final String TAG = "VisualizerBox";
    public VisualizerBox(final CardboardView cardboardView){
    }
    public void setup() {
    }
    public void preDraw() {
    }
    public void postDraw() {
    }
}
```

Integrate `VisualizerBox` into `MainActivity`, adding a `visualizerBox` variable at the top of the class. In `MainActivity`, add the following line:

```
VisualizerBox visualizerBox;
```

Initialize it in `onCreate`:

```
visualizerBox = new VisualizerBox(cardboardView);
```

Also, in `MainActivity`, call the corresponding version of each of the `IRenderBox` interface methods:

```
@Override
public void setup() {
    visualizerBox.setup();
}
@Override
public void preDraw() {
    visualizerBox.preDraw();
}
@Override
public void postDraw() {
    visualizerBox.postDraw();
}
```

Good. Now we'll set up `VisualizerBox` to let you build and use one or more visualizations. So, first let's define the abstract `Visualization` class in the `Visualization.java` file, as follows:

```
public abstract class Visualization {
    VisualizerBox visualizerBox;                //owner

    public Visualization(VisualizerBox visualizerBox){
        this.visualizerBox = visualizerBox;
    }
    public abstract void setup();
    public abstract void preDraw();
    public abstract void postDraw();
}
```

Now we have a mechanism to create a variety of visualization implementations for the app. Before we go ahead and start writing one of those, let's also provide the integration with `VisualizerBox`. At the top of the `VisualizerBox` class, add a variable to the current `activeViz` object:

```
public Visualization activeViz;
```

Then, call it from the interface methods:

```
public void setup() {
    if(activeViz != null)
        activeViz.setup();
}
public void preDraw() {
    if(activeViz != null)
        activeViz.preDraw();
}
public void postDraw() {
    if(activeViz != null)
        activeViz.postDraw();
}
```

Of course, we're not even using the Android `Visualizer` class yet and not rendering anything on the screen. That'll come next.

For now, let's create a placeholder for a visualization. Create a new folder in your project named `visualizations`. Right-click on your Java code folder (for example, `java/com/cardbookvr/visualizevr/`), go to **New | Package**, and name it `visualizations`. Then, right click on the new `visualizations` folder, go to **New | Java Class**, and name it `BlankVisualization`. Then, define it as `extends Visualization` as follows:

```
public class BlankVisualization extends Visualization {
    static final String TAG = "BlankVisualization";
    public BlankVisualization(VisualizerBox visualizerBox) {
        super(visualizerBox);
    }
    @Override
    public void setup() {
    }
    @Override
    public void preDraw() {
    }
    @Override
    public void postDraw() {
    }
}
```

We'll be able to use this as a template for specific visualizers. The purpose of each method is pretty self-explanatory:

- `setup`: This initializes variables, transforms, and materials for the visualization
- `preDraw`: This code is executed at the beginning of each frame; for example, using the current captured audio data
- `postDraw`: This code is executed at the end of each frame

Now let's add some meat to this skeleton.

Waveform data capture

As mentioned earlier, the Android `Visualizer` class lets us define callbacks to capture audio data. This data comes in two formats: waveform and FFT. We'll add just the waveform data to the `VisualizerBox` class now.

First, define the variables that we'll use for the captured audio data, as follows:

```
Visualizer visualizer;
public static int captureSize;
public static byte[] audioBytes;
```

Using the API, we can determine the minimum capture size available, and then use that as our capture sample size.

Then, initialize them in the constructor as follows. First, instantiate an Android `Visualizer`. Then set the capture size to use, and allocate our buffers:

```
public VisualizerBox(final CardboardView cardboardView) {
    visualizer = new Visualizer(0);
    captureSize = Visualizer.getCaptureSizeRange()[0];
    visualizer.setCaptureSize(captureSize);
    // capture audio data
    // Visualizer.OnDataCaptureListener captureListener = ...
    visualizer.setDataCaptureListener(captureListener,
    Visualizer.getMaxCaptureRate(), true, true);
    visualizer.setEnabled(true);
}
```

We want to use the minimum size for a variety of reasons. Firstly, it will be faster, and in VR, speed is paramount. Secondly, it organizes our FFT samples (as discussed later) into fewer buckets. This is helpful because each bucket catches more activity over a broader range of frequencies.

Note that we left a comment where we'll define the capture listener, and then set it in the visualizer. Make sure that you enable the visualizer as always listening.

Let's first write the `captureListener` object for waveform data only. We define and instantiate a new anonymous class that implements `Visualizer.OnDataCaptureListener`, and provide it with a function named `onWaveFormDataCapture`, which receives the wave form bytes and stores them for our `Visualization` code (forthcoming):

```
// capture audio data
Visualizer.OnDataCaptureListener captureListener = new
Visualizer.OnDataCaptureListener() {
    @Override
    public void onWaveFormDataCapture(Visualizer
    visualizer, byte[] bytes, int samplingRate) {
        audioBytes = bytes;
    }
    @Override
    public void onFftDataCapture(Visualizer visualizer,
    byte[] bytes, int samplingRate) {
    }
};
```

The interface still requires that we provide an `onFftDataCapture` method, but we're leaving it empty for the time being.

Now we're ready to add some graphics to this baby.

A basic geometric visualization

For our first visualization, we'll create a basic equalizer wave graphic. It'll be a rectangular block consisting of a series of cubes that are scaled according to the audio waveform data. We'll use the built-in `Cube` component already in the `RenderBox` library and its basic vertex color lighting material.

In the `visualizations/` folder, create a new Java class named `GeometricVisualization` and begin as follows:

```
public class GeometricVisualization extends Visualization {
    static final String TAG = "GeometricVisualization";
    public GeometricVisualization(VisualizerBox visualizerBox) {
        super(visualizerBox);
    }
}
```

At the top of the class, declare a `Transform` array of cube transforms and the corresponding array for `RenderObjects`:

```
Transform[] cubes;
Cube[] cubeRenderers;
```

Then, initialize them in the `setup` method. We'll allocate the array of cubes, aligned and scaled as an adjacent set of blocks, creating a 3D representation of a wavy block. The setup method can be implemented as follows:

```
public void setup() {
    cubes = new Transform[VisualizerBox.captureSize / 2];
    cubeRenderers = new Cube[VisualizerBox.captureSize / 2];

    float offset = -3f;
    float scaleFactor = (offset * -2) / cubes.length;
    for(int i = 0; i < cubes.length; i++) {
        cubeRenderers[i] = new Cube(true);
        cubes[i] = new Transform()
                .setLocalPosition(offset, -2, -5)
                .addComponent(cubeRenderers[i]);
        offset += scaleFactor;
    }
}
```

Now on each frame, we just need to modify the height of each cube based on the current waveform data from the audio source (as obtained in `VisualizerBox`). Implement the `preDraw` method as follows:

```
public void preDraw() {
    if (VisualizerBox.audioBytes != null) {
        float scaleFactor = 3f / cubes.length;
        for(int i = 0; i < cubes.length; i++) {
            cubes[i].setLocalScale(scaleFactor,
            VisualizerBox.audioBytes[i] * 0.01f, 1);
        }
    }
}

public void postDraw() {
}
```

We also need to add a stub for the `postDraw` implementation. Then, instantiate the visualization and make it the active one. In `MainActivity`, at the end of `onCreate`, add the following line of code:

```
visualizerBox.activeViz = new
GeometricVisualization(visualizerBox);
```

That's all we need for now.

Start playing some music on your phone. Then, run the app. You will see something like this:

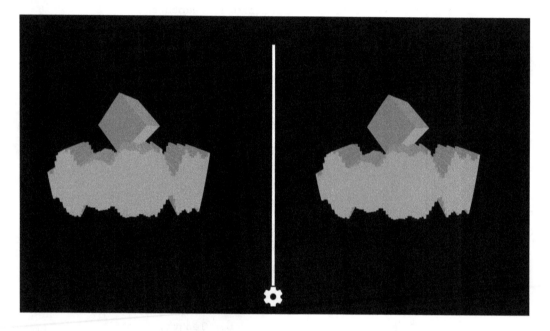

As you can see, we kept the unit cube in the scene, as it helps clarify what's going on. Each audio datum is a thin "slice" (or a flattened cube) the height of which varies with the audio value. If you're looking at a colored version of the preceding screen image, you will notice that the colored faces of the visualization cubes are like solitary cubes since they use the same object and material to render.

This visualization is a very basic example of using audio waveform data to dynamically modify 3D geometry. Let your imagination run wild to create your own. The audio bytes can control any transform parameters, including scale, position, and rotation. Remember that we're in a 3D virtual reality space, and you can use all of it—move your stuff all round, up and down, and even behind you. We have a few basic primitive geometric shapes (a cube, sphere, plane, triangle, and so on). But you can also use the audio data to parametrically generate new shapes and models. Plus, you can even integrate the ModelObject class from the previous chapter to load interesting 3D models!

In the next topic, we'll take a look at how to use the audio waveform data in texture-based material shaders.

2D texture-based visualization

The second visualization will also be a basic oscilloscope-type display of waveform data. However, previously, we used audio data to scale 3D slice cubes; this time, we'll render them all on a 2D plane using a shader that uses audio data as input.

Our RenderBox library allows us to define new materials and shaders. In the previous projects, we built materials that use bitmap images for texture mapping onto the geometry as it's rendered. In this project, we'll paint the quad using the audio bytes array, using the byte value to control the position where we set a brighter color. (Note that the Plane class was added to RenderBox lib in *Chapter 7, 360-Degree Gallery*.)

Texture generator and loader

First, let's generate a texture structure to hold our texture data. In the VisualizerBox class, add the following method to set up the texture in GLES. We can't use our normal texture pipeline, since it is designed to allocate a texture directly from image data. Our data is one-dimensional, so it may seem odd to use a Texture2D resource, but we'll set the height to one pixel:

```
public static int genTexture(){
    final int[] textureHandle = new int[1];
    GLES20.glGenTextures(1, textureHandle, 0);
    RenderBox.checkGLError("VisualizerBox GenTexture");
    if (textureHandle[0] != 0) {
        // Bind to the texture in OpenGL
        GLES20.glBindTexture(GLES20.GL_TEXTURE_2D,
        textureHandle[0]);
        // Set filtering
```

```
        GLES20.glTexParameteri(GLES20.GL_TEXTURE_2D,
        GLES20.GL_TEXTURE_MIN_FILTER, GLES20.GL_NEAREST);
        GLES20.glTexParameteri(GLES20.GL_TEXTURE_2D,
        GLES20.GL_TEXTURE_MAG_FILTER, GLES20.GL_NEAREST);
    }
    if (textureHandle[0] == 0){
        throw new RuntimeException("Error loading texture.");
    }
    return textureHandle[0];
}
```

Then add the call to setup, including a static variable to hold the generated texture handle:

```
public static int audioTexture = -1;

public void setup() {
    audioTexture = genTexture();
    if(activeViz != null)
        activeViz.setup();
}
```

Now we can populate the texture from audio byte data. In the Android Visualizer listener, add a call to loadTexture in the onWaveFormDataCapture method:

```
        public void onWaveFormDataCapture(Visualizer
        visualizer, byte[] bytes, int samplingRate){
            audioBytes = bytes;
            loadTexture(cardboardView, audioTexture, bytes);
        }
```

Let's define loadTexture as follows. It copies the audio bytes into a new array buffer and hands it off to OpenGL ES with the glBindTexture and glTexImage2D calls.

(Refer to http://stackoverflow.com/questions/14290096/how-to-create-a-opengl-texture-from-byte-array-in-android.):

```
    public static void loadTexture(CardboardView cardboardView,
    final int textureId, byte[] bytes){
        if(textureId < 0)
            return;
        final ByteBuffer buffer =
        ByteBuffer.allocateDirect(bytes.length * 4);
        final int length = bytes.length;
        buffer.order(ByteOrder.nativeOrder());
        buffer.put(bytes);
        buffer.position(0);
```

```
cardboardView.queueEvent(new Runnable() {
    @Override
    public void run() {
        GLES20.glBindTexture(GLES20.GL_TEXTURE_2D,
        textureId);
        GLES20.glTexImage2D(GLES20.GL_TEXTURE_2D, 0,
        GLES20.GL_LUMINANCE, length, 1, 0,
            GLES20.GL_LUMINANCE,
            GLES20.GL_UNSIGNED_BYTE, buffer);
    }
});
}
```

Waveform shaders

Now it's time to write the shader programs that, among other things, will dictate the parameters and attributes that need to be set in the `Material` class.

If necessary, create a resources directory for the shaders, `res/raw/`. Then, create the `waveform_vertex.shader` and `waveform_fragment.shader` files. Define them as follows.

The `waveform_vertex.shader` file is identical to the `unlit_tex_vertex` shader we were using. Strictly speaking, we can just reuse this file and specify its resource in the `createProgram` function, but it is good practice to define individual shader files unless you are explicitly following some sort of a pattern where you are using a number of variants on a given shader.

File: `res/raw/waveform_vertex.shader`:

```
uniform mat4 u_MVP;
attribute vec4 a_Position;
attribute vec2 a_TexCoordinate;
varying vec2 v_TexCoordinate;
void main() {
    // pass through the texture coordinate
    v_TexCoordinate = a_TexCoordinate;
    // final point in normalized screen coordinates
    gl_Position = u_MVP * a_Position;
}
```

For the `waveform_fragment` shader, we add variables for a solid color (`u_Color`) and threshold width (`u_Width`). And then, add a bit of logic to decide whether the *y* coordinate of the current pixel being rendered is within `u_Width` of the sample.

File: `res/raw/waveform_fragment.shader`

```
precision mediump float;        // default medium precision
uniform sampler2D u_Texture;    // the input texture
varying vec2 v_TexCoordinate;   // interpolated texture coordinate
per fragment
uniform vec4 u_Color;
uniform float u_Width;
// The entry point for our fragment shader.
void main() {
    vec4 color;
    float dist = abs(v_TexCoordinate.y - texture2D(u_Texture,
    v_TexCoordinate).r);
    if(dist < u_Width){
        color = u_Color;
    }
    gl_FragColor = color;
}
```

Basic waveform material

Now we define the `Material` class for the shaders. Create a new Java class named `WaveformMaterial` and define it as follows:

```
public class WaveformMaterial extends Material {
    private static final String TAG = "WaveformMaterial";
}
```

Add material variables for the texture ID, border, width, and color. Then, add variables for the shader program reference and buffers, as shown in the following code:

```
static int program = -1;
//Initialize to a totally invalid value for setup state
static int positionParam;
static int texCoordParam;
static int textureParam;
static int MVPParam;
static int colorParam;
static int widthParam;
```

```
public float borderWidth = 0.01f;
public float[] borderColor = new float[]{0.6549f, 0.8392f, 1f,
1f};

FloatBuffer vertexBuffer;
FloatBuffer texCoordBuffer;
ShortBuffer indexBuffer;
int numIndices;
```

Now we can add a constructor. As we saw earlier, it calls a `setupProgram` helper method that creates the shader program and obtains references to its parameters:

```
public WaveformMaterial() {
    super();
    setupProgram();
}

public static void setupProgram() {
    if(program > -1) return;
    //Create shader program
    program = createProgram( R.raw.waveform_vertex,
    R.raw.waveform_fragment );
    RenderBox.checkGLError("Bitmap GenTexture");

    //Get vertex attribute parameters
    positionParam = GLES20.glGetAttribLocation(program,
    "a_Position");
    RenderBox.checkGLError("Bitmap GenTexture");
    texCoordParam = GLES20.glGetAttribLocation(program,
    "a_TexCoordinate");
    RenderBox.checkGLError("Bitmap GenTexture");

    //Enable them (turns out this is kind of a big deal ;)
    GLES20.glEnableVertexAttribArray(positionParam);
    RenderBox.checkGLError("Bitmap GenTexture");
    GLES20.glEnableVertexAttribArray(texCoordParam);
    RenderBox.checkGLError("Bitmap GenTexture");

    //Shader-specific parameters
    textureParam = GLES20.glGetUniformLocation(program,
    "u_Texture");
    MVPParam = GLES20.glGetUniformLocation(program, "u_MVP");
    colorParam = GLES20.glGetUniformLocation(program,
    "u_Color");
    widthParam = GLES20.glGetUniformLocation(program,
    "u_Width");
    RenderBox.checkGLError("Waveform params");
}
```

Likewise, we add a `setBuffers` method to be called by the `RenderObject` component (`Plane`):

```
public WaveformMaterial setBuffers(FloatBuffer vertexBuffer,
FloatBuffer texCoordBuffer, ShortBuffer indexBuffer, int
numIndices) {
    //Associate VBO data with this instance of the material
    this.vertexBuffer = vertexBuffer;
    this.texCoordBuffer = texCoordBuffer;
    this.indexBuffer = indexBuffer;
    this.numIndices = numIndices;
    return this;
}
```

Add the `draw` code, which will be called from the `Camera` component, to render the geometry prepared in the buffers (via `setBuffers`). The `draw` method looks like this:

```
@Override
public void draw(float[] view, float[] perspective) {
    GLES20.glUseProgram(program);

    // Set the active texture unit to texture unit 0.
    GLES20.glActiveTexture(GLES20.GL_TEXTURE0);

    // Bind the texture to this unit.
    GLES20.glBindTexture(GLES20.GL_TEXTURE_2D,
    VisualizerBox.audioTexture);

    // Tell the texture uniform sampler to use this texture in
    //the shader by binding to texture unit 0.
    GLES20.glUniform1i(textureParam, 0);

    Matrix.multiplyMM(modelView, 0, view, 0,
    RenderObject.model, 0);
    Matrix.multiplyMM(modelViewProjection, 0, perspective, 0,
    modelView, 0);
    // Set the ModelViewProjection matrix for eye position.
    GLES20.glUniformMatrix4fv(MVPParam, 1, false,
    modelViewProjection, 0);

    GLES20.glUniform4fv(colorParam, 1, borderColor, 0);
    GLES20.glUniform1f(widthParam, borderWidth);
```

```
//Set vertex attributes
GLES20.glVertexAttribPointer(positionParam, 3,
GLES20.GL_FLOAT, false, 0, vertexBuffer);
GLES20.glVertexAttribPointer(texCoordParam, 2,
GLES20.GL_FLOAT, false, 0, texCoordBuffer);

GLES20.glDrawElements(GLES20.GL_TRIANGLES, numIndices,
GLES20.GL_UNSIGNED_SHORT, indexBuffer);

RenderBox.checkGLError("WaveformMaterial draw");
}
```

One more thing; let's provide a method to destroy an existing material:

```
public static void destroy(){
    program = -1;
}
```

Waveform visualization

Now we can create a new visualization object. Under the `visualizations/` folder, create a new Java class named `WaveformVisualization` and define it as `extends Visualization`:

```
public class WaveformVisualization extends Visualization {
    static final String TAG = "WaveformVisualization";
    public WaveformVisualization(VisualizerBox visualizerBox) {
        super(visualizerBox);
    }
    @Override
    public void setup() {
    }
    @Override
    public void preDraw() {
    }
    @Override
    public void postDraw() {
    }
}
```

Declare a variable for the `Plane` component we will create:

```
RenderObject plane;
```

Create it in the `setup` method as follows. Set the material to a new `WaveformMaterial`, and position it over towards the left:

```
public void setup() {
    plane = new Plane().setMaterial(new WaveformMaterial()
            .setBuffers(Plane.vertexBuffer,
            Plane.texCoordBuffer, Plane.indexBuffer,
            Plane.numIndices));

    new Transform()
            .setLocalPosition(-5, 0, 0)
            .setLocalRotation(0, 90, 0)
            .addComponent(plane);
}
```

Now in `onCreate` of `MainActivity`, replace the previous visualization with this one:

```
visualizerBox.activeViz = new
WaveformVisualization(visualizerBox);
```

When you run the project, you get a visualization like this:

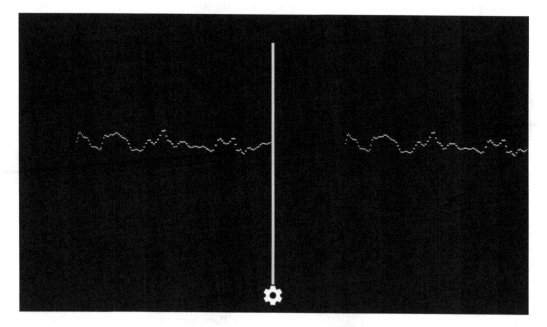

FFT visualization

For the next visualization, we'll introduce the use of FFT data (instead of waveform data). As in the previous example, we'll dynamically generate a texture from the data and write a material and shaders to render it.

Capture the FFT audio data

To begin with, we need to add that data capture to our `VisualizerBox` class. We will start by adding the variables we'll need:

```
public static byte[] fftBytes, fftNorm;
public static float[] fftPrep;
public static int fftTexture = -1;
```

We need to allocate the FFT data arrays, and to do that we need to know their size. We can ask the Android `Visualizer` API how much data it's capable of giving us. For now, we'll choose the minimum size and then allocate the arrays as follows:

```
public VisualizerBox(final CardboardView cardboardView){
    . . .
    fftPrep = new float[captureSize / 2];
    fftNorm = new byte[captureSize / 2];
    . . .
```

Capturing FFT data is similar to capturing waveform data. But we'll do some preprocessing on it before saving it. According to the Android `Visualizer` API documentation, (`http://developer.android.com/reference/android/media/audiofx/Visualizer.html#getFft(byte[])`) the `getFft` function provides data specified as follows:

- The capture is an 8-bit magnitude FFT; the frequency range covered being 0 (DC) to half of the sampling rate returned by `getSamplingRate()`

- The capture returns the real and imaginary parts of a number of frequency points equal to half of the capture size plus one

 Note that only the real part is returned for the first point (DC) and the last point (*sampling frequency/2*).

The layout in the returned byte array is as follows:

- *n* is the capture size returned by `getCaptureSize()`

- `Rfk` and `Ifk` are the real and imaginary parts of the *kth* frequency component, respectively

- If `Fs` is the sampling frequency returned by `getSamplingRate()`, the *kth* frequency is: *(k*Fs)/(n/2)*

Likewise, we'll prepare the incoming captured data into a normalized array of values between 0 and 255. Our implementation is as follows. Add the `onFftDataCapture` declaration immediately after the `onWaveFormDataCapture` method (within the `OnDataCaptureListener` instance):

```
@Override
public void onFftDataCapture(Visualizer visualizer,
byte[] bytes, int samplingRate) {
    fftBytes = bytes;
    float max = 0;
    for(int i = 0; i < fftPrep.length; i++) {
        if(fftBytes.length > i * 2) {
            fftPrep[i] = (float)Math.sqrt(fftBytes[i *
            2] * fftBytes[i * 2] + fftBytes[i * 2 + 1]
            * fftBytes[i * 2 + 1]);
            if(fftPrep[i] > max){
                max = fftPrep[i];
            }
        }
    }
    float coeff = 1 / max;
    for(int i = 0; i < fftPrep.length; i++) {
        if(fftPrep[i] < MIN_THRESHOLD){
            fftPrep[i] = 0;
        }
        fftNorm[i] = (byte)(fftPrep[i] * coeff * 255);
    }
    loadTexture(cardboardView, fftTexture, fftNorm);
}
```

Note that our algorithm uses a `MIN_THRESHOLD` value of 1.5 to filter out insignificant values:

```
final float MIN_THRESHOLD = 1.5f;
```

Now in `setup()`, initialize `fftTexture` with a generated texture, as we do for the `audioTexture` variable:

```
public void setup() {
    audioTexture = genTexture();
    fftTexture = genTexture();
    if(activeViz != null)
        activeViz.setup();
}
```

FFT shaders

Now we need to write the shader programs.

If necessary, create a resources directory for the shaders, `res/raw/`. The `fft_vertex.shader` is identical to the `waveform_vertext.shader` created earlier, so you can just duplicate it.

For the `fft_fragment` shader, we add a bit of logic to decide whether the current coordinate is being rendered. In this case, we are not specifying a width and just rendering all pixels below the value. One way to look at the difference is that our waveform shader is a line graph (well, actually a scatterplot), and our FFT shader is a bar graph.

File: `res/raw/fft_fragment.shader`

```
precision mediump float;        // default medium precision
uniform sampler2D u_Texture;    // the input texture

varying vec2 v_TexCoordinate;   // interpolated texture coordinate
per fragment
uniform vec4 u_Color;

void main() {
    vec4 color;
    if(v_TexCoordinate.y < texture2D(u_Texture,
    v_TexCoordinate).r){
        color = u_Color;
    }
    gl_FragColor = color;
}
```

Basic FFT material

The code for the `FFTMaterial` class is very similar to what we did for the `WaveformMaterial` class. So for brevity, just duplicate that file into a new one named `FFTMaterial.java`. And then, modify it as follows.

Ensure that the class name and constructor method name now read as `FFTMaterial`:

```
public class FFTMaterial extends Material {
    private static final String TAG = "FFTMaterial";
    ...

    public FFTMaterial(){
    ...
```

We decided to change the `borderColor` array to a different hue:

```
public float[] borderColor = new float[]{0.84f, 0.65f, 1f,
1f};
```

In `setupProgram`, ensure that you're referencing the `R.raw.fft_vertex` and `R.raw.fft_fragment` shaders:

```
program = createProgram( R.raw.fft_vertex,
R.raw.fft_fragment);
```

Then, make sure that the appropriate shader-specific parameters are getting set. These shaders use `u_Color` (but not a `u_Width` variable):

```
//Shader-specific parameters
textureParam = GLES20.glGetUniformLocation(program,
"u_Texture");
MVPParam = GLES20.glGetUniformLocation(program, "u_MVP");
colorParam = GLES20.glGetUniformLocation(program, "u_Color");
RenderBox.checkGLError("FFT params");
```

Now, in the `draw` method, we're going to draw with the `VisualizerBox.fftTexture` value (instead of `VisualizerBox.audioTexture`), so change the call to `GLES20.glBindTexture` as follows:

```
GLES20.glBindTexture(GLES20.GL_TEXTURE_2D,
VisualizerBox.fftTexture);
```

Ensure that the `colorParam` parameter is set (but unlike the `WaveformMaterial` class, there is no width parameter here):

```
GLES20.glUniform4fv(colorParam, 1, borderColor, 0);
```

FFT visualization

We can now add the visualization for the FFT data. In the `visualizations/` folder, duplicate the `WaveformVisualization.java` file into a new file named `FFTVisualization.java`. Ensure that it's defined as follows:

```
public class FFTVisualization extends Visualization {
```

In its `setup` method, we'll create a `Plane` component and texture it with the `FFTMaterial` class like this, (also note modifying the position and rotation values):

```
public void setup() {
    plane = new Plane().setMaterial(new FFTMaterial()
            .setBuffers(Plane.vertexBuffer,
            Plane.texCoordBuffer, Plane.indexBuffer,
            Plane.numIndices));

    new Transform()
            .setLocalPosition(5, 0, 0)
            .setLocalRotation(0, -90, 0)
            .addComponent(plane);
}
```

Now in `onCreate` of `MainActivity`, replace the previous visualization with this one:

```
visualizerBox.activeViz = new FFTVisualization(visualizerBox);
```

When you run the project, we get a visualization like this, rotated and positioned over to the right:

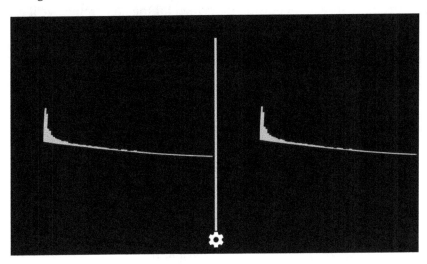

This simple example illustrates that FFT data separates spatial frequencies of the audio into discrete data values. Even without understanding the underlying mathematics (which is nontrivial), it's often sufficient to know that the data changes and flows in sync with the music. We used it here to drive a texture map. FFT can also be used like we used waveform data in the first example to drive attributes of 3D objects in the scene, including position, scale, and rotation, as well as parametrically defined geometry. In fact, it is generally a better data channel for such purposes. Each bar corresponds to an individual frequency range, so you can specify certain objects to respond to high frequencies versus low frequencies.

Trippy trails mode

If you are craving hallucinogenic simulations, we'll introduce a "trippy trails mode" to our visualizations! The implementation is added to the RenderBox library itself. If you're using the completed RenderBox library, then just toggle on the mode in your app. For example, in setup() of MainActivity, add the following line of code at the end:

```
RenderBox.mainCamera.trailsMode = true;
```

To implement it in your copy of RenderBox library, open that project (in Android Studio). In the Camera class (the components/Camera.java file), add public boolean trailsMode:

```
public boolean trailsMode;
```

Then, in onDrawEye, instead of erasing the screen for the new frame, we'll draw a full screen quad over the entire frame, with alpha transparency, thus leaving behind a ghostly faded image of the last frame. Every subsequent frame is overdrawn by more semi-transparent black, causing them to fade out over time. Define a color value as follows:

```
public static float[] customClearColor = new float[]{0,0,0,0.05f};
```

Then, modify onDrawEye, so it reads as follows:

```
public void onDrawEye(Eye eye) {
    if(trailsMode) {
        GLES20.glEnable(GLES20.GL_BLEND);
        GLES20.glBlendFunc(GLES20.GL_SRC_ALPHA,
        GLES20.GL_ONE_MINUS_SRC_ALPHA);
        customClear(customClearColor);
        GLES20.glEnable(GLES20.GL_DEPTH_TEST);
        GLES20.glClear(GLES20.GL_DEPTH_BUFFER_BIT);
    } else {
```

```
GLES20.glEnable(GLES20.GL_DEPTH_TEST);
GLES20.glClear(GLES20.GL_COLOR_BUFFER_BIT |
GLES20.GL_DEPTH_BUFFER_BIT);
}


    . . .
```

The `customClear` method skips the clear call, leaving behind the colors from the previous frame. Instead, it just draws a semitransparent full-screen black quad with transparency, slightly darkening the "old" image each frame. Before we can do this, the camera needs a shader program to draw the full screen solid color.

`fullscreen_solid_color_vertex.shader` is as follows:

```
attribute vec4 v_Position;

void main() {
    gl_Position = v_Position;
}
```

`fullscreen_solid_color_fragment.shader` is as follows:

```
precision mediump float;
uniform vec4 u_Color;

void main() {
    gl_FragColor = u_Color;
}
```

Now back to the `Camera` component. We set up the program and define a full screen quad mesh, buffers, and other variables. First, we define the variables we'll need:

```
static int program = -1;
static int positionParam, colorParam;
static boolean setup;
public static FloatBuffer vertexBuffer;
public static ShortBuffer indexBuffer;
public static final int numIndices = 6;
public boolean trailsMode;

public static final float[] COORDS = new float[] {
        -1.0f, 1.0f, 0.0f,
        1.0f, 1.0f, 0.0f,
        -1.0f, -1.0f, 0.0f,
        1.0f, -1.0f, 0.0f
};
public static final short[] INDICES = new short[] {
```

```
                0, 1, 2,
                1, 3, 2
        };
        public static float[] customClearColor = new
        float[]{0,0,0,0.05f};
```

Then, define a method to set up the program:

```
        public static void setupProgram(){
            if(program > -1)     //This means program has been set up
            //(valid program or error)
                return;
            //Create shader program
            program = Material.createProgram
            (R.raw.fullscreen_solid_color_vertex,
            R.raw.fullscreen_solid_color_fragment);

            //Get vertex attribute parameters
            positionParam = GLES20.glGetAttribLocation(program,
            "v_Position");

            //Enable vertex attribute parameters
            GLES20.glEnableVertexAttribArray(positionParam);

            //Shader-specific parameters
            colorParam = GLES20.glGetUniformLocation(program,
            "u_Color");

            RenderBox.checkGLError("Fullscreen Solid Color params");
        }
```

Define a method to allocate the buffers:

```
        public static void allocateBuffers(){
            setup = true;
            vertexBuffer = RenderObject.allocateFloatBuffer(COORDS);
            indexBuffer = RenderObject.allocateShortBuffer(INDICES);
        }
```

Then, call these from the Camera initializer:

```
        public Camera(){
            transform = new Transform();
            setupProgram();
            allocateBuffers();
        }
```

Finally, we can implement the `customClear` method:

```
public static void customClear(float[] clearColor){
    GLES20.glUseProgram(program);
    // Set the position buffer
    GLES20.glVertexAttribPointer(positionParam, 3,
    GLES20.GL_FLOAT, false, 0, vertexBuffer);
    GLES20.glUniform4fv(colorParam, 1, clearColor, 0);
    GLES20.glDrawElements(GLES20.GL_TRIANGLES, numIndices,
    GLES20.GL_UNSIGNED_SHORT, indexBuffer);
}
```

Rebuild the `RenderBox` module and copy the library file back to this `VisualizeVR` project. Don't forget to set `trailsMode` to `true`!

Now when you run the app, it looks trippy and cool!

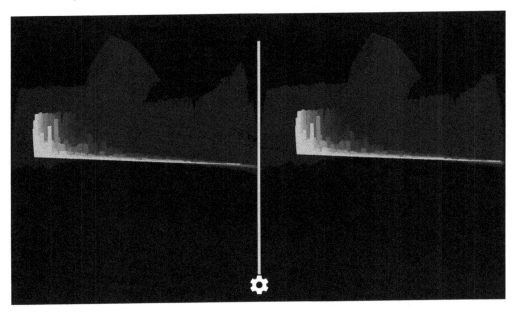

Multiple simultaneous visualizations

Now that we have a collection of visualizations, we can enhance the app to run more than one at a time and switch between them.

To support multiple concurrent visualizations, replace the `activeViz` variable in `VisualizerBox` with a list of `visualizations`:

```
public List<Visualization> visualizations = new
ArrayList<Visualization|();
```

Then, cycle through the list in each of the VisualizerBox method that use it. We always want to set up all of them, but then only draw (preDraw, postDraw) the active ones:

```
public void setup() {
    audioTexture = genTexture();
    fftTexture = genTexture();
    for (Visualization viz : visualizations) {
        viz.setup();
    }
}
public void preDraw() {
    for (Visualization viz : visualizations) {
        viz.preDraw();
    }
}
public void postDraw() {
    for (Visualization viz : visualizations) {
        viz.postDraw();
    }
}
```

We can control the scene in MainActivity. Modify the MainActivity class's onCreate method to populate the visualizations list, as follows:

```
visualizerBox = new VisualizerBox(cardboardView);
visualizerBox.visualizations.add( new
GeometricVisualization(visualizerBox));
visualizerBox.visualizations.add( new
WaveformVisualization(visualizerBox));
visualizerBox.visualizations.add( new
FFTVisualization(visualizerBox));
```

Run the project and we have a 3D scene full of visualizations!

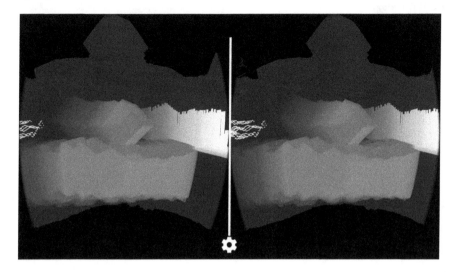

Random visualizations

We can switch between visualizations by adding and removing them over time. In the following example, we start with one active visualization and then every few seconds, toggle a random visualization on or off.

First, add an `activate` method to the abstract `Visualization` class, which takes a Boolean enabled parameter. The Boolean active variable is read-only:

```
public boolean active = true;
public abstract void activate(boolean enabled);
```

Its implementation will depend on the specific visualization. `RenderBox` library provides an `enabled` flag that's used when we render objects. The ones that instantiate a single `Plane` component are the easiest, such as `WaveformVisualization` and `FFTVisualization`. To each of these, add the following code:

```
@Override
public void activate(boolean enabled) {
    active = enabled;
    plane.enabled = enabled;
}
```

For the `GeometricVisualization` class, we can enable (and disable) each of the component cubes:

```
@Override
public void activate(boolean enabled) {
    active = enabled;
    for(int i = 0; i < cubes.length; i++) {
        cubeRenderers[i].enabled = enabled;
    }
}
```

Now we can control this within the `MainActivity` class.

Start with each of `visualizations` that are inactive. Add this initialization to `setup()` of `MainActivity`:

```
for (Visualization viz : visualizerBox.visualizations) {
    viz.activate(false);
}
```

In `preDraw` of `MainActivity`, we'll check the current time (using the `Time` class of `RenderBox` library) and toggle a random visualization after every 3 seconds. First, add a few variables to the top of the class:

```
float timeToChange = 0f;
final float CHANGE_DELAY = 3f;
final Random rand = new Random();
```

Now we can modify `preDraw` to check the time and modify the list of `visualizations`:

```
public void preDraw() {
    if (Time.getTime() > timeToChange) {
        int idx = rand.nextInt
        ( visualizerBox.visualizations.size() );
        Visualization viz = visualizerBox.
        visualizations.get(idx);
        viz.activate(!viz.active);
        timeToChange += CHANGE_DELAY;
    }
    visualizerBox.preDraw();
}
```

A similar kind of time control structure (or delta time) can be used to implement many kinds of animation, such as changing the visualization object's position, rotation, and/or scale, or evolving the geometry itself over time.

Further enhancements

We hope that we've given you some tools to get you going with your own music visualizations. As we've suggested throughout this chapter, the options are infinite. Unfortunately, space prohibits us from having too much fun coding more and more stuff here.

- **Animations**: We have applied the simplest transformations to each of our visualizations: a simple position, scale, and perhaps 90-degree rotations. Naturally, the position, rotation, and scale can be animated, that is, updated for each frame in coordination with the music, or independent of the music using `Time.deltaTime`. Stuff can be virtually flying all around you!

- **Advanced textures and shaders**: Our shaders and data-driven textures are the most basic: fundamentally rendering a single color pixel corresponding to the audio byte value. The audio data can be fed into much more complex and interesting algorithms to generate new patterns and color and/or be used to morph preloaded textures.

- **Texture mapping**: The texture materials in the project are simply mapped onto a flat plane. Hey man, this is VR! Map the textures onto a photosphere or other geometry and totally immerse your users in it.

- **Render to texture**: Our trails mode looks alright for these visualizations, but will probably become a mess for anything sufficiently complex. Instead, you could use it exclusively within the surface of your textured planes. Setting up RTs is complex and beyond the scope of this book. Essentially, you introduce another camera to your scene, direct OpenGL to render subsequent draw calls to a new surface that you've created, and use that surface as the texture buffer for the objects you want to render it onto. RT is a powerful concept, enabling techniques such as reflection and in-game security cameras. Furthermore, you can apply transformations to the surface to make the trails appear to fly off into the distance, which is a popular effect among traditional visualizers such as MilkDrop (`https://en.wikipedia.org/wiki/MilkDrop`).

- **Parametric geometry**: Audio data can be used to drive the definition and rendering of 3D geometric models of varying complexity. Think of fractals, crystals, and 3D polyhedra. Take a look at Goldberg polyhedra (refer to `http://schoengeometry.com/`) and Sacred geometry (refer to `http://www.geometrycode.com/sacred-geometry/`) for inspiration.

A community invite

We invite you to share your own visualizations with other readers of this book and the Cardboard community at large. One way to do this is via our GitHub repository. If you create a new visualization, submit it as a pull request to the project at `https://github.com/cardbookvr/visualizevr`, or create your own fork of the entire project!

Summary

In this chapter, we built a music visualizer that runs as a Cardboard VR application. We designed a general architecture that lets you define multiple visualizations, plug them into the app, and transition between them. The app uses the Android `Visualization` API to capture the waveform and FFT data from the phone's current audio player.

First, we defined the `VisualizerBox` class responsible for the activity and callback functions to the Android `Visualizer` API. Then, we defined an abstract `Visualization` class to implement a variety of visualizations. We then added waveform audio data capture to `VisualizerBox` and used it to parametrically animate a series of cubes to make a 3D wavy box. Next, we wrote a second visualizer; this time using waveform data to dynamically generate a texture that is rendered with material shader programs. And lastly, we captured the FFT audio data and used it for a third visualization. Then, we added more fun with a trippy trails mode and multiple concurrent visualizations that transition in and out randomly.

We acknowledge that the visual examples are pretty simplistic, but hopefully they'll fuel your imagination. We challenge you to build your own 3D virtual reality music visualizations that perhaps utilize a combination of the techniques in this project as well as other things from this book.

Onward to the future

We hope you've enjoyed this introduction to and journey through Cardboard virtual reality development for Android. Throughout this book, we have explored the Google Cardboard Java SDK, OpenGL ES 2.0 graphics, and Android development in general. We touched on a number of VR best practices and saw the limitations of low-level graphics development on a mobile platform. Still, if you followed along, you've succeeded in implementing a reasonable general purpose library for 3D graphics and VR development. You created a wide variety of VR applications, including an app launcher, a Solar System simulation, a 360-degree media gallery, a 3D model viewer, and music visualizers.

Naturally, we expect the Cardboard Java SDK to change, evolve, and mature from this point forward. No one really knows what the future holds, perhaps not even Google. Yet here we are, at the precipice of a bold new future. The best way to predict the future is to help invent it. Now it's your turn!

Index

Symbols

2D texture-based visualization
  about 335
  basic waveform material 338-341
  texture generator 335, 336
  texture loader 335, 336
  waveform shaders 337
  waveform visualization 341, 342
3D camera 67
3D models
  about 305
  center 317
  extents 316
  rotating teapot model, viewing 319, 320
  scaling 317
  teapot model, viewing 317-319
3D model viewer project
  intent, launching with 322, 323
  practical and production ready 324
  setting up 306, 307
  threading, adding 321
360-degree gallery 239
360-degree photo
  background image, using 246
  sample photosphere, viewing 244, 245
  viewing 242-244

A

activity_main.xml file 45
aidl tool 26
Android API Reference
  URL 47
Android app
  about 23, 24
  APK files 24
  Gradle build process 24-26
  Java compiler 26
Android Asset Packaging Tool (aapt) 26
Android Interface Definition Language 26
AndroidManifest.xml file
  about 40-45
  URL 41
Android OpenGL ES API Guide
  URL 60
Android project structure
  about 26-29
  URL 27
Android SDK Getting Started page
  URL 32
Android Studio
  about 29
  developers page 29
  installing 29
  user interface 29-33
Android Virtual Device (AVD) 24
APK files 24
apps, for Cardboard
  developing 16
  developing, Unity used 16-18
audio data
  capturing 327

B

basic geometric visualization 332-334
border frame
  border material 254-256
  border material, using 256, 257
  border shaders 252, 253
  putting, on image 252

C

Camera component 159-161
camera location
  changing 234
Cardboard 1-3
Cardboard Android demo app
  URL 32
Cardboard apps
  360-degree photo viewing 10
  cartoonish 3D games 11
  creepy scary stuff 11
  educational experiences 11
  first person shooter games 11
  launching, trigger used 122, 123
  listing 115, 116
  marketing experiences 11
  queries 116
  roller coasters and thrill rides 11
  Shortcut class, creating 117
  shortcuts, adding to OverlayView 117
  video and cinema viewing 10
  view lists, using in OverlayEye 118-120
Cardboard devices 11-14
Cardboard Java SDK
  adding 37-40
Cardboard project
  creating 33-37
Cardboard SDK for Android
  reference 16
Cardboard SDK for Unity
  reference 16
Cardboard viewer
  about 12-14
  configuring 14, 15
Cardboard VR app
  creating 99, 100
  further enhancements 123
  new project, creating 100, 101
compileShaders method 63
Component class 149
cube
  about 75
  animating 172, 173
  code 77-79

model data 75, 76
  spinning 88
Cube RenderObject component 152-155
cube, with face normals 164, 165
culling 56
current shortcut
  highlighting 120, 121

D

Dalvik virtual machine (DVM) 26
day and night material
  about 212
  DayNightMaterial class 215-217
  day/night shader 212-214
  rendering with 218
depth masking 303
draw method 156

E

Earth
  fine tuning 232
Earth texture material
  adding 201
  camera position, changing 211
  diffuse lighting material 205-208
  diffuse lighting shaders 203-205
  diffuse lighting texture,
    adding to Sphere component 209
  texture file, loading 202, 203
  viewing 209, 210
Embedded Systems 59
enhancements, music visualizer project
  advanced textures and shaders 355
  animations 355
  community invite 356
  parametric geometry 355
  render to texture 355
  texture mapping 355
entity component pattern
  URL 126
equirectangular projection
  reference 243

F

FFT visualization
  about 343, 347, 348
  basic FFT Material 346
  FFT audio data, capturing 343, 344
  FFT shaders 345
field of view (FOV) 14
fine tuning, Earth
  about 232
  axis tilt and wobble 234
  night texture 233
floor
  about 89
  drawFloor 94
  initializeScene 92
  model data 91
  onCreate 92
  onDrawEye 94
  onSurfaceCreated 92
  prepareRenderingFloor 93
  shaders 89
  variables 91
frequency 327
front-facing 56

G

Gallery360 project
  enhancements 303, 304
  launching, with intent 294-296
  RenderBox library, updating 302, 303
  setting up 240-242
gateway to VR 6, 7
gaze, loading
  about 278
  events, queuing 280, 281
  gaze-based highlights 278, 279
  photos, displaying 279
  photos, selecting 279
  vibrator, using 281
Gekkopod
  URL 74
geometry 55-57
Goldberg polyhedra
  reference 355

Google Cardboard SDK guide
  URL 18
**Google Developers Cardboard Getting
    Started page**
  URL 38
Google Expeditions
  reference 9
Gradle build process
  about 24-26
  URL 24
graphics processor (GPU) 126
grid
  showing/hiding,
    with tilt-up gestures 297-300

H

head look
  responding to 111-113
head-mounted displays (HMD) 5
head rotation 67
heads-up display (HUD) 101
Hello Virtual World text overlay
  adding 101
  overlay view, controlling from
    MainActivity 108, 109
  simple text overlay 101, 102
  stereoscopic views,
    creating for each eye 105-108
  text, centering with child view 103-105

I

icon
  adding, to view 113-115
**IDE (integrated development
    environment) 29**
image gallery user interface
  about 272, 273
  features 272
  photo screen, positioning on left 274
Image.loadLock 288
IntelliJ IDEA
  URL 31
intent 295, 322
intent metadata 42, 43
isLookingAtObject method 95-98

J

Java compiler 26
Java Virtual Machine (JVM) 137

L

LauncherLobby 99
Light component 165, 166
lighting and shading. *See* shaders
low-end VR 9, 10

M

MainActivity.cancelUpdate 288
MainActivity class
  about 46-48
  building 49, 50
  Default onCreate 48, 49
  running 49, 50
MainActivity gridUpdateLock 288
map projections and spherical distortions
  reference 242
materials
  about 133
  abstract material 134-136
  shaders 134
  textured material 134
Math package
  about 137
  MathUtils 137
  Matrix4 138
  quaternion 138, 139
  Vector2 139
  Vector3 140, 141
MathUtils variables 137
matrix
  about 67, 68
  URL 68
Matrix4 class 138
MilkDrop
  reference 355
ModelObject class
  creating 309
model-view-perspective (MVP)
    transformation matrices 159

multiple simultaneous
    visualizations 351, 352
music visualizer project
  enhancements 355
  setting up 326, 327
MVP vertex shader 70

N

normal vector 82
numeric literals 81

O

objects
  detecting 174, 175
OBJ file format
  about 307, 308
  reference 307
OBJ models
  buildBuffers 315, 316
  parsing 310-315
onDrawEye 65, 66
OpenGL ES 2.0 58-60
OpenGL rendering pipeline
  URL 60

P

parent methods
  about 144
  setParent 143
  unParent 143, 144
perspective
  about 67
  app, building 73
  app, running 74
  render 71-73
  viewing matrices, setting up 70, 71
photo image
  correct orientation, rotating to 263-265
  dimensions, for correcting width
    and height 266
  displaying 257
  image class, defining 258
  image, displaying on screen 262

image load texture 260
images, reading into app 259, 260
loading 257
sample image down to size 267-269
photosphere image
  displaying 270, 271
  loading 270, 271
Photosphere mode 270
Planet class
  creating 224-226
position methods
  getPosition 144
  setPosition 144
postDraw 331
preDraw 331
prepareRenderingTriangle method 63-65
profile generator tools
  reference 14
project
  creating 54, 55

Q

quaternion
  about 138
  references 139

R

random visualizations 353, 354
regular photo
  allocating buffers, defining 247, 248
  image screen, adding to scene 249-251
  materials, adding to Plane component 249
  Plane component, defining 247
  viewing 247
RenderBox
  about 125-128
  empty RenderBox class, creating 130-132
  IRenderBox interface, adding 132, 133
  new project, creating 128, 129
  RenderBox package folder, creating 129
RenderBox library
  updating 236
RenderBox methods 161, 162

RenderBox package
  exporting 176
  RenderBoxLib module, building 177-181
  RenderBox test app 181
  RenderBox, using in future projects 182-185
RenderObject component 150-152
rotation methods
  setRotation 146

S

Sacred geometry
  reference 355
sampler function 205
scale methods
  setScale 147
scrolling, enabling
  about 282
  scroll buttons, interacting with 285
  scrolling method, implementing 286, 287
  Triangle component, creating 282-284
  triangles, adding to UI 284, 285
setBuffers method 156
setup 331
setupProgram method 156
shaders
  about 80
  adding 80, 81
  app, building 88
  app, running 88
  cube normals and colors 82-84
  light source, adding 87
  preparing 85, 86
  vertex buffers, preparing 84
shading 77
simple box scene 163
smooth shading 82
software development kit (SDK) 3
Solar System project
  camera's planet view 230
  creating 188, 189
  enhancements 235
  formation 226, 227
  heavenly bodies, animating 231

planets, setting up in
    MainActivity 227-229
solid color lighted sphere
  about 195
  Material, adding to Sphere 200
  solid color lighting material 197-199
  solid color lighting shaders 195
  Sphere, viewing 200, 201
spectrum, VR devices
  Cardboard, as mobile VR 4
  desktop VR 5, 6
  old fashioned stereoscopes 3
Sphere component
  creating 189-194
spherical thumbnails
  about 300
  sphere, adding to
    Thumbnail class 300-302
starry sky dome 231, 232
Sun
  adding 223, 224
  creating 219
  unlit texture material 220, 221
  unlit texture, rendering with 222
  unlit texture shaders 219, 220
Surround Shot 270

T

threading 292-294
threads
  using 287-292
Thumbnail class 275
thumbnail grid 276-278
thumbnail image 274
thumbnails
  displaying, in grid 274
tilt damper feature 300
tilt-up gestures
  for showing/hiding grid 297-300
Tissot's Indicatrix
  reference 242

Titans of Space
  URL 230
Transform class
  about 141-143
  drawMatrices method 149
  drawMatrix() function 148
  identity matrix, transforming 148, 149
  parent methods 143, 144
  position methods 144, 145
  rotation methods 146
  scale methods 147
translation, rotation, and scale (TRS) 142
Treasure Hunt 33, 53
triangle
  about 55
  app, building 66, 67
  app, running 66, 67
  compileShaders method 63
  geometry 55-57
  onDrawEye 65, 66
  onSurfaceCreated 58
  OpenGL ES 2.0 58-60
  prepareRenderingTriangle method 63-65
  repositioning 74, 75
  simple shaders 61, 62
  variables 57
trigger
  used, for picking and
    launching app 122, 123
trippy trails mode 348-350

U

Unity
  about 16
  reference 16
  using 16
Unity 3D game engine
  URL 3

V

VBO (Vertex Buffer Object) 59
Vector2 139
Vector3 140, 141
vertex color lighting material 167-172
vertex color lighting shaders 167-172
VertexColorMaterial class 156-159
VertexColorMaterial instance
  defining 155
vertex color shaders 155, 156
ViewMaster brand VR/AR viewer
  URL 4
virtual screen
  using 109-111

VisualizerBox architecture 328-330
VR best practices
  overview 19, 20
VR devices
  spectrum 3

W

waveform 327
waveform data capture 331, 332
Wearality viewer
  URL 14

www.ingramcontent.com/pod-product-compliance
Lightning Source LLC
Chambersburg PA
CBHW062045050326

40690CB00016B/2991